THE UNCIVIL WAR

THE UNCIVIL WAR
ALABAMA vs. AUBURN, 1981–1994

SCOTT BROWN AND WILL COLLIER

RUTLEDGE HILL PRESS

NASHVILLE, TENNESSEE

Published in Nashville, Tennessee, by Rutledge Hill Press, 211 Seventh Avenue North, Nashville, Tennessee 37219.

Typography by E. T. Lowe, Nashville, Tennessee.

Library of Congress Cataloging-in-Publication Data

Brown, Scott, 1969–
    The uncivil war : Alabama vs. Auburn, 1981–1994 / Scott Brown and
Will Collier.
        p.   cm.
    ISBN 1–55853–354–0
    1. Auburn University—Football—History.   2. Alabama Crimson
Tide (Football team)—History.   3. University of Alabama—Football—
History.   I. Collier, Will, 1968–   .   II. Title.
GV958.A92B76   1995   95–31628
796.332'62'09761—dc20   CIP

Printed in the United States of America.

1 2 3 4 5 6 7 8 9—99 98 97 96 95

For our families and friends and, most of all, our parents, who helped us attend the schools that we love so much. Thank you for filling our lives and our autumns with joy.

CONTENTS

ACKNOWLEDGMENTS

WE WOULD like to thank the staffs of the Ralph Brown Draughon Library at Auburn University, the Auburn University Archives, the Montgomery Public Library, the Peachtree Corners (Georgia) Public Library, the Birmingham Public Library, the Paul W. Bryant Museum, and the University of Alabama in Birmingham Library for their assistance in our research.

The help of Auburn sports information director Kent Partridge was invaluable. We would like to thank Kent and the entire Auburn Athletic Department staff for taking time to work with us during the busiest days of the 1994 season.

We would like to express our sincere gratitude to the following Alabama and Auburn players, coaches, and officials for sparing time they didn't have to talk to us. Our book could not have been completed without them: Marco Battle, Terry Bowden, Kurt Crain, Wayne Hall, Gary Hollingsworth, David Housel, and Bobby Humphrey.

Videotapes of several of the Games recounted in this book were supplied to us by Alabama and Auburn fans from all over the South. We would like to thank the following people for entrusting their irreplaceable cassettes to us during our work: Dr. and Mrs. Wayne Palestini, Mike Palestini, Pete Pappas, James Nolin Sr., and Beth Gasperini.

Dr. Elly Welt, Auburn University's writer-in-residence, and George Littleton, president of Owl Bay Publishing, offered invaluable editorial suggestions and criticism. Jeff Etheridge, Tina Gottesman, and the staff of Auburn University Photographic Services were patient, diligent, and extremely generous with their assistance and outstanding pictures. Rich Addicks, photographer at the *Atlanta Journal-Constitution*;Taylor Watson, archivist of the Paul W. Bryant Museum; and Larry White, Alabama's sports information director, were of tremendous help in securing photographic sources.

And, of course, this work would not have been possible without the support and understanding of our families and friends.

INTRODUCTION

THE BATTLE THAT NEVER ENDS

COLLEGE FOOTBALL is a violent combination of rivalry and tradition everywhere it is played. For the last century the sport has flourished in the Deep South, a region that knows something of tradition, rivalry, and violence. In the middle of the old Confederacy, the nation's strongest league—the Southeastern Conference—dominates the bowls and national rankings season after season.

In Alabama, the state known as the Heart of Dixie, the sport reaches its highest levels of excellence and fanaticism. A small, largely rural state of four million, bearing two medium-sized state colleges and a multitude of smaller schools, Alabama rarely crosses the screens of the nation's mass media . . . except during the waning months of each year. It is long into October before the air cools and the leaves change in this state, but the colors of the University of Alabama and Auburn University are visible every day, reaching their highest concentrations during the fall. Situated in the geographic center of the Southeastern Conference, Auburn and Alabama have collected between them a host of championships and All-Americans during the last hundred years. But these things are not the heart of the story. Alabamians consider these national and conference honors only as secondary objectives. The real prize is the state championship, the game that comes at the end of the season, the battle that makes it all worthwhile. Or futile.

Former Auburn coach Ralph "Shug" Jordan named the annual Auburn-Alabama game the Iron Bowl during his twenty-five-year tenure as the leader of the Tigers. His friend and nemesis, Paul "Bear" Bryant, saw eye-to-eye with Jordan on few matters, but in this case the two legends were in complete agreement. Jordan was referring not only to the iron ore of the Birmingham hills, but to the nature of the Game itself. It is a hard game, but its metal is tempered in a fire of the hottest forge—in the hearts of the teams and the people that follow their every move.

Coaches and players who have participated in football spectacles and other regional rivalries agree that nothing comes close to the grudge match between Auburn and Alabama. No other game strikes a deeper chord within the participants and the fans, no other game generates such intense loyalties or hatreds, and no other game dominates the lives of a region as completely as this one. To win means a day of joy and a year of glory. To lose can mean days of dark depression, endless weeks of recrimination, and, worst of all, a year of unending torture from the other side's fans on the radio, in the boardrooms and offices and factories and playgrounds, and sometimes across the dinner table.

The divisions run deep, and they can be found at every level of society in Alabama. The University of Alabama produces the majority of the state's attorneys and politicians, and a banker in this state likely holds a diploma from Tuscaloosa. Auburn is the home school for most of the state's engineers and boasts one of the nation's premier veterinary schools. Auburn is historically the state's agriculture school, and even though today that curriculum attracts a tiny fraction of Auburn's twenty-two thousand students, Alabama fans and alumni have always delighted in calling AU a "cow college." There are, of course, lawyers from Auburn and engineers from Alabama, but these professions are still radically tilted toward the traditional roles of the two schools. The blue-collar people who are the real backbone of the state choose their loyalties in much the same way as the professionals, based on their family's leanings, where they live, and, in some cases, on who is winning this year. The last group, known as "I-65 alums," from the north-south highway that bisects the state, are held in contempt by both camps, except, of course, when they happen to be fans of *our* team.

Rivalry and enmity do not end on the field. For more than twenty years it was rumored that Bear Bryant and Shug Jordan maintained a gentlemen's agreement regarding the NCAA. This mutual nonaggression pact assured that neither school would turn in the other for rules violations. Soon after Jordan's retirement, however, Bryant seized an opportunity to bury his greatest foe and reported Auburn for recruiting infractions, for which the school received two years' probation. Many Auburn voices protested that Bryant's clout had produced an overly harsh sentence for the Tigers and was protection for the Tide from a similar fate. Auburn people had complained for years that the NCAA was afraid of

Bryant's power and did not move on accusations made against Alabama during his tenure.

More than a decade later, a former Auburn player, Eric Ramsey, accused Auburn coaches and boosters of providing him with illegal benefits. He produced a provocative collection of audiotapes to back his claims. After two years of accusations, investigations, resignations, and a media circus that many Auburn followers believed was instigated by pro-Alabama forces, Auburn was again placed on probation by the NCAA. It was (and still is) widely believed in AU circles that Alabama money had paid Ramsey's bills throughout the affair.

The story didn't end with Auburn's probation. Indeed, the Auburn faithful licked their wounds and suggested ominously that they would not go down alone. In November 1992, a year before Auburn's sentence was sent down, Gene Jelks, a former Tide star, accused Alabama coaches and boosters of providing him with illegal benefits going as far back as his high school days. Jelks, taking a cue from Ramsey, offered tape recordings and cashed checks as hard evidence. In turn, Alabama supporters claimed that Auburn was behind the whole thing. Subsequently, a Tiger booster acknowledged supporting Jelks during the controversy. A three-year NCAA investigation followed. It uncovered other violations and led to sanctions, the first in the university's history. It is not enough, with the rivalry on and off the field being as strong as it is, simply to win; some devotees seek to destroy the opposing program.

Coaches, players, school officials, reporters, and especially fans contribute daily to this intrastate squabbling, and they all collide once a year in the spectacle referred to as "the Game." It is a game that is discussed every day of the year, from last year's to next year's to the Game years ago when tornado warnings were given over the public-address system. Coaches are judged by whether or not they win the Game; players are remembered with relish if they win and scorned forever, or at best forgotten, if they lose. The rivalry is as alive in the statehouse and courts and hospitals and employment offices as it is within the confines of Jordan-Hare Stadium and Legion Field. School budgets are affected by it, jobs and contracts are won or lost based on the allegiances of the parties concerned, and sometimes even marriages fail to survive the passions of the Game.

There have been innumerable articles, newspaper columns, and even a few books about this contest that means so much to so many. To our knowledge, however, there has never been a book about the Game written by two people who have lived through both sides of this uncivil war. We have been fans of the Game and followers of our respective schools since infancy. We have graduated from these universities. We have experienced the childhood, student, and alumni worlds of this cultural phenomenon.

We grew up together in Enterprise, Alabama, a small town in the southeastern corner of a state that is as obsessed with football as any community in America. Enterprise has produced two state champions in the top division of high school football—a feat unheard of for such a small city—and has sent many of its young men on to glory (or ignominy) at Auburn, Alabama, and many other schools. Will was raised in the Tiger tradition, and in 1992 he became the third generation of his family to graduate from Auburn University. His father and grandfather saw to his brainwashing early, taking him to his first Auburn game at the tender age of three. Scott was born in Virginia. When his family moved to Enterprise in 1971, he was initiated into the world of Bear Bryant and the Crimson Tide. We have been rivals as long as we have been friends, and when it comes to football we agree on only one thing: the Auburn-Alabama rivalry is the greatest story in college football.

We have selected ten Games that span several distinct coaching eras during perhaps the most competitive period of this storied series. The chapters that follow, like this introduction, are divided into three sections. The first is a bipartisan look at the Game and the season that preceded it. Written in collaboration, each chapter was wrangled over bitterly to ensure that the narrative contained as little bias as possible. They read like the lead story of the Sunday morning sports page, with the following sections resembling editorials and having little regard for the niceties of unbiased discourse. We have given ourselves license to recount stories on and off the field from our own admittedly biased and slanted perspectives—and we have had a great time doing it. They are the honest memories and reactions of fans and, yes, our excuses and miseries.

ROLL TIDE

Alabama Getaway

EVERYONE EXPOSED to the power of the Game has to make a decision early in life. I was no exception. I know my choice was the right one because, short of a good shot of brandy, nothing warms my heart more than Alabama beating Auburn in the Game. That's just the way it is in Alabama. I spent the first twenty-five years of my life in the various reaches of the state, and the only thing worse than losing to Auburn is having to hear "the faithful" praise their Tigers for handling those evil rich boys from Tuscaloosa. Moreover, victory in the Iron Bowl affords us Tide followers the opportunity to be just as obnoxious while denigrating those illiterate farm hands on the Plains. I joined in writing this book because I have never felt anything more intense than the hatred between Alabama and Auburn. Period.

That intensity is the driving force behind this book. No other subject, be it sports in general, politics, or even religion, can come close in this state to being a sure-fire conversation starter. If you're getting your hair cut in February, you might have to endure a few desultory remarks about the weather, but sooner or later someone will want to talk about football recruiting. If you call a family member in May, you'll end up talking about the alleged changes "Coach" is making to the team this year. Of course, from September through December (and sometimes beyond), weekly game talk dominates even the most cordial chat. Naturally, mid-November is the most feverish time of all, because the Iron Bowl is fast approaching. Normal life is put on hold, and the Heart of Dixie becomes a virtual battle zone for the followers of the University of Alabama and Auburn University. Brash predictions, fond reminiscing of past outcomes, and last-minute bragging about last year's Game (in case this year's doesn't work out so well) become the standard discourse. Finally it's Gameday morning. The fans file in hours before kickoff, the players charge onto the field, and it's time . . .

Many people (myself included) have wondered why this rivalry is so much stronger than others. Some feuds, such as Texas-Oklahoma, fall out of the running early because the fans involved don't have to live with each other on a daily basis. But why do Alabama and Auburn people make life so much more difficult for each other than, for instance, Georgia and Georgia Tech people? What does this rivalry have that UCLA-USC doesn't? What about Florida and Florida State?

First and most important are the perceptions of the people. In general, Alabama people think of Auburn followers as low-class rednecks lucky to have the Crimson Tide on their schedule. Auburn, in turn, views Bama as a bunch of spoiled smoke-blowers living off Daddy's money. Obviously, neither perception is true, but a deep socially based resentment between the two camps has existed since the beginning. The infamous 1987 pre-Game rendition of the Auburn alma mater illustrates this, as many Tide fans shouted the words from "Old McDonald" in accompaniment to the Tiger band's melody. I must say I was hoarse for days after that one.

A second factor is Bear Bryant. The Bear consistently pounded Auburn for most of his twenty-five years in Tuscaloosa. To this day, veteran Tiger fans long to emerge from the pall Bryant cast over their fortunes. From the mid-1960s through the 1970s, a convenient way for Auburn followers to overlook their mediocrity was to root against Alabama at every opportunity. This pastime continued even after Pat Dye had pulled the Tigers equal to (and often beyond) the hated Tide. Bryant's dominance, as well as his casual disregard for everything Auburn stood for, sparked a lot of bitterness. Make no mistake: bitterness is at the heart of this never-ending battle.

Third, the Alabama-Auburn rivalry is great because both teams traditionally boast spectacular athletes who raise the level of play on the field. Joe Namath, Pat Sullivan, Bo Jackson, and Cornelius Bennett are just a few of the many tremendous talents who have contributed to this series. Great players usually make great teams. Therefore, this game pits two superior squads against each other in a struggle that typically means something more than just bragging rights. Oftentimes, a berth in the Sugar Bowl is at stake.

It makes sense to compare the Alabama-Auburn rivalry to that of Florida and Florida State, because that series is the only one even remotely comparable in terms of talent and proximity. Obviously, both Florida and FSU have produced a number of gifted players, and their game usually has significance beyond "bragging rights." But there are several differences. If you live in Florida, you've got a lot of options to vie for your spare time. For example, there's professional baseball, basketball, football, and hockey. Starting this year, the Sunshine State will have *three* NFL teams. Alabama once had a USFL team, the Birmingham Stallions, that had to sign up truckloads of Tide and Tiger players just to be mentioned in the local sports sections.

Also, neither Florida nor FSU has a legacy to match that which Bear Bryant left the University of Alabama. Consequently, neither team has polarized young football fans in the state to the degree found in Alabama. In Alabama, you either love the Crimson Tide or you live to see them lose to someone like Louisville. In Florida, you're not a Gator fan simply because you hate the Seminoles (or vice versa). Gator and Seminole fans genuinely love their teams—they just hate Miami.

Additionally, if you asked the Florida and Florida State players who they would want to beat if they could only go 1–10 in a season, I'd wager that most of the FSU players would say Miami in a flash, and the Florida players would probably be divided among Auburn, Georgia, and Florida State, depending on where they grew up in the state. Think about it. In any given year, *the* game in Florida could be FSU-Miami, FSU-UF, UF-Miami, or all three. In Alabama, the Iron Bowl is the only Game in town. Sure, Alabama has a fantastic rivalry with Tennessee, and Auburn's series with Georgia is itself worthy of a book. As a Tide fan, I personally enjoy watching Auburn play Florida because it's a nasty rivalry and I really hate both schools. Still, none of those contests compares to the Game.

Don't fool yourself. Bo Jackson didn't go to Auburn with visions of knocking off the Florida Gators. Mike Shula isn't remembered for his first game in 1985 (a heroic last-second charge against Georgia), but for his eleventh (which, believe me, will receive the proper coverage later in the book). Auburn fans don't buy bumper stickers that say Honk If You Hate Southern Mississippi, and Bill Curry wasn't forced out of Tuscaloosa because he couldn't beat Memphis State (although losing to them in 1987 didn't help). In Alabama, players, coaches, and fans alike live for the Iron Bowl. Nothing can compare to it.

This is why I took part in this project. This and it was a good excuse to watch Van Tiffin's kick over and over and over and . . .—S.B.

WAR EAGLE

More Than Just a Game

MY FAVORITE Auburn-Alabama fan story says all you need to know about the nature of this rivalry. My younger sister and I were both delivered by cesarean sections. When Kitty's birth was imminent, it was two weeks into November 1969. Auburn's team was winning big behind the legendary arm of Pat Sullivan. The Game that year would be huge and is still remembered as one of Auburn's all-time great victories. The delivering surgeon, an Alabama graduate, and my father agreed that an untimely birth would wreck their chances to see the Iron Bowl. So in the true spirit of sportsmanship, they arranged to have my sister born on the open date prior to the Game. Needless to say, Dad made the kickoff.

I can't remember a time when Auburn wasn't a part of my life. My parents' home is filled with photographs from my childhood, and I am wearing an Auburn jersey in most of them. My father (Class of '61) and my grandfather (Class of '29) carried me to my first game at what was then Cliff Hare Stadium when I was three years old. Throughout my entire life, the autumns have been marked by Saturday journeys to Auburn, and every year included the pilgrimage to the Auburn-Alabama game.

It wasn't easy to grow up as an Auburn fan in the 1970s. Alabama was enjoying its greatest decade ever. With the exception of a few bright moments, Auburn struggled. I was attacked continually by Alabama fans young and old, even from within parts of my own family, with the insulting question, Why are you for *Auburn?* The implication was that only a fool would associate himself with such a lowly institution. The question was generally followed by some variation of "Auburn's *awful!*" Imagine hearing that on a daily basis throughout your childhood. Hearing it from your neighbors, your playmates, even occasionally from your teachers. Either you give up and give in, or you bow up and fire back. Being an Auburn fan means that you never give up. Being me means I learned to fire back.

Before the 1989 Game, ESPN announcer Beano Cook observed, "Auburn and Alabama hate each other every day of the year—including Christmas." He was right. The rivalry could not exist without loving your school and hating the other side. I'm not afraid to admit it. I hate the University of Alabama. Nothing would make me happier than to see them go 0–11 every season. I hate the sight of those obnoxious fans with their red and white polyester. I hate that braying fight song. I hate the arrogant attitude that permeates Alabama football. And I'm proud to hate it all.

I have just infuriated half the people who will read this book. There are many people in the state who, with a straight face, claim to cheer for the other side in every game but the last one. In south Alabama, we have a name for people who say things like that. We call them liars.

Many sportswriters have written that football is a religion in Alabama. Some meant this as an insult, others considered it a fitting label for something that means so much to so many. Nonetheless, they're correct, regardless of their motives. Football is a religion to us, to my people. The Game is our high holy day. It's Christmas, Easter, the Fourth of July, and a jihad all rolled into one. Show me another event that draws pilgrims from every corner of a great nation, one that results in an outpouring of such pure emotion, and I'll show you a religious holiday in the Middle East.

My favorite part of every Game every year is the playing of the national anthem just before the battle begins. The stadium is always packed beyond capacity. The fans have been shouting at the players during warmups for about two hours and at each other for days, weeks, even months. And then, for a brief moment, all fall silent as the band on the field plays "The Star-Spangled Banner." You can hear the wind as it wraps around the bowl of the arena where a moment earlier you would have been lucky to hear yourself screaming. You can hear the sound of the American flag whipping in that wind as it is raised above the throng. You look out at the vast gathering standing in expectant silence, and you realize that it is not hate that has brought them to this place, to this cathedral of grass and concrete and steel. You realize that this game, this experience, is a reaffirmation of what we really are. It is a statement of family, of state, of country, and, yes, of religion. You take a deep breath of the cool southern wind, and in that magical pause you see all the things that bring us together and you look far beyond the things that tear us apart.

The anthem ends, and you roar out your school's battle cry at the top of your lungs, and the uncivil war is on for another Game and another year. But you are always left with that warm stillness, filled with giddy anticipation. Whether you win or lose, that feeling will always be with you—until you come back next year and experience it again. That's what draws us back, year after year, that's what keeps us thinking about this larger than life THING that happens once every twelve months.—W.C.

1981

A COLLISION OF ERAS

A S THE 1981 SEASON approached, Paul "Bear" Bryant had Amos Alonzo Stagg's record as the winningest collegiate football coach of all time squarely in his sights. In typical style, Bryant shrugged off the significance of the milestone. He preferred to talk about his football team, and it was easy to understand why. Most of his 1980 squad, which had gone 10–2 and humbled Baylor in the Cotton Bowl, was back. Had it not been for a quiet freshman named Herschel Walker, who powered the University of Georgia to the national championship, Bear's 1980 squad would have been his fourth in a row to visit the Sugar Bowl. There were murmurs among Bama loyalists that the Bear was also gunning for his umpteenth national championship.

But the national press didn't care about that. All they knew was that Bear Bryant had won 306 football games and that he could pass Stagg on November 6, against Mississippi State. Ironically, the NCAA in 1993 posthumously credited an additional six victories to Pop Warner, then third on the all-time list, vaulting him above Stagg with a total of 319 career wins. Naturally, this change in the record books would have made a considerable difference to the teams, the coaches, and the media of 1981, but at that time the mark to reach was still 315.

21

The prospect of beating the Bulldogs to reach that peak represented potential sweet revenge. One year earlier, State had upset the Tide, 6–3, snapping a twenty-eight-game Bama winning streak. But for Bryant, even being asked about such a scenario—which assumed Alabama would be 8–0 when the Bulldogs rolled into Birmingham—was ridiculous. There were just too many good football teams lying in wait for those first eight games, and at the moment Bryant had other matters on his mind. For one, things were shaking to the east.

PATRICK FAIN DYE HAD been introduced as the new head coach at Auburn University on the second day of 1981. The original choice was Auburn alumnus Vince Dooley, who was coming off a national championship at Georgia. Dooley's former teammate and current governor of Alabama, Fob James, nearly persuaded him to take the job, but at the last moment the former Tiger quarterback chose to stay in Athens. Many coaches scrambled for the position, including Bobby Bowden, Ray Perkins, Jackie Sherrill, and Dan Reeves, but the search committee chose Pat Dye, the head coach at Wyoming. Dye wanted the Auburn job badly. After interviewing with the committee, but before he was offered the Auburn job, the Wyoming administration gave Dye an ultimatum: drop out of the Auburn race or be fired. Dye tendered his resignation and waited ten agonizing days before being hired by Auburn.

The decision did not meet with universal acclaim from the Auburn faithful. Dye had graduated from Georgia and worked as an assistant at Alabama from 1965 to 1973. Few knew that Dye had family connections to Shug Jordan or were aware of his conservative South Georgia upbringing. It didn't help any when Dye committed the faux pas of recalling the past glories of "the University of Auburn" at his introductory press conference.

Nevertheless, Dye's head coaching tenures at East Carolina and Wyoming had earned him a reputation as a coach who could rebuild a program. His demeanor and his boot-camp style of discipline were proof positive of his apprenticeship under Bryant.

The new coach received his most remarkable endorsement before he ever set foot in Auburn. A few days before his hiring, Dye received a phone call in his Wyoming home from the Bear.

"You aren't going to take that job," Bryant said.

"I am if they offer it," Dye replied.

Bryant countered, "You're going to get this one [at Alabama]."

"If I come to Alabama . . . I'd be trying to maintain what you've already done. At Auburn, I can build a program," Dye explained.

"Well, you're not gonna beat me," Bryant warned.

"Maybe not, but the one that follows you, I'm gonna beat him like a stepson," Dye promised.

The first spring practices under Dye have assumed legendary status. As Randy Campbell, who would quarterback Auburn's 1982 and 1983 teams, put it, "[Dye's staff] came in and really got after us, I mean there were . . . bodies flying here and there . . . coaches jumpin' on fumbles, and it was almost like the coaches were saying, 'If you don't pick it up, we'll put on the pads ourselves and come out here and whip your butt.' But we all learned how to work. And we learned something about being accountable, about being responsible, and I guess that was the start of learning how to win."

Auburn people embraced Dye with a mixture of hope and frustration. Doug Barfield had come and gone as the successor to Shug Jordan. Jordan was a southern gentleman of the old school, who would have been a national legend had he worked in a state not containing Bear Bryant. His handpicked heir, Barfield, was personable, but he wasn't the man Auburn was looking for. What Auburn needed, clearly, was someone who embodied the work ethic and spirit of the Auburn people, and Pat Dye was that man.

BEAR BRYANT had a record to break, and his season began in a most inhospitable environment: Baton Rouge, Louisiana. Initially, Alabama was scheduled to play LSU in November, and Number 315 could have been reached, again assuming perfection, against the Bengal Tigers rather than Mississippi State. But ABC enticed the two schools to move up the LSU game and capture a prime-time Labor Day audience. Bama proved ready, dispatching the Bayou Bengals of Jerry Stovall, 24–7. It was a nice way for the Tide to begin the year and to familiarize the rest of the nation with the record Bryant was nearing. It looked like destiny would be calling on Legion Field in November. That much would be true, but Mississippi State would not mark the end of Bryant's quest.

Georgia Tech, an old foe of both the Tide and the Tigers, came into Birmingham with little regard for Bryant or the Alabama mystique and stunned the Tide, 24–21. Suddenly, it was clear that a perfect season did not lie at the end of 1981's rainbow. Perhaps that realization affected the Tide's mediocre performance the next week against Kentucky in Lexington. It took the foot of Peter Kim, who nailed four field goals, to subdue the Wildcats, 19–10, in a game Jerry Claiborne's troops controlled until late. Then came whippings of long-time patsies Vanderbilt (28–7) and Ole Miss

(38–7). At 4–1, the Tide was still in the running for the national title and definitely for the Southeastern Conference crown.

But Southern Miss dealt Bryant another setback, a 13–13 tie in Tuscaloosa. Clearly, national title hopes had gone from slim to minuscule, and a trip to highly ranked Penn State lurked later in the schedule. Even worse for Bama, Johnny Majors and the Tennessee Volunteers were headed toward Legion Field for the traditional Third-Saturday-in-October showdown with the Tide. The Vols were still smarting from the 27–0 waxing Bryant's squad applied in 1980, when both teams had entered the Knoxville rain undefeated. This time the Big Orange made things interesting but were eventually worn down, 38–19. Rutgers supplied the Homecoming entertainment the following week, falling 31–7.

And now the Tide was playing Mississippi State. If Bama had

PAUL W. BRYANT MUSEUM

Bear Bryant, the legend from Moro Bottom, Arkansas, strikes a familiar pose.

revenge on their minds, they certainly didn't show it on the field, holding off a late Bulldog charge to struggle to another win, 13–10. Unhappy with his team's lackluster performance against MSU, Bryant used the open date to whip the squad into shape, and Alabama played its best game of the year against Penn State in Happy Valley. Sophomore quarterback Walter Lewis was the catalyst, hooking up with Jesse Bendross early and often, giving the Tide a 24–3 halftime edge against the stunned Nittany Lions. The game also featured a thrilling goal-line stand that kept the Lions from getting within striking distance, reminiscent of the 1979 Sugar Bowl. The game ended Penn State's run for the top, 31–16, and Bear Bryant had tied Stagg's record. In the process, Alabama had climbed to 8–1–1, manhandled the number four team in the country, positioned itself to win at least a share of both the

Pat Dye left Wyoming to become Auburn's head coach in 1981.

league and national titles, and beaten some Yankees.

PAT DYE'S first game as coach of Auburn University came against the Texas Christian Horned Frogs. Ron O'Neal, a heavyset freshman fullback, scored two touchdowns, and although the defense gave up 354 total yards to TCU, Dye passed the test, 24–16, and walked away from Jordan-Hare Stadium a winner his first time out. But three painful losses followed, starting when Wake Forest took advantage of turnovers by the young Tigers and emerged on top, 24–21.

A trip to Knoxville afforded Dye a chance at his first road victory, and his team nearly upset the Vols in front of ninety-five thousand fans. But time ran out on Auburn three yards short of the end zone, and Tennessee took the win, 10–7. It was a terrible, heartbreaking defeat for a young team that had come a long way in a short time. The new coach's speech to his players after the loss set the tone for the entire Dye era at Auburn. In the visitor's locker room the worn-out team watched as the coach paced, struggling for a way to bring something positive out of an almost win.

"That's life," Dye said. "There's gonna be a lot of days when you lay your guts on the line, and you come away empty-handed. Ain't a damn thing you can do about it but go back and lay 'em on the line again. And again, and again. . . . If you'll keep fightin' like you did today, if you keep playin' like that, you can build a foundation that we can live a long, long time on at Auburn."

Then came a challenge from a national superpower, a trip to Lincoln, Nebraska, to face Tom Osborne's Cornhuskers. Auburn played a remarkably strong game, leading at the half, 3–0. Yet once again mistakes killed the Tigers, who fumbled twice inside their own ten-yard line. Those two turnovers led to two Nebraska touchdowns as the Cornhuskers handed Auburn a 17–3 defeat. Dye unveiled a rotating quarterback offense for a surprisingly easy 19–7 win over LSU in Auburn. A big win over traditional rival Georgia Tech (31–7) followed and evened the Auburn record at three wins and three losses.

A bitter home loss to Mississippi State, 21–17, was made worse by the presence of former Auburn coach Doug Barfield, now the Bulldogs' offensive coordinator. Dye's team was below .500 again. Auburn responded with an emotional 14–12 victory in Jordan-Hare over Charley Pell's Florida Gators and a desultory 20–0 Homecoming win over North Texas State.

Herschel Walker and the Georgia Bulldogs were waiting in Athens. A win would have guaranteed a winning season for Dye's first team and a probable bowl berth. But in 1981 Auburn was not ready for Georgia. After trailing early, the Bulldogs pulled away behind Walker, winning 24–13, cementing a berth in the Sugar Bowl (although Alabama could have tied the Bulldogs for the league title, Georgia was ranked higher than the Tide, and the Sugar Bowl Committee, exercising its right to choose the league representative, picked the Dawgs). So Auburn was 5–5, still with a chance for a winning season by beating Alabama.

THE STAKES for the Game were high on both sides. For fourth-ranked Alabama, beating Auburn would make their record 9–1–1 going into the Cotton Bowl against Texas. A win over the Longhorns and the right combination of other outcomes on New Year's Day would give Bama legitimate claim to at least a share of the national title. And, of course, Bryant would have broken the game's most cherished coaching record against his archrival, which over the years had supplied 18 of his previous 314 wins.

For Auburn, Dye would likely achieve sainthood by upstaging the Bear and knocking off Alabama in his first attempt. Auburn would be appearing on national television for the first time in two years due to previous NCAA probation, which would surely pump up the Tigers. And the pupil had a chance to school the teacher. But Dye had history going against him: former Bryant assistants had lost twenty-eight in a row to the Old Man.

Bryant's preference for a run-oriented offense had rubbed off on Dye: while Alabama entered the game averaging 288 yards per game on the ground—fifth in the nation—the Tigers were churning out 211. Clearly, the forty-sixth renewal of the series would be decided on the line of scrimmage.

The edge in depth at running back and at virtually every position went to Alabama, which is why the Tide was a twelve-point favorite. In Dye's words, his backfield contained "a wide receiver at halfback, a midget at the other halfback, and a nose guard at fullback." Auburn's best chance at pulling off the upset, conventional wisdom held, was to build an early lead and hold it. Otherwise, the Tigers would be little more than the entrée at the Bear's coronation feast.

SATURDAY BROKE cloudless and cool in Birmingham, and the eyes of America were on Legion Field. The pre-Game hype centered, predictably, on Bryant and Bama. The state's sportswriters, following the oddsmakers, gave Auburn virtually no chance to win. Dye was a year or two away, they seemed to agree. In their opening comments, ABC's Keith Jackson and Frank Broyles, in addition to focusing on the milestone Bryant was approaching, mentioned the similarities between Bryant and Dye and the enthusiasm that Dye had brought to his new position. What they did not discuss were the Tigers' chances for pulling off the upset. Still, the Alabama fans in the stands noticed that their Auburn counterparts weren't as intimidated as they thought Auburn ought to be.

But if Bear Bryant was as confident as the Bama fans seemed to be, he certainly wasn't showing it. Asked by Keith Jackson about his feelings, he simply said, "I'm scared to death."

Alabama won the toss, taking the opening kickoff and starting the first offensive series from its 23. Alan Gray, one of three quarterbacks Bryant played on a regular basis, led the team against an inspired Auburn defense. Three running plays netted one yard, forcing a punt. Tiger Chuck Clanton fielded the ball at the Auburn 32, picked up a few good blocks, and jetted down the right sideline to Bama's 14, electrifying the Auburn faithful.

Auburn, however, had no more success with the wishbone than the Tide had had on their first possession. Lacking an outstanding player at quarterback, Dye was using a "designated quarterback" system, substituting three costarters—Joe Sullivan, Ken Hobby, and Clayton Beauford—on a play-by-play basis. This rotation system misfired on the first series, and three plays later Al Del Greco missed a 25-yard field goal, wide right. It was not the last time that afternoon the Tigers would fail to exploit an excellent scoring opportunity.

On Bama's second possession, quarterback Gray broke through on an option play and went for 63 yards to the Auburn 21. Paul Ott Carruth, who would be a solid four-year contributor for the Tide, then picked up another first down at the Auburn 10. Two plays later, Carruth took a pitch from Gray and was stopped just short of the goal line by standout Tiger freshman Gregg Carr. On the next play, Gray dove for the end zone, just breaking the plane of the goal line. Peter Kim added the point after, and the score was 7–0, Alabama.

After an exchange of punts, the Tigers took over on their own 30. Ken Hobby and Clayton Beauford, Auburn's best running quarterback, split time under center. On third down Hobby connected with Ed West for a new series of downs. Then Joe Sullivan, Auburn's third quarterback and younger brother of Heisman winner Pat Sullivan, somehow avoided the Bama rush and found West for another big play, this time to the Bama 19. George Peoples, who would have a huge day, powered his way to the seven for another first down. But on first and goal, Hobby threw for West and All-American Bama defensive back Tommy Wilcox outjumped the tight end for a momentum-crushing interception.

As the first quarter ended, Bama was backed up inside its own five and had to punt. The Tigers started on their 48. Flanker Chris Woods gained ten yards on a reverse. The drive ended with another failed field goal attempt, again wide right.

The two teams traded punts, and Bama was once again on its own five-yard line. This time the Alabama offense fared better. Lewis, avoiding a sack and a safety, scrambled to the 14. On the next play Joe Carter was able to get the first down. The next series of downs, however, led to a punt, and Auburn took the ball at its own 37.

Following the interception and the missed field goal, down by seven, Auburn badly needed to score. On the first play, Peoples plowed through the Bama line, broke free, and carried a defender with him five yards into the end zone for a 63-yard touchdown. It was an electrifying run, giving Auburn a badly needed lift after the offensive sputters of the first quarter. Del Greco added the point after. With a little more than three minutes left in the first half, the Game was tied at 7–7.

On the ensuing kickoff, Auburn again pinned Bama inside its own 20, this time at the 12. On the next play, Dorminey pounded Gray, forcing a fumble that Tiger Zac Hardy recovered at the 10. Auburn threatened to score again and take the lead. Willie Howell carried the ball to the six. On second down, Peoples was stuffed after a one-yard gain. Lionel James took a third-down pitch from Hobby and angled for the corner of the end zone, but he was stopped by linebackers Thomas Boyd and Robbie Jones. The field goal unit came on the field, Del Greco determined to make amends for his two early misses. Sullivan, the holder, however, bobbled the ball, jumped up,

AUBURN UNIVERSITY ARCHIVES/OPELIKA-AUBURN NEWS

Auburn sophomore kicker Al Del Greco had a frustrating afternoon against Alabama, making only one of four field goal attempts.

and threw a wobbly pass to an ineligible receiver, adding insult to injury with a penalty. Alabama was awarded the ball at its own 26, and Auburn had missed a golden opportunity.

With less than a minute in the half, Lewis threw deep down the middle for Jones, who was well covered. The ball was deflected by David King and intercepted by Dorminey at the Auburn 23. Sullivan and Tommy Carroll connected on a twenty-six-yard pass to set Auburn up at the Alabama 47 with 26 seconds left in the half. On his next attempt, Sullivan overthrew his man and was nearly intercepted. Sullivan threw three more prayers into the end zone, but all three fell harmlessly to the turf. Both teams went to the locker rooms at the half, tied 7–7.

Auburn had missed two field goals, muffed another by a bobbled snap, and been intercepted in the end zone. The faithful saw that their Tigers could have led Alabama by the improbable score of 23–7. Instead, they had managed only a tie at the break. Bear Bryant saw the possibility too, saying in a halftime interview with ABC's Verne Lundquist that his team was playing like it was "afraid of hurtin' somebody's feelin's." One can imagine he expressed his sentiments a bit more emphatically in the locker room. It was hard to argue with him: the Tide had been outgained 200 yards to 86 in total offense in the first half, 127 to 82 on the ground, and 73 to 4 through the air. Put simply, 5–5 Auburn was dominating the fourth-ranked Crimson Tide statistically.

Auburn's Joe Sullivan (5) endured a solid pass rush throughout the afternoon, here supplied by Alabama's Randy Edwards (96) and Tommy Wilcox (15).

AUBURN TOOK the second-half kickoff and started on its own 17, but the offense couldn't advance and barely avoided disaster when a poor Sullivan pass was dropped by Bama's Bennie Perrin. Had Perrin held on to the ball, he could have easily scored. A fair catch set up Bama at its own 45. Ken Coley came in at quarterback for the Tide for the first time in the Game and carried the ball on three consecutive downs. Although he failed to convert the down, Auburn was flagged for a facemask penalty. From the Tiger 32, freshman Ricky Moore rumbled for a gain of five yards. Coley carried on second down for two more yards, but on third down he mishandled the snap and ended up short of the first. With a fourth and one at the 23, Bryant called on Moore, who hurdled over the top for two yards and a first down. The fourth-down gamble paid off. Two plays later, after a motion penalty had cost the Tide five yards, on second and fifteen from the 26, Coley flipped a shovel pass to Bendross, who followed the blocking of Moore and Jones around left end and glided—untouched—into the end zone. Bama was back on top, 14–7, with just under ten minutes left in the third quarter.

Auburn's offense again stumbled, but the ensuing punt was probably the Game's most bizarre play. Bama's usually sure-handed punt returner, Joey Jones, dropped the ball at his own 42. It bounced 10 yards closer to the Bama end zone, then Clanton batted it even closer, never gaining possession of the ball until he ultimately fell on it at the Alabama two-yard line. Two plays later, Lionel James took a short pitchout from Hobby and dove into the right corner of the end zone. It was not the last time that James would throw his miniature frame into the gears of the Bryant machine. With Del Greco's extra point, the Game was tied again, 14–14, with seven minutes left in the third quarter.

Jones was determined to redeem himself on the following kickoff, returning the ball to the Bama 25. But three plays later, the Tide had to relinquish the ball, and Auburn went on the offense from its own 33.

Peoples continued to slam his huge frame up the middle of the Bama defense, carrying for five yards, then four more, just shy of the first down. Hobby kept the ball on a sneak and covered just enough real estate to move the chains. Keeping the ball on the ground, Peoples ran again for nine. Believing the Bama defense was focused entirely on stopping Peoples and the running game, Hobby tried a long pass to Woods. The completion, however, was to an Alabama player. Perrin held on to this one and brought it back to the Tide 35-yard line.

Lewis gave to Moore, who took off behind the blocking of Doug Vickers for 13 yards. Moore, responding to People's heroics, went for five more, then four. On third down, Lewis pitched to Mickey Guinyard, Bama's tenth ball carrier of the day. But Guinyard fumbled on the Auburn 33, where the ball was recovered by Tiger Tim Drinkard.

Auburn's offensive woes returned, but once again a Bama miscue—another muffed punt reception by Jones—was recovered by Auburn deep in Alabama territory, this time at the Tide 33-yard line. While Bama faltered on turnovers, Auburn was haunted by penalties. Every other play seemed to end with an Auburn penalty. A holding call, a clip. Nevertheless, the Tiger offense inched closer to the end zone. The third quarter ended with Auburn threatening to break the tie and gaining momentum. The Tide was self-destructing on turnovers, and Auburn was hindered by offensive problems.

The sun had set, but on whose fortunes? Despite Auburn's apparent momentum, Alabama's depth chart was legendary. Would the Bear make the right substitutions in face of the hard-hitting and tiring Auburn players? Auburn could have been well ahead on the scoreboard. Despite an amazing five turnovers, unheard of for a Bear Bryant team, the Tide had managed to keep things close.

On the first play of the fourth quarter, Bama was flagged for a facemask penalty, giving Auburn a third-and-one situation on the Bama 13-yard line. The Tigers converted and took the ball to the five-yard line, but then the Bama defense stiffened. Auburn lost two yards on first down, gained two on second, and ran for two more on third, setting the ball up between the hash-marks for a Del Greco field goal attempt. On his previous tries, the offense had given Del Greco difficult angles toward the goalposts. This time his kick pierced the uprights. With thirteen minutes left in the Game, Auburn led for the first time, 17–14.

In the stands, the Auburn faithful were roaring. This was what they had envisioned for every Iron Bowl—a chance to knock off the Bear in a Game that was particularly important to Bryant personally. The significance of this particular Game, however, was not lost on the Alabama players. They weren't about to disappoint the coach in his quest for the record.

Starting at its own 25-yard line, the Bama offense slowly marched down the field. Several critical third-down plays had to be converted in the process. On the first, Lewis connected with Bendross at the Alabama 41 to keep the drive alive. It was a simple out route, but for the Tide it might well have been the biggest play of the game. Short of the completion, Bama would have gone three and out and the resolve of the Auburn players might have stiffened to sense that the Game was theirs.

Three plays later, it looked as if the Tigers had held the Tide, but a defensive holding call gave Bama a new series of downs. It was a crucial mistake. On the next play, Bendross lined up as a tight end and burned

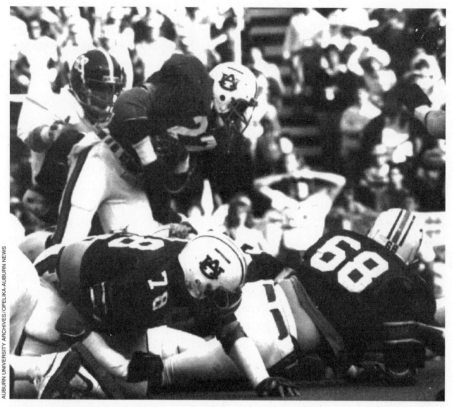

AUBURN UNIVERSITY ARCHIVES/OPELIKA-AUBURN NEWS

Auburn's George Peoples had one of the best afternoons of his career in the 1981 Game, gaining more than 150 yards.

Dorminey for a picture-perfect 38-yard score. Bama was back up on the scoreboard, 21–17, with ten minutes to play.

Momentum now rested on the shoulders of the Tide, and Bama held the Tigers to a single series of downs, forcing a punt. Bryant's offense began its next series from Auburn's own 49-yard line.

On first down, Linnie Patrick demonstrated the most remarkable individual effort of the Game, bouncing off five potential tacklers for a 32-yard gain. The talent of Alabama's players was beginning to tell, as the Auburn defense suddenly ran out of steam. Two plays later, the sophomore Patrick fended off three more defenders for 15 yards and a touchdown. With 7:07 remaining in the Game, Alabama led, 28–17.

Starting at its own 31, Auburn's offense tried to put together a drive. After gaining a first down and threatening to cross the midfield stripe, the Bama defense hurled Sullivan for a ten-yard loss and harassed Hobby into a third-down incompletion. When Auburn punted, the Tide placed every man on the line and allowed the ball to go through the end zone.

The Tigers held the Bama offense to three plays and a punt, receiving the ball at their own 38. Down by eleven points, conventional wisdom would have conceded that victory was beyond Auburn's grasp, but stranger things have happened on the gridiron in less time than the Plainsmen faced, particularly when state pride is involved.

Auburn's passing offense took the ball to the Bama 48 with 2:30 left in the game. After a sack, Hobby connected with Tommy Carroll at the Tide 35. Peoples then charged for nine yards. On his final carry of the contest, he carried for two yards. He ended the day with 155 yards on 26 carries. The drive stalled at the Alabama 31-yard line. Auburn's last pass was intercepted and returned to the Alabama 44. The Tide ran the clock out and the deed was done.

Alabama 28, Auburn 17.

Paul W. Bryant was now the all-time winningest coach in college football, and he had beaten Auburn for a ninth consecutive time. He graciously talked to ABC's Lundquist underneath the Legion Field stands before heading into the dressing room: "It looked like the good Lord wasn't gonna let us win for a while. . . . It's one of the greatest games I've ever been involved in." Bryant received congratulatory phone calls from President Ronald Reagan and former President Jimmy Carter.

IN THE other Legion Field locker room, Pat Dye, who had just completed his first year at Auburn, told his young players to keep their heads up, be prepared to work hard, and expect great things. They had been uninvited guests at Bear Bryant's party, but they knew, on a day not too far in the future, they would be holding a few celebrations of their own. Dye apologized to the seniors for not bringing them a victory to take home after four years of toil. He told the young men that what he had taught them would win, not just in football, but in life.

In the post-Game press conference, Dye praised his former mentor, and his sincerity was obvious. Bryant sauntered in as Dye finished and jokingly asked, "What the hell are you doing up here speaking?" Dye grimaced, exchanged a few quiet words with the Bear, and went back to his players. Bryant made it a point to speak well of Auburn's team, particularly George Peoples, and Auburn's new coach, saying that Dye had done "a great job and had a great year. It's a good start, but I don't want him to get 'biggety'!"

It was a vintage Bryant performance, par for the course from a man who had raised intimidation to an art form. But Pat Dye was a young coach with a young team, and this was the first losing season he had ever experienced. You could tell by the look in his eyes that he didn't plan on having any more.

Alabama went on to lose a heartbreaker to the Texas Longhorns, 14–12, in the Cotton Bowl. Any hopes for a national title were gone, and Clemson wrapped up the mythical throne by beating Nebraska in the Orange Bowl. But the year, for better or for worse, was Bear Bryant's.

ROLL TIDE

Records Are Meant to Be Broken

THERE HAS never been, nor will there ever be, another college football coach like Bear Bryant. His impact on the game is so obvious and so well chronicled that to dwell on it borders on the tedious.

As the Old Man approached his 315th victory, it was hard to tell whether this singular accomplishment added to or detracted from the atmosphere surrounding the 1981 Iron Bowl. At first glance, it seemed that "The Record" was an added incentive for the Tide to whip Auburn for an amazing ninth consecutive time. But the pressure on the Bama players easily outweighed the emotional boost of gaining Bryant's milestone. What if Auburn, with Bryant disciple Pat Dye at the controls, upstaged the Bear at his own coronation? Were the Bama players so caught up in the numbers that they forgot they had to overcome their most bitter rivals to get there?

Fortunately, of course, this did not keep the Tide from dealing Auburn yet another losing season and Bear Bryant his rightful place as the winningest coach of all time. But I think it's regrettable that Number 315 dominated the usual fortnightly hype that traditionally surrounds this series. Had it not been for that early season loss to Georgia Tech or the tie to Southern Miss, the record could have been dispensed with and Alabama could have beaten Auburn just for the sake of beating Auburn.

Don't get me wrong: it's easy now to say that the record made beating the Tigers even sweeter. That's the approach most fans have taken over the years. But when I look back at this game, my foremost thought is not of Bear Bryant. I remember Alan Gray, Linnie Patrick, Tommy Wilcox, and all the players who made it happen. To simply refer to '81 as "The 315 Game" is to overlook how hard this team had to play to make it happen. True enough, Bama had more talent than Auburn, but the Tigers, just like anyone else who senses they've shown up at their own funeral, almost turned the Bear away.

Of course, Auburn had some help in keeping things close. The Tide was altogether too willing to give up the ball, and who's to say all the hoopla surrounding Bryant had nothing to do with that? In fact, Dye's team could have had Bama on the ropes had they converted their opportunities in the first half. But, of course, they didn't, and once again the orange and blue left Legion Field wondering what if?

Neither team in this Game played up to its potential. So, like it almost always does, it came down to the fourth quarter, where Alabama pulled ahead, not because of Bear Bryant, but because he had the better players. I firmly believe that the opportunity to tie the record, which had occurred two weeks earlier, was the spark the Tide needed to manhandle a great Penn State team. But the Iron Bowl, even in 1981, had its own particular ambiance. And I think it's too bad that the game was billed as little more than Bear's victory parade. For one thing, with the win over Penn State, Bama still had a legitimate shot at the national title. While brief reference was made to this, it was clear that the "history in the making" angle was first and foremost on ABC's collective mind that fall afternoon at Legion Field.

The Bear's detractors—namely Auburn people—love to point out that Eddie Robinson took the title as winningest collegiate coach of all time from Bryant in 1985. But life in the Division I-AA Southwestern Athletic Conference simply does not compare and never has to the Southeastern Conference. Paul Bryant is in a category all by himself. Consider how many of today's coaches studied at the foot of the master. Stroll through the Bryant Museum to glimpse what the Old Man in the Hat did in his lifetime. Eddie Robinson can have the record. We had the Bear.

When you recall the 1981 Iron Bowl, don't just think of the record book. Think of blood and guts. Think of being behind 17–14 in the fourth quarter. Think of Walter Lewis and Jesse Bendross, Mike Pitts and Jim Bob Harris. Think Alabama. The Bear would have wanted it that way.—S.B.

WAR EAGLE
Things Past, Things to Come

BEFORE WE reviewed 1981 for this book, I have to admit that I didn't remember much about the Game, even though I had been there at Legion Field. To be honest, my memories were colored by the general perception that Auburn had hung in there for a while on breaks and was eventually overwhelmed. That had been the script for the majority of Alabama's nine-Game streak, with a couple of blowout exceptions. Upon reading the articles and statistics, and particularly after watching a tape of the Game, I was reminded of just how well Auburn had played. For once, the score was nowhere near indicative of just how close this Game really was.

For my transgression, I apologize. I apologize to George Peoples for forgetting what a great runner he was. I apologize to Chuck Clanton for not remembering his spectacular punt returns. I apologize to Alan Bollinger, Danny Skutack, and Edmund Nelson for disregarding their remarkable contributions. I apologize to Doug Barfield for all the times I've said that the cupboard was bare when Pat Dye came to the Plains. For all the abuse that has been heaped upon Barfield over the last decade, the most undeserved complaint was that he couldn't recruit against the Bear.

Auburn folks were as susceptible to the 1981 Bryant hype as anybody, and I vividly remember following the count as 315 crept closer. A loss here, a win there, a tie of all things, and damned if it wasn't going to come down to the Game. I didn't want Auburn to have anything to do with that record. I was cheering for Penn State all the way so the record would have nothing to do with the Iron Bowl (if Alabama played Iraq, I'd probably root for the Iraqis). Alabama's emotions surrounding that fateful first shot at the record would surely be tremendous. It is all the more remarkable to me today that an Auburn team that had been wholly discounted by the "experts" came as close as it did to inspiring bumper stickers reading "314 And Holding."

Still, in many ways, this Game was more of the same for Auburn. How many times had we come close and seen it all slip away? (Five of the previous nine, but, hey, who's counting?) Auburn hadn't won since 1972, which was the greatest comeback in the history of the series and arguably one of the most incredible in the history of college football. Were the football gods exacting a long-term price for that day when their magical lightning struck twice?

Whatever the reasons, this Auburn defeat was tough to take. Paul Bryant had lorded it over the Tigers for far too long. Surely, *surely*, Auburn would get a chance to beat him one last time before he shuffled off to the old coaches' home and not let him escape the fate that Shug Jordan had suffered, losing in his last Game. Pat Dye had brought great hope to Auburn with his tough talk and tougher actions, but here we were, 5–6 again.

We couldn't know what great times were ahead, but maybe we should have seen them coming. The Tigers had not backed down before Bryant's onslaught of the record. Auburn had acquitted itself well, earning the respect of those who had tuned in idly to watch a historic but dull blowout.

Dye had fire in his eyes, lacking only the means with which to blaze a trail across the face of the Southeastern Conference and the nation. Those days were coming, but in the dark December of 1981, watching the hated UAT masses whoop it up in Legion Field, they looked a long way off. How could we have known that the fuel for that fire was waiting for us, just a few miles down the road in Bessemer?

Darkness before the dawn, indeed.—W.C.

1982

THE END . . . AND THE BEGINNING

AS THE EMOTION OF Bryant's 315th victory died down, a sixty-eight-year-old legend began to crumble. Stories began to circulate about discipline problems in Tuscaloosa and players running wild. The Old Man, the stories said, was out of touch. He had reached his mountaintop, and he was content to let his assistants run the show.

Still, the Bear was not without his bite. The recruiting year yielded, among others, two of his finest linemen ever in Jon Hand and Wes Neighbors. But this had not been a typical year for Alabama on the recruiting field. For years the Tide had been living on its reputation and prestige. After the national attention accorded Bryant in 1981, the Bear and his assistants acted as if they needed only to drop their nets and wait for the prize fish to jump in. The pitch was simple: We are Alabama. Sign with us and we will allow you to share in our glory. But we will win with you, or we will win without you. The technique had been successful for many years. This time, the approach cost them one of the biggest catches of all time.

The 1982 recruiting season was the most hotly contested in many years, perhaps the most competitive since Bryant began his great run of 1971–79. Pat Dye and his young staff hit the road and began to out-Bear the Bear. They went into the farmhouses and the projects, the fields and the high schools. They met with the parents, and they offered the players a very different message. Come to us and together we will build a dynasty. If you have the talent and the guts and the will, you stand an even chance of starting, not in two or three years, but maybe in just a few *months*. The Old Man won't be there forever, they whispered. In 1983, the state's mandatory retirement laws will kick in. Come to Auburn, Dye told them. It won't be easy, but I'm gonna be here for a long, long time. He looked them in the eyes and told them he was going to win. And a lot of them believed.

Of that freshman class, many names would blaze across the Auburn sky and some would go on to greatness in the NFL: Tommy Powell, Tommie Agee, Steve Wallace, Ron Middleton. The most highly recruited of them all, a running back from Enterprise named Alan Evans, washed out in two years. If Auburn had needed to make a choice, if it could only sign one running back that year, Auburn would have taken Evans and let another player, unheralded by the press and the recruiters, find some other school to play football. And baseball. And run track. And win the Heisman Trophy.

Virtually unknown outside of Alabama, this player was a quiet, stuttering boy from a rough neighborhood just thirty miles east of Tuscaloosa. His name was Vincent "Bo" Jackson, and he made only one official visit—to Auburn. Bear Bryant did not bother to visit Jackson personally. Assistant coach Ken Donahue recruited Jackson, and he gave Bo the standard Alabama pitch. He told Bo that if he were lucky, he might be able to play by his junior year. Donahue knew that Dye was recruiting Jackson heavily, and he warned that if the young man went to Auburn, if he had the temerity to deny the siren song of the Capstone, then he would never beat Alabama. Bo would never go to the Sugar Bowl. He would be forgotten, even ridiculed for his stupidity, if he did not grasp the opportunity being granted to him by the mighty Crimson Tide. Donahue's critical mistake was to tell Bo Jackson that Bo couldn't do something. Bo signed with Auburn.

WHEN THE 1982 season began, most of the national and state sports pundits picked Alabama to win the conference. Some said that the Tide was the favorite to win another national championship. Alabama was deep and talent rich, returning many of the players who had won nine games in 1981, including Walter Lewis, Joey Jones, Doug Vickers, Jeremiah Castille, and Tommy Wilcox. The schedule was favorable, with the toughest test likely to come from Penn State midway through the season. Riding the crest of

Bryant's image and aura, Bama fans expected great things from the 1982 edition of the Crimson Tide.

A couple of hours down the road in Auburn, the faithful had more modest hopes, but Tiger fans were imbued with a new spirit the likes of which had been missing since 1974. Pat Dye had spent the offseason traversing the state on the alumni and booster club circuit, preaching the gospel of his young, tough team and his lofty ambitions for the future. Dye was a commanding presence in those early appearances, rarely speaking above a whisper but radiating an air of rugged country-boy surety that stirred the blood of long-suffering Auburn fans. They looked at each other and said to themselves that this man looked like a winner, he talked like a winner, and he acted like a winner. Optimism has never been in short supply at Auburn, but Dye was adding something that Auburn had been sorely lacking: confidence.

Alabama opened the season with a 45–7 demolishing of Georgia Tech, avenging the previous year's upset. Ole Miss fell next, 42–14, in Jackson, then Vanderbilt put up a valiant struggle before losing in Tuscaloosa, 24–21. Arkansas State was walloped, 34–7, setting up a huge clash with Penn State in Legion Field. That game ended as a 42–21 Tide shellacking of the eventual national champion Nittany Lions. Bama was ranked number two in the nation and looked unstoppable. Talk of Bear Bryant's "best team ever" permeated the local and national press, and a trip to the Sugar Bowl seemed a foregone conclusion.

Still, some wondered if this version of the Tide was worthy of its hype. Their suspicions were confirmed when Johnny Majors and Tennessee broke an eleven-year drought by beating the Tide, 35–28, in Birmingham on the Third Saturday in October. Two lackluster wins against weak Cincinnati (21–3) and Mississippi State (20–12) barely served to allay the concerns of Tide fans. Then, in two disastrous weeks, Alabama's invulnerability was shattered.

First, LSU mimicked Tennessee by avenging eleven straight losses with a 20–10 humbling of the Tide in Birmingham. Yet this embarrassing loss to an old conference foe was not as stunning to Alabama's morale as what came next. Southern Miss had been known forever as the place for players not quite good enough for Auburn or Alabama, a scrappy team that couldn't quite put it all together when it counted. This time, however, tough little Southern Miss came to Bryant-Denny Stadium and handed the Tide its once-proud head in a 38–29 game that wasn't as close as the score indicated. Prior to that day, Alabama had won fifty-seven straight in Tuscaloosa. The Bama backers were beside themselves.

AUBURN'S SEASON followed the same ups and downs as Bama's, but the atti-
tude of the faithful was exactly opposite that of their counterparts. Auburn
opened with three wins, including victories over Wake Forest (28–10) and
Tennessee (21–14). But then the Tigers ran headlong into Mike Rozier and
Nebraska. Auburn was on the rise, but Dye's young players were overwhelmed by the talent and depth of the Cornhuskers. After holding
Nebraska to a 7–7 tie at halftime, the Tigers were blown out, 41–7, at home.
It was a sign of how far Auburn had come that the Tigers did not fold their
tents following the crushing defeat. The team rebounded to win three con-
secutive games: Kentucky (18–3), Georgia Tech (24–0), and Mississippi
State (35–17). The team faltered briefly on a road trip to Gainesville when
a controversial ruling on an onside kick led to a 19–17 loss to Florida.

After dispatching a punchless Rutgers for Homecoming, 30–7, the
Tigers faced their oldest foe, the top-ranked Georgia Bulldogs. It was one of
the most pivotal games in Auburn history, which is all the more remarkable
because Vince Dooley's Dawgs prevailed. Most observers had predicted a
repeat of the Nebraska debacle: Georgia still had Herschel Walker, the
most electrifying player in America. The Dawgs had only lost twice since
Walker had first set foot in Athens three years earlier. Behind the inspired
play of quarterback Randy Campbell, an unheralded redshirt junior, and
running back Lionel James, Auburn actually led at one point, 14–13, and
was driving toward the Georgia end zone when the clock ran out on a
19–14 Georgia victory.

It was a loss, but Auburn had come within a play or two of beating the
nation's top team in a toe-to-toe slugfest. The Tigers had not feared the Bulldogs, and Dye's players had entered the contest believing they were about to
knock off Dooley's troops. In another year, in another place, a heartbreaking loss such as this would have killed the spirit of a team. But this year, in
this place, something very special happened.

Dye would talk about it a week later in a speech to the Birmingham
Touchdown Club: "We'd just lost to Georgia and the kids are in the dress-
ing room dying. Tears are rolling down their faces and I'm trying to find the
right words to say. I walk into the dressing room and it's quiet and still and
I really don't have a talk ready for losing. Then, outside, there's 60,000
Auburn fans cheering, 'It's great to be an Auburn Tiger! It's great to be an
Auburn Tiger!'"

It had been a magic moment. Auburn had lost the biggest game yet of
the season, but the fans would not leave the stadium. They were not in
shock; they did not stand in mute disbelief. They stood in defiance and pride
and yelled out to the world that Auburn was back and would not be hum-

bled again. The team heard the fans and took strength from their faith. It was the rarest of occasions in the emotional world of college football, a defeat that gave the losing side a new strength of commitment and hope. It was a loss in the record books, but the 1982 Georgia game might have been the most important contest of Pat Dye's career. Auburn had lost to Georgia, but the Tigers had vanquished a much mightier foe—their own despair.

AFTER THE loss to LSU, Bear Bryant said, "We need to make some changes, need to start at the top." The comment unleashed the greatest barrage of retirement rumors in Bryant's career. The only Bear that retired though was the complacent Bear. Bama's practices became more intense, as did the Bear. Citing a "lack of a winning attitude," he removed three players from the team. The Bear's growl was getting louder as the Game approached.

In Auburn, Dye thought that he had enough talent to beat Alabama if the first strings went head to head, but he knew that the Tigers' depth chart didn't compare to the Tide's. With Lionel James and Bo Jackson being his only productive running backs and knowing how difficult it is for a wishbone team to come from behind to win, Dye decided to throw a new wrinkle into his offense. Auburn practices were not only closed but moved to "The Bubble," AU's indoor practice facility. Once inside, Dye and offensive coordinator Jack Crowe installed the I-formation, intending to surprise Bryant and his staff and as an insurance policy in case one of the halfbacks was injured. Still smarting from the could-have-been loss to Georgia, Dye intended to walk into Legion Field loaded for, well, Bear.

On November 27, the Birmingham sky was a leaden gray, but as the fans poured into Legion Field and the players began to warm up on the worn AstroTurf, the spirits of both sides were undampened by the dreary atmosphere. For this Game, which looked to be more competitive than any in years, the demeanor of the fans for both sides was noticeably changed from years past. The Alabama partisans were as confident as ever. After nine consecutive victories, it was hard to believe they could ever again lose to Auburn. But there was an edge of nervousness that hadn't been present in a while. The loss to Southern Miss still had them rattled, and Auburn's strong season had them worried.

On the Auburn side, the hope was still there, but this time it was augmented by the moral victory of the Georgia game and the knowledge that Alabama was no Goliath this season. The faithful shared a deep feeling that this, at long last, would be the year. But a fear gnawed at them, suspecting that somehow Alabama would find a way to dash their hopes once again.

Alabama was designated the home team. The Tide took the field first in their accustomed style, Bryant walking at his usual slow pace, checking the crowd and eyeing the other sideline. Auburn came onto the field at a higher pace. As Dye jogged with his team to the visitor's sideline, the look in his eyes caused ABC's Keith Jackson to note, "I get the feeling today that Paul Bryant is more worried about Pat Dye than Pat Dye is worried about Paul Bryant."

Auburn won the toss and, after the deafening roar of the kickoff, took the ball on its own 20. After three running plays by James and Jackson, the Tigers fell inches short of a first down and punted. Bama moved the ball fairly well, mixing runs and passes well, but their first drive bogged down at the Tiger 42, and they kicked it away.

The Tiger offense found the running tough going. Bama's defense, led by linebacker Eddie Lowe, was swarming ball carriers and holding the line of scrimmage. Auburn's initial first down came on a twenty-yard pass from Randy Campbell to Chris Woods, and rugged running from Campbell and Jackson brought the Tigers to a fourth-and-inches situation at the Auburn 49.

It was Dye's first major decision of the Game, and he felt that he needed a show of strength early to spark his struggling young offense. He called for a quarterback sneak, but Alabama rose to the occasion and stopped Campbell short of the first down. The Tigers appeared to lose a little confidence, but not much. Every player knew how Auburn had squandered its opportunities the previous year.

Bama took over and marched down the field with precision and power. Following a short gain, Bryant called for a reverse. The Tigers covered the play, but Joey Jones accelerated and made the first down at the Auburn 34. Three plays later the Bear called Jones's number again for one of the most spectacular plays of the Game. Walter Lewis found Jones running along the back of the end zone just to the right of the goalposts. The pass was high, but Jones leaped, grabbed the ball, and, with the instincts of a great receiver, dragged his leg just enough to be in bounds. An official was on top of the play and Bama was ahead, 7–0.

The Tiger offense faltered and relinquished the ball to a very confident Tide, which rolled to the Auburn 30. In one of the most fortuitous plays in Auburn football history, Bama's Joe Carter carried the ball to the left side of the line for what looked like a big gain; that is, until Auburn's Mark Dorminey hit him, knocking the football up and into the hands of surprised cornerback Tim Drinkard. There were no red shirts anywhere near the Auburn senior, and he ran for the opposite end zone as the Tiger faithful went berserk. Drinkard's athletic gifts did not include blazing speed, and Walter Lewis was able to pull Drinkard down after a sixty-two-yard return to the Bama 14.

Auburn's offense gained nothing on two plays, and it looked like the most the Tigers could hope for would be a field goal. On third and ten, however, James broke through the right side and headed for the goal line. On paper there was no way for a five-seven, 170-pound halfback like James to get past Bama's great Jeremiah Castille, but he did. Al Del Greco added the extra point, and the Game was tied.

For Alabama's next series, the Bear changed to Ken Coley at quarterback but stayed with the running game. After a long drive, all on the ground, the Tide found themselves with a fourth-and-inches situation of their own. Bryant chose to try for the first rather than take the field goal. Auburn held but could not capitalize on the good defensive play and gave the ball up after three snaps. The Tide regained possession on their own 16.

Bryant reinserted Walter Lewis as quarterback, and he moved the ball quickly to the Auburn 22 on two pass plays. The drive stalled, however, and Peter Kim successfully kicked a field goal. Alabama led again, 10–7. The

Randy Campbell (14) ran the Auburn wishbone to perfection.

Tide had fallen short of the end zone, but they were moving the ball easily between the 20-yard lines.

On its next possession, Auburn's offense appeared in the new I-formation. It was good enough for a first down, but that was all. Alabama took over on offense at its own 27. On the second play of the drive, Lewis was hit just as he released the ball. According to announcer Keith Jackson, the pass "just came fluttering out there like an old lame-legged turkey," right into the arms of Auburn's Bob Harris at the Alabama 25, who returned it to the 23.

The Tigers' offense took over, making it interesting on first down, with a near interception. On the next play, Campbell hit split end Mike Edwards in the numbers for a fourteen-yard gain to the nine. James scrambled for six more. Fullback Ron O'Neil carried to the two. On third down, Campbell found daylight and backed into the end zone. Del Greco added the point after, and Auburn led, 14–10, with just less than three minutes to go in the half.

On the Alabama side, Bryant and his staff were probably asking themselves just what the hell was going on. By the numbers, Alabama was blowing Auburn off the field, running and passing the ball with great success, and stuffing Auburn's vaunted running game for less than a hundred yards in the first half. By rights, the Tide should have been leading by at least a couple of touchdowns. But there it was on the decrepit Legion Field scoreboard, Auburn leading by four and gaining confidence with every play.

Alabama again switched quarterbacks. Coley ran the offense well, but the half was running out. Depending on one's perspective, Bama was either punishing the Tigers with a very physical style of football by keeping the ball on the ground or foolishly wasting the remaining time before the half. Whatever their intent, Coley ran the wishbone effectively and threw two short passes to move the ball to the Auburn 40.

With nineteen seconds remaining, Bryant pulled Coley and reinstalled Lewis. His quarterback promptly found Daryl White at the 15 but never saw a wide-open Jesse Bendross in the end zone. With no time-outs and only a few seconds on the clock, Kim converted the short field goal to cut Auburn's intermission lead to 14–13.

WHEN DYE reviewed the halftime statistics, he saw that his team had managed only four first downs to Alabama's fourteen and had gained a paltry 99 yards of combined offense compared to Bama's 284. Bryant more likely saw red as he looked over those same figures. His team was playing well enough to win easily, but the Tide's offensive mistakes had given Auburn all its scoring opportunities. Whatever the Bear said at the half must have taken hold, because his team came out roaring in the third quarter and completely dominated Auburn.

Walter Lewis performed brilliantly in the third period. The Tide's initial series was a textbook example of Alabama power football, with the only unsuccessful play coming on a reverse flea flicker screen that gained two yards. For the remainder of the possession, Alabama continued a straight-up running attack and high-percentage short passes. The drive culminated with a toss sweep to Paul Ott Carruth from the Auburn 10, and Bama was in the lead again. It looked easy. Bryant consulted his famous roll of game-preparation papers and called for a two-point conversion. Like the rest of the Alabama drive, it looked like the perfect play, but Carruth slipped and couldn't hold on to Lewis's pass. The score remained 19–14, Alabama.

Auburn's first possession of the second half began on its 20. The offense ran from the I-formation with Bo Jackson at fullback. The freshman took the ball for nine yards on the first snap. James followed with another nine-yard run for a new set of downs. The two runs were a sign of things to come for Auburn, but the Alabama defense stiffened and forced a punt, although the Tide went on offense at its own five-yard line.

After some tough inside running from Ricky Moore and a typically spectacular Joey Jones catch for a forty-yard gain, Alabama faced another fourth-and-inches situation at its own 49. Reaching into his bag of tricks, Bryant sent Lewis in to punt, but he then jogged forward to the line of scrimmage to take the snap. Unnerved by this, Auburn's defense jumped offsides and gave Bama a free first down. Coley came in to spell Lewis, shifted the formation, and ran for a first down at the Auburn 35. Two plays later, Coley tried to take the option left, found nothing, reversed his field, and darted for another first down at the 20. After a delay-of-game penalty, halfback Joe Carter and fullback Ricky Moore powered the ball to the five. On third-and-goal, Coley was stopped just short of the end zone. Bryant chose to kick the field goal instead of try to punch the ball in. It looked like a reasonable decision—three easy points. The kick was good, but Auburn was flagged for an offsides penalty. The Bear chose not to take the points off the scoreboard. The tally was now 22–14 and things looked grim for Auburn.

Before the end of the quarter, Auburn began to march forward on the running of Jackson and James. Three plays later the quarter ended for the exultant Tide and the weary Tigers. The familiar four fingers were raised into the air as the teams switched sides, and the Auburn crowd held its breath in nervous anticipation. This was it. The last chance for another year. The fire of hope still flickered within them, but how many times had they felt that before, only to see it snuffed out by Bryant's fourth-quarter magic? Yet the feeling from the beginning of the Game was still alive. Something could still happen. *Anything* could happen.

The Alabama side breathed a sigh of relief and anticipation. Finally, the fourth quarter began and Auburn wasn't even close. Sensing that fatigue was beginning to set in on the other side, the Tide expected to wear the Tigers out. With Auburn down by slightly more than a touchdown and having little offensive consistency to show for the afternoon, the Game looked out of reach. Bama was now playing to form. The Southern Miss debacle was a faint memory.

The beginning of the fourth quarter looked a lot like the third for Auburn, with the Tigers' most effective weapon being their punter, Alan Bollinger, who kept Alabama deep in its side of the field. Through three quarters, Alabama had gained 221 yards on the ground and 219 through the air; Auburn had managed only 132 yards total offense.

Coley took over for Alabama at the 12, and behind his running and that of Linnie Patrick, it looked like the kind of clock-killing drive that would end the final period quickly. But the Auburn defense finally stiffened, and Bama had to punt with 11:23 left.

Auburn came back out in the wishbone. After a short gain by James, Auburn finally found the break it had been looking for all day. Jackson slipped through the line, broke a tackle, and ran to the Tide 13 before he was pushed out of bounds by Jeremiah Castille and Tommy Wilcox. Fullback Greg Pratt powered the ball to the nine. On third down, Campbell took it to the five. Without hesitation, Dye called for the field goal. Del Greco drilled it, and Auburn closed the gap to five points, 22–17.

Following the kickoff, the Tide took over on its own 20. After an impressive Carruth run for a first down, the Tiger defense rose to the occasion. Lewis failed to connect with any receivers on two attempts, and Bama had to relinquish the ball.

Starting from its own 33 with 7:06 remaining, Auburn began a historic drive with Jackson taking an option toss for three yards. Campbell then threw a perfect pass to Chris Woods for a first down. James found a seam in the Alabama line and ducked through for four yards. On the next play, Dye tried a trick play of his own, but it backfired, drawing a five-yard penalty for illegal motion. On third and seven, Jackson rumbled through the line for what looked like a first down, but the ball was spotted just inside the first-down marker. Dye had no choice. With 5:16 left to play, the Tigers had to go for it. Jackson hurdled over the line for the desperately needed first down. On the next play, he managed another four yards. On second down, Campbell was sacked. On third and fourteen, the Auburn quarterback rifled a perfect spiral to Mike Edwards on the sideline at the Alabama 31. It was just enough for the first down. The clock showed only 3:31 left to play.

By this time, the spectators were on their feet for good. This was getting too close for comfort for Alabama, too good to be true for Auburn. After missing Edwards on a first-down pass, Campbell threw over the middle for Chris Woods, who was being covered by the All-American Jeremiah Castille. At the last possible moment, Castille crossed in front of Woods, shoving the Auburn player out of the way and intercepting the pass at the nine-yard line. He returned the ball to the 28. It looked as if the old Bear magic had done its work again. Auburn had fought the good fight to fall short at the hands of the Tide. But Castille was flagged for interference.

At that time, defensive interference meant the offense received the ball and a first down at the spot of the foul. Castille's game-winning pick suddenly turned into a game-winning opportunity for Auburn. There were still nine yards to go, however.

Auburn jumped offsides on first down. Facing first and fourteen, Campbell threw for Woods in the corner of the end zone. Castille's coverage was perfect, however, and the pass sailed out of bounds. On the next play, Jackson took the ball to the nine. The Tigers were back where they had started. Facing third down, they were down to two plays.

Campbell dropped back as Jackson broke through the line to the five, wide open. Campbell threw him the ball, and Bo turned toward the end zone. He saw Bama's Castille and Wilcox, the two best players on the Tide defense, running toward him at the goal line. Instead of trying to power through the two All-Americans, Bo did what he is wont to do—something incredible. Just before being tackled between the oncoming defenders, he leaped. Castille and Wilcox ran into each other with jarring force. Bo somersaulted over them and fell on his back at the goal line. The ball crossed the line, but not before his right shoulder touched down a foot short of the end zone. Fourth and goal, 2:30 left to play.

Wilcox had been shaken up by the collision with Castille, and the officials called a time-out to get him off the field. The Bear watched the scene with concern. His team had played far too well to be this close to a loss. While he looked for answers, Dye became more animated on the Auburn sideline. This was the opportunity he had been seeking his entire life, a chance to vault into the ranks of major college coaches, a chance to see a team that he had built from the ground up win a big one, a chance to beat the Bear at his own game.

Dye summoned Jackson once more, calling a play that had not failed the Tigers all season. Jackson took the ball and hurled himself, twisting in the air, over center. He stretched out, extended the football, and fell toward the pile of linemen. The stretch was just enough, the ball barely but clearly in the end zone—touchdown. The play was called Number 43, but the Auburn offense had a more appropriate name, one that would be etched into the collective memory of the Tiger faithful forever after. They knew it as Bo Over the Top. The score set off a roar and a celebration as intense as any ever seen in this storied rivalry.

The Auburn fans and players went crazy. They jumped up and down, they high-fived each other, they hugged each other, they screamed and hollered, and they watched Bama's Russ Wood stop Campbell well short on the two-point conversion. Now they held their breath, because the Tide would be getting the ball back with plenty of time on the clock to come back. The score was 23–22 in Auburn's favor, but Bama still had almost two and a half minutes.

Lewis stepped in and fired a bullet toward Bendross that fell incomplete. Moore ran for four yards and left the Game injured. Lewis then hit Bendross in the numbers, but his receiver couldn't hold on to it. On fourth down and desperate, Lewis threw again, but his pass fell like a wounded duck into Bob Harris's hands, his second interception of the Game. Harris fell to the turf and cradled the ball under his body. The Auburn faithful exploded, their anxiety giving way to jubilation. Dye was swarmed by his delirious players. With 1:45 left, all Auburn had to do was hold on to the ball through Alabama's time-outs, and it would all be over.

James ran for five yards, and Bama used its first time-out. With 1:26 remaining, James took the ball again and managed four more yards. The second Tide time-out was expended at 1:13. Dye called for Bo Over the Top once more for the first down to seal the win. He said, "Tell Bo to squeeze the ball!" Like an instant replay, Jackson vaulted over the top. Unlike an instant replay, he held the ball out, away from his body, and it came down on the helmet of an Alabama defender. Russ Wood fell on the fumbled ball at the Alabama 21, and the mighty mojo of the Bear struck fear into Auburn hearts once again.

Bryant sent Lewis in with a simple mandate. We've got 1:09 to get in field goal range. Get there, and get there fast. Lewis responded with a fifteen-yard strike to Bendross at the Bama 47. He followed that with an eleven-yard completion to Bendross. With forty-six seconds left to play, Lewis rolled out, looking for Bendross once more, but the pass went incomplete. Thirty-five seconds remained on the clock. Lewis faced a heavy pass rush and grounded the ball. The penalty cost Alabama ten precious yards and a loss of down. Lewis was pressured again and nearly sacked on third

AUBURN UNIVERSITY PHOTOGRAPHIC SERVICES

His name was Bo Jackson, and he introduced the Iron Bowl to one of the most famous plays in Auburn football history—Bo Over the Top.

down, but he dumped the ball off to Craig Turner for a short gain. Twenty seconds left. On fourth down from the Alabama 30, under pressure again for the last time, Lewis tried desperately to find an open receiver. As he went down, he lobbed a wobbly pass in the direction of Turner, but the receiver was nowhere near the ball, which fell incomplete.

The Tiger side of the field became a wall of noise, about nine years' worth. Dye struggled to maintain his composure as he sent his offense onto the field to take a knee. There were tears in his eyes, tears of joy as the monumental meaning of the victory to Auburn sank in, tears of sadness for his former teacher, who looked at the scoreboard like a man who'd lost a child. Campbell took the snap, crumpled to the ground, and the clock ran unheeded.

The teams came out to the center of the field for the traditional handshakes, and the Auburn fans stormed onto the turf, swarming around the goalposts at the south end zone. The coaches embraced, their words to each other lost in the roar. As they went to the locker rooms, the goalpost fell under the weight of delirious Auburn students and fans, just as the Tide had fallen at long last to the Tigers. A huge chunk of the hated Legion Field AstroTurf was ripped up and parceled out for souvenirs. The Alabama fans left quietly, somberly, many in disbelief. The Tiger fans had no intention of leaving. As it turned out, neither did the players.

Bear Bryant rarely allowed television cameras into his locker room and certainly never showed his postgame talk to the team on his Sunday play-back show, but Pat Dye did. The footage from that locker room is some of the most stirring ever shown on *The Auburn Football Review*. Aired without commentary, the images from that afternoon show the coach and his play-ers embracing, yelling, weeping with joy in the immediate aftermath. When they were all together and the doors were closed, the Tigers knelt for an emotional prayer. After it was over, Dye called for silence and made a stir-ring request to his team. The scene is electric, even many years later. It still raises goose bumps on those who bleed orange and blue as Dye stands, points at the door to the field, and says, "What I'd like for you to do, I'd like for you, the ones that want to, I'm gonna go back out there, and thank our people." The sound of the players' response alone makes you want to strap on the pads and play football.

They poured back out onto the field and stayed there for nearly an hour, celebrating with the raucous fans. Some questioned if Dye were rub-bing it in by returning to the field. In his own words, "I didn't send our play-ers back on the field, and I didn't go out there myself to put on a big show, or anything like that. I wanted our players to get the true feelings and emo-tions of winning a big, big football game. It's going to come down to having to win one like that to win a national championship one of these days." On that day, Dye received the highest compliment that Auburn could bestow on somebody who had attended another school. They proclaimed him an Auburn man, now and forever.

Auburn went on to win in the Tangerine Bowl, beating Boston Col-lege, 33–26, in a game that featured two future Heisman Trophy winners, Bo Jackson and Doug Flutie. Alabama went to the Liberty Bowl and defeated Illinois, 21–15, in a game that would have been relatively meaningless, except for one small detail.

NOBODY WILL ever know if the loss to Auburn in 1982 caused Paul Bryant to announce his retirement two weeks later. Pat Dye, who was as close as an Auburn coach could possibly be to the Bear, believed that Bryant had made the decision halfway through the season when he lost then-recruit Ben Tam-burello to Dye (Tamburello had visited Tuscaloosa over the weekend of the embarrassing Tide loss to Southern Miss, and the Bear was not in a charming mood, barely acknowledging the prospect's presence). He stepped down on December 15 and named Ray Perkins, a former Alabama player and future head coach of the New York Giants, to take his place. Bryant's words were typically direct and humble: "There comes a time in every profession when you need to hang it up, and that time has come for me as head football coach at the University of Alabama. . . . This is my school, my alma mater, and I love it. And I love the players, but in my opinion they deserve better coaching than they've been getting from me this year, and my stepping down is an effort to see that they get better coaching from someone else."

At the time Bryant said his health was not an issue. Dye noted on the day of the announcement that the Bear "looked as good as I've seen him in a long, long time." Perhaps they both meant it, perhaps not, but they were both proven wrong on January 28, 1983. Just as he had once jokingly predicted, Bear Bryant died from a massive heart attack in Tuscaloosa within a month of his retiring from coaching.

The outpouring of grief was astounding. Alabama fans and many Auburn people as well lined the overpasses along the interstate to pay their last respects as the funeral procession made its way from Tuscaloosa to a quiet suburban cemetery in Birmingham. Regular traffic on I-59 pulled off to the side of the road to salute the Bear's final journey. By written estimates, more than half a million people attended the funeral service or viewed the motorcade. After twenty-five years, the Bryant era at Alabama was over and the future was uncertain for all concerned. Bama fans wondered how their beloved team would go on without the Old Man. Auburn folks wondered how things would change now that the big bad Bear was gone.

For better or for worse, everything was different in 1983.

ROLL TIDE

Can You Get Sweet Tea in Canada?

CONVENTIONAL WISDOM claims that time heals all wounds. Not so. I still find the memory of the 1982 Iron Bowl as unpalatable as I did when the final seconds ticked off the clock on that overcast November afternoon. Ah, 1982, how do I hate thee? Let me count the ways.

First, I hate looking back on this game because of the effect it had on the coaches involved. It meant that Bear Bryant would close out his career with a loss to Auburn and a trip to the Liberty Bowl. Hardly a fitting farewell for the man who molded the sport of football in the state of Alabama. Pat Dye would begin a long tradition of acting childishly in the face of success, in this case sending his players back out on the field to "thank ahhh people."

He even dropped hints that Auburn would win a national championship under his guidance. Pretty big talk for a coach whose team had lost to Nebraska by 34 points at home.

Second, 1982 is unsavory to me because of the way some Auburn fans acted afterward at Legion Field, yelling and running like they were about to loot a tractor store. The allure of tearing up a patch of artificial turf is far beyond me. Tearing down goalposts is not only pointless and stupid, it's also dangerous, as has been proven on numerous campuses throughout the country. Besides, what do you do with goalposts once you've taken them down? Cover them with the artificial turf and call the thing a Christmas tree?

Another burr in my saddle is the fact that Alabama could have had this Game wrapped up by halftime. Apart from the earlier thrashing of eventual national champ Penn State on the same field, this was the most impressive showing by the Tide all year. Two plays were the difference in the game: the first-half fumble return and Bo Jackson's long run early in the fourth quarter. Without the return, on which the most impressive effort was Walter Lewis's touchdown-saving tackle, Bo's heroics would have been meaningless. As Florida's Errict Rhett would say after a similarly miraculous upset years later, "I'm still trying to figure out what happened."

Most unbearable of all is the memory of having to face all those born-again Auburn fans for the next 365 days. How far would Bama people have to go to be out of earshot? A couple of time zones? Mexico? The moon? Hey, Canada's got a football league; that'll work. Tiger folks were every bit as awful as I knew they'd be, and it only got worse a few weeks later when they began patting themselves on the back for "forcing" Bear Bryant into retirement. It was the perfect opportunity for even the more docile among their ranks to stick out their chests and raise their voices. Throw in those walking megaphones that characterize the Auburn "spirit," and you're talking about a traumatic experience for a young Bama fan with no previous recollection of defeat in the Iron Bowl.

No other Game covered in this book will ever come close to matching this one in terms of sheer pain and frustration for Bama fans. The images of a diving Bo Jackson and that of Bear Bryant walking off Legion Field for the final time just bring back too much misery to handle. Time, I promise you, has done nothing to change that.—S.B.

WAR EAGLE

One Second and Forever

I AM OFTEN asked, "Why pay the money and go to the trouble of going to a football game when you can just stay at home and watch it on television?" Before I answer, I think about this Game.

In 1982, I was fourteen years old and had attended every Game since 1975. In all of those contests, Auburn had not been closer than seven points to Alabama in the final score. Every time I had walked into Legion Field believing that this would be "next year," and every time I had walked out with the nauseating sounds of Alabama celebrations echoing in my ears for another twelve months.

Today I can watch the aging videotape of this Game and get excited in the fourth quarter, even though I've probably seen it a hundred times. I can watch the Auburn highlight film or the tape of the Dye show and revel and remember. The sight of the fans' reactions, carrying Randy Campbell like a war hero, passing Lionel James like an ecstatic doll above their heads, the sight of Bo Jackson and his mother embracing in tears. If you can watch that and not be moved, you're either dead or an Alabama fan or both.

For all their power, the two-dimensional images of that Game are but a poor reflection of the glorious reality of November 27, 1982. For me and so many others it validated some very old Auburn beliefs. It was proof that faith, loyalty, hope, and love do, in the end, conquer all. It was proof that if you work hard enough, if you believe hard enough, if you hang in there and go the distance, the long road will lead you to the promised land. It was proof that the tide can turn.

What do I remember about 1982? I remember my dad trying to find a way to tell me that we were going to lose, when things looked bad in the third quarter. I remember my emotional rejection of his comfort. I remember running out onto the field when it was over, joining the delirious students and fans and eventually the players, all of us transported by the joy of the moment. I remember getting a chunk of ratty Legion Field AstroTurf from an older kid who was tearing it up with a pocketknife. I remember waiting in front of the stadium to buy a bumper sticker with the score.

I remember the look on the face of my grandfather, Baxter Collier, who was every bit as excited as I was. It was my first time to see Auburn win the Game. It was his last. When I think about 1982, I will always be most thankful that it happened before he died and that he could be there to experience it.

Nineteen eighty-two was everything that we hoped for and more. This time the old Alabama luck wasn't enough, and that made it sweet. The sweetest memory, however, was that the Bear would retire and never coach an Alabama team over the Tigers again. The Bryant record ended with a loss to Auburn, and that was history.

When the Bear died a month later, we mourned his passing, too. All of our posturing and braggadocio aside, this is just a football game. That doesn't forgive the Bear for the torment he put Auburn through during his twenty-five years in Tuscaloosa. Tiger fans respected Bryant as an opponent, only a fool wouldn't, but we weren't ever fond of the man. As an Auburn man, I can't forgive him for a lifetime of lambasting my alma mater.

The emotion in Legion Field on that damp, cloudy, wonderful day was like a living thing that flowed around us and lifted the team and the fans above the overcast and into the sunshine. There would be no more grousing about "next year" for us. Next year was here.

There will probably never be another Game like this one. Even the championships and tremendous victories on our home soil in the years to come didn't achieve the emotional heights we all felt in 1982. It's somehow fitting that this was an event never to be repeated, because this game was a new beginning. As the last seconds ticked away on November 27, the bright sun of success was beginning to dawn over Auburn. Indeed, the last seconds never really ticked off the clock.

After Auburn's last play, Alabama called a time-out with six seconds left. That was close enough for the Auburn fans, who surged over the fence and onto the field to celebrate with their heroes and claim the spoils of victory. An official made his way to Bear Bryant and asked the old coach if he wanted to clear the field for another play. Bryant looked out at what had once been his undisputed domain and shook his head, deciding that it wasn't worth the trouble to postpone the inevitable. As the coaches made their way to the center of the field, the clock wound down to one second and stopped.

For so many of us who were there, for the ones who watched in their living rooms and dorms, for the faithful listening to their radios on the highways and at their military postings overseas, that last second has never really run off the grimy, barely functioning Legion Field scoreboard. Those last moments of glory and joy are still with us, and they will never pass away. They live in our hearts and memories as if they are still going on today. We will have 23–22 with us for as long as Auburn University exists. No loss, no hardship, no words or deeds can ever take it away from us.

It was Auburn's day, and we will have that last second forever. What could be sweeter?—W.C.

1983

INDIVIDUAL EFFORT

WERE IT NOT FOR the epochal coaching change in Tuscaloosa, 1983's preseason media attention would have been dominated by Auburn. The Tigers were the consensus preseason pick for the SEC title. *Playboy*'s Anson Mount picked Auburn to win the national championship, and Bo Jackson was beginning to turn heads on the national scene. It was a heady time for a team that had been playing under .500 football just two years earlier. The enthusiasm of the Auburn fans was scarcely dampened when the NCAA pronounced the 1983 Tiger schedule the toughest in the nation. The Tigers would face no less than eight 1982 bowl teams, the first five of which would have at least two weeks to prepare for Auburn.

On paper and on the field, it was easy to see how Auburn could rate such high hopes. Pat Dye and defensive coordinator Frank Orgel had four of the best down linemen in the long, powerful history of Auburn defense. Doug Smith, Donnie Humphrey, Ben Thomas, and Dowe Aughtman represented a fast and daunting challenge to any opponent, and Gregg Carr returned at defensive end. Of these five, all except Thomas had been named All-SEC at some point prior to the 1983 season. The secondary, however, was as young and inexperienced as any in the conference, but Vic Beasley, Tommy Powell, David King, and Jimmie Warren were all talented players, and Dye's defensive staff felt that they all could be up to speed in time for the season.

The offense was deep, talented, and experienced. On the offensive line, Pat Arrington, David Jordan, and Jeff Lott were all solid players, and Steve Wallace was All-SEC and on his way to starting four Super Bowls for the San Francisco 49ers. Ben Tamburello would start as a freshman. Ed West was touted as the best tight end in the conference, and the reliable Chris Woods returned for another season at wide receiver. But it was the wishbone backfield that formed the real heart of this Auburn team, and it was perhaps the best ever to play in the formation. Georgia's Herschel Walker had departed early for the short-lived USFL, making Bo Jackson the SEC's most prominent runner. With Lionel James at the other halfback, proven winner Randy Campbell at quarterback, and Greg Pratt returning at fullback, the Tiger running game looked unstoppable—until a dark day during preseason drills.

On August 20, the players were running through a series of diagnostic 440-yard sprints. The coaches noticed that Pratt was having trouble on his last lap. When the sprints were over, the big senior collapsed. He was quickly packed in ice by a frantic training staff, but he died of heat stroke before an ambulance arrived. The world of football was suddenly forgotten. Death and sudden loss had descended like a thunderbolt. There was nothing to explain it, nothing to ease the pain, only a numbing funeral and a quiet return to work. It was a long summer for Auburn.

RAY PERKINS settled into his new roles as Alabama's coach and athletic director with predictable resistance. During the last quarter century, Alabama football and Bear Bryant had become indistinguishable. Some state sportswriters publicly wondered how many of the Tide's huge following were Alabama fans and how many were Bryant fans. Perkins, to his credit, made no attempt to cling to the outward trappings of the Bryant era. He immediately laid down the law to his staff and his players, replacing Bryant stalwarts with his own assistants. He set his own standards about who went where and did what in the Alabama athletic department, shutting out many of the old guard. He had the Bear's famous tower removed from the Alabama practice field and consigned to a scrap yard. Perkins chose to follow Bryant in one important arena: he would stand or fall on his record, critics be damned. Unfortunately for Perkins and for every Alabama coach who would follow him, his record would be compared daily to Paul Bryant's.

Perkins's first team was similar to the Bear's last, with a couple of notable exceptions. Walter Lewis, Jessie Bendross, and Joey Jones returned

PAUL W. BRYANT MUSEUM

Ray Perkins accepted the head man's job at Alabama following the retirement of Bear Bryant.

for their senior season, forming a passing attack that demanded their opponents' respect. Linnie Patrick and Ricky Moore were back, joined by the first member of the "Goode dynasty" to play for the Tide, freshman Kerry Goode, at running back. Center Wes Neighbors would start for the first of four years, accompanied by the talented Doug Vickers, Mike Adcock, and Willard Scissum on the offensive front.

Much of Bryant's defense returned, including seniors Steve Booker, Randy Edwards, Mike Rodriguez, and Stan Gay, but the most significant defender would play his first set of downs for the Tide in 1983. Freshman Cornelius Bennett would have a huge impact on Alabama's fortunes for the next four years.

AUBURN'S SEASON finally began with Southern Miss at home, and the Tigers were more than ready, blowing out the Golden Eagles, 24–3. Then came one of the biggest games on the Auburn campus in years and one of Auburn's greatest disappointments. CBS and a national television audience followed the Texas Longhorns into Jordan-Hare Stadium. When it was over, Texas carried a 20–7 victory back to Austin, and Auburn had to lick its wounds and fly to Knoxville the next week. There the Tigers walked away with a rare big win in Knoxville, 37–14. Bobby Bowden came to Auburn with his Florida State Seminoles the next Saturday, and returned to Tallahassee in defeat, 27–24. Several years of high drama followed to color the Dye-Bowden rivalry.

The following weekend against Kentucky in Lexington, Auburn coasted to a 49–21 win. Kentucky was the last of five straight teams to have a week off before playing Auburn, but the Tigers themselves would not see an open date for another four weeks. Dye was worried about a letdown against Georgia Tech in Atlanta, but his team exploded in the second half for a 31–13 win. The Tigers followed up by smoking Mississippi State, 28–13, in a game that saw the scoring debut of freshman running back Brent Fullwood.

The MSU game was barely over before Dye and his players started talking about Florida. This game featured no less than fifty players who eventually signed pro contracts, and the Gators came to Auburn looking for their first ever SEC championship. It was not to be. Bo Jackson ran for two touchdowns, including an eighty-yard run following a controversial Florida fumble, to lead Auburn to a 28–21 victory. Florida had been ranked fifth in the nation before the game, Auburn was the number four team. The Tigers would go on to face two more top-ten teams in the next two weeks, but now they had the confidence that they could play the nation's best and come out on top.

Auburn's Homecoming opponent was no patsy. The Maryland Terrapins were led by Boomer Esiason and were ranked seventh in the nation. Auburn, however, came up with another huge win, 35–23.

Athens was the site for Auburn's next duel with a top-five opponent, and there was plenty on the line. Georgia was undefeated, ranked fourth (Auburn had since moved up to number three), and this game would decide the SEC representative to the Sugar Bowl. The Dawgs seemed on the verge of buying permanent training space in New Orleans, having owned the SEC for three consecutive years. Friends and foes alike considered this *the* crucial game for Auburn. In an intense defensive battle, the Tigers prevailed, 13–7. As the sun set orange and blue over Sanford Stadium, Auburn clinched no less than a share of the SEC championship, but it would take a win in the Iron Bowl to claim the title outright.

ALABAMA OPENED the Ray Perkins era with a show of strength, beating Georgia Tech, 20–7. It was an important win for Perkins and his team. Although it had left the Southeastern Conference many years ago, Tech was still reviled by the old guards of Alabama and Auburn. Taking out the Yellow Jackets and Perkins's old friend and NFL teammate Bill Curry with ease set a comforting tone for the Tide faithful. Ole Miss had been a power of the conference in decades past, but in the 1980s they were more often than not a doormat, and Alabama coasted with a 40–0 thrashing. Vanderbilt has never been a power within the conference or anywhere else, so Tide fans were upset, to say the least, when the Commodores leaped out to a 17–0 lead in Nashville. But Alabama came back powerfully and won going away, 44–24. Memphis State visited Tuscaloosa the next week and was dispatched, 44–13, and the soft opening of Bama's 1983 schedule was over. The Tide was ranked fourth in the nation, and Ray Perkins was the toast of Tuscaloosa and Birmingham, but the real tests were still ahead.

The Tide traveled to Happy Valley to face Penn State, and Joe Paterno's Lions were gunning for revenge after the 42–21 humbling suffered in Legion Field the previous year. Alabama was ranked higher and a slight favorite this time around and looked the part in claiming an early 7–0 lead on an 80-yard drive. Penn State, the defending national champions, dominated the next two quarters, building a stunning and seemingly insurmountable 34–7 lead early in the fourth quarter.

Finally, senior Walter Lewis, playing on the field where he had helped Bear Bryant become a part of history in 1981, led Bama back from the dead, scoring three touchdowns to pull within six points, 34–28, and moving the Tide again to a first and goal at the Nittany Lion five-yard line. On third and goal, Lewis made a Herculean effort to avoid State's pass rush, spinning out of the defenders' grasp and firing desperately in the direction of tight end Preston Gothard at the back of the end zone. Replays would show that Gothard had both control of the ball and one foot in bounds, but the officials ruled it incomplete. Just as in 1982, when the Lions were awarded a dubious game-winning touchdown reception against Nebraska that allowed them to go on their championship run, the referees in 1983 supplied Paterno with some timely home cooking. Thus, rather than kicking an extra point for the lead, the Tide was faced with fourth and goal, and Kerry Goode was stacked up for a loss, ending Alabama's gallant attempt at a last-second comeback.

The ancient rites of the Third Saturday in October were played out next in Birmingham. Tennessee coach Johnny Majors had no intention of letting his 1982 victory over the Tide be a one-time only affair. Following Penn State's lead, the Volunteers exploited the Alabama defense. The Tide, despite scoring high and moving the ball well, limped out of Legion Field a 41–34 loser. The back-to-back losses eliminated Alabama as a national championship contender, and the single setback in the conference had greatly damaged the Tide's chances to win the conference (no team has ever won the SEC title with two losses). The defeats also evoked a barrage of criticism against Perkins. He was reviled by many fans and derided by sportswriters, apparently for committing the unforgivable sin of not being Bear Bryant. Most of the critics forgot or chose to ignore the fact that Bryant himself had failed to beat Tennessee the year before, with practically the same players.

The stoic Perkins soldiered on, and Alabama topped Mississippi State easily, 35–18. Bama then traveled to Cajun country for a game with LSU.

Tiger Stadium is considered one of the most inhospitable arenas in the SEC, but Alabama usually defies conventional wisdom in a series oddly dominated by the visiting team. It was close, and the Bengal Tigers had a chance to win late in the game, but Alabama escaped with a victory, 32–26. Southern Miss came to Tuscaloosa hoping for an unprecedented two consecutive wins over the Tide, but the Tide whipped the Golden Eagles, 28–16. Juggling the schedule to accommodate CBS coverage of the game, Perkins moved the season's penultimate match, a contest at Boston College, to the week before the Iron Bowl.

The weather in Foxboro, Massachusetts, was less than inviting for a Southeastern Conference team as snow, sleet, and freezing rain awaited the Tide. During the third period, a transformer blew, knocking out the power for the stadium, the scoreboard, and the telecast for the duration of the quarter. Doug Flutie, a year away from winning the Heisman Trophy, passed for 198 yards and a touchdown, a solid, but not exactly career-making performance. The game ended with a 20–13 BC victory. Alabama could still manage a tie for the conference title and earn a berth in the Sun Bowl, but none of these would save Perkins from the barbs of the critics during the pre-Game week.

FOLLOWING THE loss to Boston College, Perkins revealed to a surprised press corps (and a stunned Auburn coaching staff) that his team had practiced their Auburn game plan several times before flying to Massachusetts. This wasn't all that unusual. No Alabama coach had ever been fired for losing to Boston College, and Perkins knew which game should be his highest priority. The coach was cut from the whole cloth of Alabama football in his dedication to fierce recruiting, his insistence on intense preparation, and his deep-seated contempt for Auburn. While he had a studied presence before the media, there was something in Perkins's demeanor that suggested he was more than a little insulted by the suggestion that he was going to lose to Auburn, even a 9–1 Auburn. The Alabama head man also had notoriously thin skin. When asked in a pre-Game press conference whether or not his wife had questioned his coaching decisions, Perkins snapped, "Sure. Everybody else is going to. Why shouldn't she?"

Auburn had the luxury of a three-week layoff following the Georgia win, and the Tigers needed the rest. They had played all but one game of the nation's toughest schedule without an open date. The rigorous schedule, however, had generated a rhythm of preparation, execution, and confidence that the extra long lull threatened to break. Dye was concerned that his third-ranked Tigers would dismiss the Tide lightly.

In the meantime, the *New York Times* issued a computer-generated poll naming Auburn as the nation's top squad, in defiance of the national sportswriters who were falling over themselves to designate Nebraska as the greatest college football team of all time. The *Times* poll found that Nebraska's opponents averaged losing their games by 1.4 points, while Auburn's opponents were winning by more than a touchdown, giving additional credibility to the Tigers' hard-earned 9–1 record.

THE FORECAST for Saturday afternoon, December 3, was less than encouraging for a pass-oriented team. Heavy thunderstorms and a squall line had moved across Arkansas and Mississippi early in the day. Seven inches of rain had fallen on Legion Field during the high school state championship game the night before, but at kickoff time for the Game the sky was only partly cloudy, and the sun shone brilliantly onto the recently replaced AstroTurf of Legion Field.

This was a very different Game day. The Auburn fans were confident entering the stadium. They knew that they should win, that Auburn (at least on paper) was a better team than Alabama. For the first time in a long time, they thought they would not have to pin their hopes on a miracle or a bizarre play or to just hang in there until the fourth quarter. Auburn was riding high, and Bama didn't compare to three or four of the teams that the Tigers had already vanquished during the season.

Bama fans saw things differently. Luck had been the deciding factor in the previous Iron Bowl. The Tide had been just two plays from being undefeated. Hell, we're *supposed* to beat Auburn, they rationalized.

Alabama kicked off and Auburn's first drive, which was powerful on the ground and useless through the air, ended with no points—a bungled field goal attempt. But Cornelius Bennett and Bo Jackson had met. The Tide offense was even less effective with a three plays and out series. Neither side moved the ball well during the first quarter, and the wind wreaked havoc with both the passing and the kicking games. The only offensive threat occurred late in the quarter with Bama moving the ball to the Auburn 34, but the quarter ended and the teams exchanged sides.

At the start of the second quarter, Van Tiffin came out for his first Iron Bowl field goal attempt. It was short and wide right, and Auburn took over on the 29. On the Tigers' first play, Bo Jackson was given the ball and ran into a stack of linemen on the left side. He reversed direction and whirled around the right side to acres of open turf. Following key blocks from Randy Campbell and Chris Woods, Bo went all the way to the end zone. Two plays into the second quarter and it was Auburn, or maybe Bo, 7–0.

AUBURN UNIVERSITY PHOTOGRAPHIC SERVICES

Bo Jackson was making a habit of finding the Alabama end zone in his second Iron Bowl appearance.

The Bama offense responded with a textbook drive of pass-and-run football. An eighty-five-yard, eight-play drive, to be exact, culminating with a twenty-yard scoring toss from Walter Lewis to Joey Jones. It was classic Tide football with Jones darting toward the back line of the end zone and pulling down the pass with one foot in bounds. The Game was tied, 7–7.

The Tigers and Tide traded punts on two desultory series. On Auburn's third possession of the quarter, the Tigers kept the ball mostly on the ground and advanced from their 45 to the Alabama 10. Al Del Greco nailed a twenty-seven-yard chip shot, handing the lead back to Auburn, 10–7. Again the points were mostly thanks to the prowess of Jackson.

Jackson's performance also inspired the Tide's runners to match him. Beginning at its own 20, Bama took the ball and marched down the field. The Tide's running game functioned beautifully, picking up yardage in large and small chunks. Playing in the last minutes of the half, Perkins found the draw was his most effective play. When he did call for the pass, his quarter-back's nimble feet guaranteed that the Auburn defense had to cover both the Bama receivers and their quarterback. On the eighth play of the drive, it looked as if the Tigers had finally caught up with Lewis as he searched for an open man, but the senior tucked in the ball, dodged three tacklers, and darted downfield to the Auburn 14. Three plays later the Tide had a first and goal on the one-yard line. On the twelfth play of the drive, with fifty-one seconds left in the half, Lewis found Joe Carter open in the flat, and Bama took its first lead of the game, 14–10. This wasn't supposed to happen. Auburn down?

Trying to run out the clock, Auburn's Tommie Agee, spinning away from a tackle, was stripped of the football. Alabama recovered and magically had another chance to score before the half expired. Starting from the Auburn 35, Perkins called for two passes. One was broken up on a great play by Alvin Briggs, the other was short of the first down. With eight seconds left, Tiffin returned for a field goal attempt from the Auburn 26. His attempt was identical to his first try, wide right. The half ended with Campbell taking a knee.

As INTERMISSION began, heavy clouds blanketed the sky over Birmingham. Perkins took a phone call from one of his people still in Tuscaloosa. Extremely severe thunderstorms were currently pelting the UA campus; he could expect to see the storm hit Birmingham within the hour. The greatest opportunity would be early in the third quarter; after that, his quarterback would be lucky to see the nose guard through the sheets of rain.

Perkins had good reason to feel confident about the second half. Auburn had been contained, notwithstanding Jackson's one long run, and his offense was having one of its best games of the season, embarrassing the SEC's top defense with outside runs and opening up pass routes.

On the Auburn side, Dye was nonplused. He was first and foremost a coach of tough defense, and Alabama had just executed two impressive scoring drives against minimal resistance. The long layoff had dulled his defensive players. They were missing far too many tackles. Offensively, Campbell and his receivers had lost their timing. On the positive side, this wasn't the first time his team had been behind in a game that season. The talent and desire to come back were certainly there on offense, and they could win this game if his defensive line and linebackers could exert more pressure on the Tide's Lewis. Of course, Dye had the same weather reports as Perkins, and Lewis did not have a good reputation in bad weather. Even if Lewis did manage to overcome the elements, Dye knew that his wishbone running game was far more likely to be effective in a downpour than Bama's pro-style passing attack.

ALABAMA'S FIRST possession of the half ended after three plays and a punt. The Auburn offense accepted the ball at its own 25 and began to execute a seventy-five-yard, twelve-play scoring drive. Jackson and James carried the ball downfield, and Campbell connected with Woods on a twenty-one-yard completion, taking the ball to the Tide 24. The Bama defense stiffened, however, and Del Greco came out to nail the chip shot. The Tigers had moved the ball impressively on their opening possession, but Alabama still led, 14–13, with 7:11 left in the quarter.

The weather worsened and the stadium announcer, Carl Stephens, made one of the most memorable pronouncements in the history of this or any other series. The sellout crowd of seventy-eight thousand fans was informed that the National Weather Service had issued a tornado warning for Jefferson County. This was serious, since it indicates that a twister has been sighted in the area. For the first and probably only time in the history of the Iron Bowl, the partisans at the Game forgot about the contest on the field for a moment. Birmingham's Legion Field is a historic venue for football, but its steel construction does not inspire confidence in some situations, and a tornado is one of them. The upper deck, suspended in the air by slender girders, was already swaying slightly but noticeably in the strong winds. The idea of a whirlwind hitting the stadium was frightening, to say the least. Fortunately, the tornado blew itself out before getting near the arena and caused little damage. Still, nobody at the stadium knew that at the time. It says something about this rivalry that very few left Legion Field before the clock expired.

Meanwhile, Alabama took over at the 20. Lewis threw two incompletions, one to a wide open receiver and the other out of frustration in the face of a furious pass rush. On third down, Lewis was blind-sided by Gerald Robinson, who also stripped the ball loose. The faithful held their breath as the ball rolled out of bounds at the nine, and Alabama retained possession. The ensuing punt was a disaster. The ball was caught up in the oncoming storm winds and fell like a wounded duck at the Alabama 25.

The Game's momentum, which had been Alabama's in the first half, now belonged to Auburn. Despite prescient defensive play calling by Alabama, six plays later Del Greco came on the field to try a twenty-seven-yard field goal. He converted, and Auburn regained the lead, 16–14.

The subsequent Alabama possession lifted the Tide offense out of the doldrums into which it had fallen at halftime. Bama runners slowly worked the ball downfield in three plays, setting up the ball on their own 43-yard line. On a second-and-three play, Ricky Moore hit the line and blew past Auburn's blitzing linebackers. He rambled virtually untouched into the end zone, fifty-seven yards away. Perkins called for a two-point conversion. Lewis tried to pass into the end zone, but the ball fell incomplete, and the Tide led the Game, 20–16. Moore's sudden blast had shifted the Game's momentum again. Many on the Auburn side were wondering if all those field goals would cost them this Game.

In answer to the unstated question, a legend was born. Just as he had done earlier in the season in the Florida game, Bo Jackson answered the call for a badly needed big play.

On Auburn's first snap, Jackson cut through a hole on the left side and streaked down the sidelines, aided by timely blocking from Agee and Woods. Freddie Robinson was the only Tide player to lay a hand on Bo,

Ricky Moore (26) sprinted through the Auburn secondary pursued by Gregg Carr (54), showing that the Bama backs were not going to quietly surrender the field to Auburn's Bo Jackson.

diving at his feet, but Jackson kicked out of his grasp, turned on the speed, and was gone for a seventy-one-yard touchdown. In one blinding play, the Game had turned around again, negating Moore's heroics of only moments before. Adding the extra point, Auburn had trailed for only twenty seconds on the clock. The score was 23–20, and two minutes were left in the third quarter.

The two teams were giving the best they had to give. In answer to Jackson's electrifying/disheartening run, Alabama kept the ball on the ground and tried to piece together another march toward the Auburn goal. The first series of downs was converted entirely on the ground. For a moment, it looked as if the Tide had the answer to Jackson's run through some tough running of their own. Then Lewis fumbled the handoff on the fourth play of the drive, and the ball was cradled by Tiger Gregg Carr.

Auburn took over at the Alabama 24, but the Tigers failed to exploit the opportunity. They ran a disastrous reverse that lost thirteen yards as the Tide blitzed everyone and the quarter ended. As if on cue, the long-awaited rain began to drench the field, accompanied by a swirling wind. The Tigers kept the ball on the ground, but they came nowhere near the first-down marker. Again Del Greco came onto the field. And again the snap was mishandled and the opportunity lost. Auburn relinquished the ball at the Bama 33, and Alabama had dodged the bullet.

The Tide held onto the ball for five plays before having to punt it away to the Auburn 26. Then the bottom dropped out of the sky and the rain fell so hard that the stadium's upper deck was barely visible from the press box side of Legion Field.

Auburn's runners—Jackson, Agee, Campbell, and James—entered the downpour and carried the ball from their 26 to Alabama's 41 before the eight-play drive stalled. Water was gathering into huge puddles on the artificial surface. The Tigers lined up for a field goal attempt with 6:30 left on the clock, but Dye decided to punt instead. The ball bounced out of bounds perfectly at the Alabama five-yard line.

Ninety-five yards from the Tiger end zone, the look on Perkins's face could probably have killed anything within twenty yards. After two plays and a defensive penalty, the Tide gave the ball up on an interception. Auburn had the ball at the Alabama 11, but promptly fumbled it back to Bama at the seven-yard line with 5:04 left.

The rain dampened the Tide's chances as Lewis failed to complete a pass to a teammate for the rest of the game. From the seven-yard line, Bama made no offensive progress and had to kick the ball to Auburn, who took over at the Tide's 36-yard line. The field was submerged now, and the Tigers elected to keep the ball on the ground. Three plays later they faced a fourth-down situation. Dye recalled his mixed success with field goal snaps and decided to run a play on fourth and three from the Alabama 30. Those who considered Dye an overly conservative coach were shocked when Campbell faked to Jackson and dropped back to pass. His receiver, however, ran over a Tide defender, drawing an offensive pass interference penalty. The consequence was that Alabama had the football on the Auburn 44 with 2:26 left in the Game.

On the first play of the series, Lewis's pass was knocked to the ground. Goode carried on the next play for a first down. Lewis attempted to pass on the following play and threw the ball down the middle to Preston Gothard. Auburn's Tommy Powell, however, jumped in front of the receiver, knocking the ball out of Gothard's hands. It fell toward the flooded turf, surely an incomplete pass, but Vic Beasley dove down at the football and reeled in his second interception of the game. The rain was coming down harder, but no one on the Auburn side of Legion Field seemed to care. They were warmed to the bone by the knowledge that all they had to do was hold on

Auburn's Victor Beasley intercepted Walter Lewis to seal the 23–20 victory.

to the ball for a little less than two minutes and the SEC championship would be theirs alone.

The end was swift and merciful. There was some celebrating on the Auburn side before the fans left, but not much. They wouldn't feel their wet clothes for some time, but that didn't mean that they meant to stay out in the typhoon any longer than absolutely necessary.

The most memorable scene from the 1983 post-Game was not a set of goalposts being carried off, but of the Game's hero, Bo Jackson, lying in a puddle of water, waving his arms and legs in delight. He had come to Auburn with the promise of failure from an Alabama coach ringing in his ears, but after just two years he had proven that coach doubly wrong and led his own team to claim the championship of the nation's toughest conference. He had earned his playing time, gaining an incredible 256 yards on 20 carries. Yet when asked later about his Heisman prospects, Jackson refused to talk about himself, referring instead to his great offensive line.

The Tide's Randy Edwards encapsulated his team's frustration and the vitality of the rivalry when he said: "This is something that I will have to live with for the rest of my life. . . . Today was my last chance to hit somebody from Auburn and not go to jail for it."

ALABAMA TOOK the first of several trips to the Sun Bowl in El Paso that Christmas and embarrassed Southern Methodist University, 28–7. The win would help to ease the pain of the second consecutive loss to Auburn. Not much, but it would help.

Auburn went on to play Michigan as the host team in the fiftieth Sugar Bowl, winning 9–7. Bo Schembechler's Wolverines kept Auburn out of the end zone for the duration of the game, allowing only field goals. With five seconds left on the clock, Del Greco was called on one last time to knock in the win. The senior from Key Biscayne finished his Auburn career by splitting the uprights and making Auburn 11–1 for the season. Bo Jackson was named the most valuable player, but he refused the honor, giving the trophy to his friend and mentor, Lionel James, who was graduating.

The win was almost enough to add one more trophy to Auburn's 1983 haul, which already included the Southeastern Conference and the Sugar Bowl championships, as well as national coach of the year honors for Pat Dye. The two teams ranked ahead of Auburn, Nebraska and Texas, lost their bowl games to Miami and Georgia, respectively. Normally, that would have moved Auburn into the top spot and the national championship. But 1983 was not an ordinary year. Nebraska had been lauded all season as the best team of all time by the national media. Miami had pulled off the win on its home field in the Orange Bowl when Tom Osborne's team couldn't convert a two-point play in the final seconds. Miami, despite being whipped by Florida during the regular season, vaulted from number five to number one, and media darling Nebraska dropped only to number two.

Coach Dye was understandably disappointed, but philosophical. "There comes a time in everybody's life when you're going to get screwed over," he said. "And this was our time."

ROLL TIDE

Letting It Slip Away

THE DECK was stacked against Ray Perkins, without a doubt. It was bad enough taking over for a legend, but it was even worse that Auburn had just won its first Game in ten years. Dye's recruiting was paying dividends, and Bama's lackadaisical recruiting style was behind the turn in the Tide's fortunes. It wasn't Perkins's fault, but before long everyone in the state was going to start acting like it was.

Nevertheless, Perkins came in and laid down the law, and you have to respect him for that. He knew there were going to be problems, and he was doing all that he could to correct them. It was simply going to take time.

It was hard to accept losing two in a row to Auburn. It was harder, still, to watch Bo Jackson run up and down the field, knowing that he could have done the same thing for Alabama had things been handled differently. But there he was, the difference in the Game, leading the Tigers to the Sugar Bowl and sticking Bama with its fourth loss of the year.

The 1982 Game was such a fluke that there was no need to worry at the time about Auburn's making a run at Alabama's string of dominance. When Bear Bryant retired, though, it made everyone wonder what was in store for the state. Then Auburn came into the 1983 Game at 9–1, a heavy favorite. Bama, clearly, was a step behind for the first time in memory.

When this one was over, nothing remained but a strange feeling of gloom. It wasn't as shocking as the year before; 9–1 teams don't shock people very often by winning. It was clear, however, that the balance of power had swung decisively. For a lot of us, we had never known this before. *Auburn*, going to New Orleans? Well, that just wasn't right. It was confirmation that the days were growing dark. There was a strange sound to it, this playing second fiddle.—S.B.

WAR EAGLE
Most Valuable Players

YOU CANNOT talk about the 1983 Game without talking about Bo Jackson. I don't think I've ever seen an individual player take control of a game like that before or since (with the possible exception of a *Monday Night Football* game featuring Bo four years later).

As good as Bo was, he had a lot of help from his teammates and coaches, including my personal favorite football player of all time, Lionel James, "the Little Train." The story goes that Lionel wore number 6 because his jersey wasn't big enough for two digits. You couldn't watch this diminutive back running around out there with all those behemoths without being alternately thrilled and scared to death. The fact that he could stand up again after one hit, much less start in a wishbone backfield—the toughest place to be a runner in college football—was nothing short of amazing, and we all loved to see him play. He went out in style, with a championship ring. Like many others, Lionel's story didn't end in New Orleans. He went on to have a successful career in the NFL, and after he retired, he returned to Auburn to earn his degree. I understand he's a teacher today. Wherever he is now, those are some very lucky students.

Randy Campbell is also one of my favorites. He ran on guts and brains and heart, but he had enough guts for ten quarterbacks, enough brains for ten teams, and enough heart for ten lifetimes. There has never been a better director of the wishbone and there may never be a better triple-option quarterback than Number 14.

There were more, dozens more. The kicking of Al Del Greco and Lewis Colbert was phenomenal. Donnie Humphrey, Dowe Aughtman, Doug Smith, Gregg Carr, and Ben Thomas terrorized offenses from the kickoff to the closing buzzer, week in and week out. Chris Woods was as dependable a receiver as you'll ever see. Let's not forget Steve Wallace, the perennial All-Pro, or his partners, Pat Arrington, Jeff Lott, and David Jordan. These guys were among the very best to play at their respective positions.

I think Auburn people will always remember the 1983 team as one of the greatest ever, because they came so far, so fast. In the eyes of the "experts," this was a team of misfits, a bunch of players that nobody else wanted. For everybody else in the world, this was a team of champions. To hell with Miami. This was the best damn football team in America.—W.C.

1984

A SENSE OF DIRECTION

IN THE SUMMER OF 1984, a powerful feeling of euphoria swept across America. The Summer Olympics were being held in Los Angeles. Larry Bird and Magic Johnson were finally getting to square off against one another in what would become a classic rendition of the NBA Finals. And the Chicago Cubs were on a drive for the National League pennant (only to fall short, once again, of the World Series). A wave of patriotism carried Ronald Reagan to a forty-nine-state reelection landslide.

This good feeling was particularly discernible in east Alabama, as Pat Dye's Auburn Tigers entered the 1984 season ranked number one in the Associated Press poll. Bo Jackson was considered a contender for the Heisman Trophy, and expectations were obviously high for Dye's fourth campaign at Auburn. Meanwhile, Ray Perkins entered his second year in Tuscaloosa seeking to move farther from the daunting shadow of Paul Bryant, whose legacy did not include a large number of experienced players. Perkins had a talented but young team in 1984, and it was now up to him and his staff to fill the confines of Bryant Hall with quality players. Perkins didn't try to lower expectations for this team, claiming to have future All-Americans at several positions.

Auburn had to justify the high regard of pollsters from the start. The Miami Hurricanes—who had used their home-field advantage to knock off the supposedly invincible Nebraska Cornhuskers, 31–30, in the Orange Bowl to win the 1983 national title—awaited the Tigers in the second annual Kickoff Classic at New Jersey's Meadowlands. Dye started fifth-year senior Mike Mann at quarterback, taking the place of graduated hero Randy Campbell, but pulled Mann halfway through the second quarter. His replacement, junior Pat Washington, played a strong game, keeping Auburn in contention throughout, but a Brent Fullwood fumble killed a late rally, and the Tigers fell, 20–18.

Next came a trip to Austin, Texas, for a rematch with the powerful Longhorns. Bo Jackson was expected to be a major factor in the game, but having sprained an ankle against Miami, the injury-slowed Jackson badly separated his shoulder against Texas. The game ended with the Longhorns on top, 35–27, and Auburn had plummeted from the top-ranked team in the country to 0–2.

Alabama kicked off 1984 at home with Boston College, which had handed the Tide a maddening loss in the Foxboro snow the previous year. The rematch began as a showcase for Alabama sophomore running back Kerry Goode, who scored two first-half touchdowns and returned the second-half kickoff for another score. The Eagles, however, had their own savior, quarterback Doug Flutie, the Heisman winner-to-be. Goode was lost to a season-ending knee injury late in the third quarter. Leaving the field, Goode's numbers for the game were outstanding—295 combined offensive yards. Flutie led BC scoring drives to first tie the game, then pull ahead, and Alabama dropped its opener, 38–31.

After the tough loss, Bama faced the Yellow Jackets of Georgia Tech, in Atlanta's Grant Field. Bill Curry's Engineers controlled the game from start to finish and coasted to a 16–6 triumph, avenging Ray Perkins's first win as Alabama head coach.

Euphoria was in short supply in the state of Alabama by mid-September 1984. The two major state schools had begun their seasons a collective 0–4. If misery loves company, fans of both schools could take solace in the fact that the other side had suffered as much damage in as little time. The similarities, however, quickly ended.

Dye rallied his troops, and the monumental loss of Bo Jackson was slowly overcome. Auburn returned to the winner's circle with a 35–12 home win over Southern Miss, followed by a 28–10 trouncing of Tennessee, also at home. Ole Miss was a more trying opponent as the Tiger offense struggled in Oxford, but Auburn came back to win, 17–13. The next week in Tallahassee produced what Dye called "the wildest game I've ever coached in, or even seen." Untelevised, the 1984 Auburn–Florida State game has gone down in the collective memories of both schools as one of the greatest offensive shootouts ever played. The game was run-and-gun from the opening whistle and ended with an incredible score of 42–41, a huge win for the Tigers.

Auburn managed a high-scoring win over Georgia Tech, 48–35, nearly blowing a 41–0 halftime lead. Place-kicker Robert McGinty supplied the winning margin in a last-second come-from-behind victory over Mississippi State, 24–21. The Tigers fell, however, to the fired-up Florida Gators in Gainesville, led by freshman quarterback Kerwin Bell, 24–3. The loss to Florida was particularly galling in that it marked Bo Jackson's return to the field after a six-game layoff, but the Gators had one of their great all-time teams in 1984. Cincinnati paid the price for Florida's sins in a 60–0 Homecoming thrashing. Sophomore fullback Tommie Agee led the way for a 21–12 win over Georgia at home, keeping the Tigers in the race for the SEC championship. After a season of breathtaking highs and horrible lows, Auburn still was a front-runner for the host's spot in the Sugar Bowl.

ALABAMA, CONVERSELY, plunged to depths uncharted in more than twenty-five years. A lackluster win over Southwestern Louisiana supplied short-term salve to the pain of the season's beginning, but back-to-back losses of 24–14 to Georgia and 30–21 to Vanderbilt put the Tide at 1–4, and Ray Perkins was at the center of a firestorm. Fortunately, Joe Paterno brought an unusually weak Penn State squad to Tuscaloosa, and the Tide defense stubbornly regained some lost pride, shutting down the feeble Nittany attack and prevailing, 6–0, ironically on the same day that Auburn and Florida State held their eighty-three-point scoring festival in Tallahassee.

As inspiring as the Penn State win was, the following week's loss to Tennessee was surely the toughest for Perkins and his team to endure. The Tide controlled the Volunteers in Knoxville for three and a half quarters. Tennessee's brilliant quarterback Tony Robinson brought the Vols back to a 28–27 victory, dropping Perkins to 2–5 and 0–2 against Tennessee. The rivalry between the two schools has always been very heated, and for a proud man such as Perkins the loss was a crushing blow.

The next week the Tide rebounded well enough to handle Mississippi State, 24–20, in Jackson and improved to 3–5. An opportunity to regain more respect against Louisiana State University followed in Birmingham. Clearly, the Tide was showing signs of life on both sides of the ball. A stern test against a solid Bengal Tiger team would be a fine gauge of where the Tide stood. Bama dominated the game statistically, holding the ball for more than forty minutes and gaining more than twice as many offensive yards as the twelfth-ranked Tigers. Alabama was intercepted three times, and the visitors prevailed in the rain, 14–10, writing the first dark chapter in Perkins's tumultuous personal rivalry with LSU.

This, it seemed, was the loss for which everyone had been waiting. Here was hallowed Alabama, at 3–6, guaranteed of a losing season for the first time since 1957, the year before Bear Bryant's arrival in Tuscaloosa. Remarkably, the Tide defense would end the season as the best overall in the Southeastern Conference. Calls for Perkins's dismissal (and head) were at a fever pitch across the state. Here was a man nobody was really sure they liked in the first place, trying to replace a crimson deity and failing miserably in the process. Worst of all, in Auburn, the Tigers seemed to be improving markedly, and Bo Jackson's health was getting better. A rout in Birmingham at the hands of the plowboys would surely be the coup de grâce for Perkins.

A remarkably desultory performance against Cincinnati set the stage for Perkins's possible last stand. The Tide slept through a 29–7 beating of the Bearcats in frigid Riverfront Stadium, raising team spirits at least a bit but doing absolutely nothing in the eyes of observers. More interesting than the game itself was something Perkins said when it was over. He told his players in the dressing room that the Tide was entering "a new era." Perhaps the coach was starting to feel confidence in his young team, a group made up almost entirely of his own recruits, and attempting to give them a sense of purpose. Perkins was playing freshmen and sophomores in this horrid losing season because he had no choice, and evidently he liked what he was beginning to see in them.

Whatever the reasons for Perkins's claim, it was ridiculed in most circles. After all, Alabama, at 4–6 and playing for little more than pride and contract security, was headed for Legion Field to take on Auburn, which was 8–3 with a moderately healthy Bo Jackson, as well as additional incentive for whipping the Tide. A simple demolition of those bumbling snobs, and the Tigers would head back to New Orleans for a date with Nebraska in another Sugar Bowl. When asked if this would serve as extra motivation for beating Alabama, Dye said, "That may be an added incentive, but I think the big motivation is just playing Alabama for the state championship. That means a lot more to these kids than anything else surrounding the game. And that's the reason that this is such a great game for fans across the country to see."

Perhaps this is as strong a testimonial to the strength of the Alabama-Auburn rivalry as can be found, that a bunch of nineteen- and twenty-year-old young men were more concerned about winning this game for the sake of state supremacy than for the right to spend New Year's weekend in New Orleans. Priorities are often different in the state of Alabama.

SATURDAY MORNING ushered in December and the forty-ninth renewal of the Iron Bowl. The kickoff came in the late morning, early enough for ABC to broadcast a more ratings-friendly matchup, Florida–Florida State, in the afternoon.

A much-publicized sidelight in the mid-1980s Tide-Tiger rivalry gained notoriety well before the ball was teed up. For the second straight year, Perkins and Dye did not exchange the usual deferential banter that coaches share before a game, and each time it was Perkins who was being unsociable. This snubbing clearly bothered Dye, who made several remarks about this breach of gentlemanly tradition when it first happened in 1983, and Perkins did nothing this time around to make amends. The Alabama coach later downplayed the incidents and "made up" for them personally a year later, but at the time they only served to enhance the public image of Perkins as cold and arrogant.

Alabama returned the opening kickoff to the Auburn 32, sparking hope for a quick score. The Tide converted their first series of downs but faltered and gave the ball to Auburn at the Tiger 20 following a touchback. The Auburn offense took the field with a healthy Bo Jackson, primed to run the ball. They climaxed the eighty-yard, eleven-play drive with a two-yard

Auburn's Jackson scored from short yardage, giving the Tigers an early lead.

Jackson carry for the touchdown. It was Bo's fourth career touchdown against the Tide.

Any more machinelike drives from Jackson and Company, and Perkins's second Iron Bowl as Alabama coach would be his last. Of course, this was what Auburn fans had been wanting for years. Their team seemed ready to take control early, and many anticipated a blowout.

The next few minutes marked a high point of the season for the Alabama offense, which prior to the Game was bringing up the rear in the SEC. Behind the quarterbacking of Mike Shula and the running of Paul Ott Carruth and Ricky Moore, the Tide covered eighty yards in thirteen plays, with Carruth carrying on a six-yard scoring run. The score worked wonders for the psyche of the 4–6 team picked by many to be crushed by the Auburn Goliath. It was a drive that Bear Bryant would have loved.

The Alabama faithful on hand seemed to have a certain electricity about them this day, much as that which those dressed in orange and blue had possessed two years earlier, when Bama's nine-game streak of dominance finally came to a halt. For the first time in a long while, the Bama fans seemed to put aside their usual pretentious attitude and focus all their energy on salvaging pride and retrieving state bragging rights from the surging Tigers.

In the second quarter, aside from punts, neither team could move the football in four successive series. As expected, this edition of the series was becoming a defensive struggle. Finally, Auburn's offense took over on its own 42 and began to assemble a drive. Jackson and Agee seemed to have solved the Bama defensive puzzle. With just less than three minutes to go before the half, quarterback Pat Washington overthrew his receiver and was intercepted at the Bama 28 by David Valletto, an otherwise obscure figure in Tide lore.

The Tide failed to convert the turnover and returned the ball to the Tigers at the Auburn 27. Mike Mann, Dye's passing specialist, replaced Washington at quarterback. Alabama's defenders sacked him on his first play. Offensive coordinator Jack Crowe chose to exploit Bama's anticipation of the pass and called a draw play to Jackson, who exploded up the middle of the field to the Alabama 48. Two plays later Mann connected with Trey Gainous, taking the ball out of bounds and stopping the clock after gaining the first down. Strangely, the Tigers used their second time-out with the clock already stopped. Mann threw two incompletions, and the Tide caught Agee for a loss on a draw, pushing the Tigers back to the Bama 40.

Auburn called its last time-out. Mann found Freddie Weygand on the sideline at the Alabama 23, but the officials ruled that the receiver had not gotten out of bounds. With one second remaining in the half, the Tigers rushed their kicking team on the field and snapped the ball as soon as it was spotted. Mann, holding for McGinty on the forty-yard field goal attempt, mishandled the snap and lobbed the ball toward the end zone and Ron Middleton. The pass fell incomplete. Had Middleton made the reception the play would not have stood, as the Tigers were flagged for an ineligible receiver. The halftime score remained 7–7.

ALABAMA KICKED off, but Auburn could only run three plays and punt the ball back to the Tide, which began its first possession at the Bama 31. Initially, the Tigers contained the Tide running game, but Shula took the ball himself nineteen yards down the sideline. Dropping back to pass, he connected with Greg Richardson for seventeen more down the middle. Carruth went off left tackle and charged thirty yards downfield to the Auburn four-yard line. On the next play, Carruth, playing his last game for the Tide, carried the ball on a sweep to the left and into the end zone for his second score. Alabama had gone sixty-nine yards in only five plays and taken the lead, 14–7, with 11:51 left in the third quarter.

Auburn failed to make a first down on its next possession and returned the ball to Bama. Starting from their own 28, Perkins placed the burden on his running backs. After four productive runs, Shula dropped back to pass and found Richardson at the Auburn 39. The Tide was keeping the Tiger defense off balance and returned to the ground game. A holding penalty, however, pushed Alabama back. Shula connected with fullback Ricky Moore, who moved the ball inside the 35 but lost it on the tackle. Luck smiled on the Tide as the ball rolled backwards and out of bounds at the Tiger 42, ending up as a Bama gain of three yards. Shula dropped back again, this time finding his tight end, Preston Gothard, who took the ball as far as the Auburn 35. It was short of the first down but within place-kicker Van Tiffin's range. The sophomore nailed the fifty-two-yarder, increasing Alabama's lead to 17–7, with 5:09 to go in the third period. The Tigers had given up seventeen unanswered points since their initial score.

For a third time Auburn failed to move the chains and returned the ball to Alabama, this time at the Bama 47. The Tide, however, had little success with this possession. The Tigers closed down the run. Shula was able to convert one third-and-long situation, but a second similar situation resolved itself differently. With Bama needing eight yards for the first, Auburn defensive coordinator Wayne Hall gambled and blitzed his safety, Arthur Johnson. Johnson disrupted the play sufficiently and almost sacked Shula, who threw incomplete and was taken to the turf. He picked himself off the field, holding his ribs. It had been the last play of the quarter. When the final period began, Perkins chose not to try the fifty-one-yard field goal, noting that although Tiffin had made a fifty-two yarder earlier, it had been with the wind, and he now faced the wind. His punter tried to pin Auburn within the ten-yard line, but the ball went through the end zone for a touchback.

Auburn failed to produce again on offense, and the two teams traded punts and played for field position. With 11:24 to play, Auburn had the ball again at the Tiger 20. Pat Washington returned as Dye's quarterback. Two plays and one penalty later the Tigers faced a third-and-four situation. This time the ball went to Jackson. He ran a sweep and darted to the Auburn 37 for the Tigers' initial earned first down in the second half. An incompletion and a short run set up third down and seven. While usually a passing situation, Auburn stayed with the wishbone. Washington pitched the ball to sophomore Brent Fullwood, who had been held in check all afternoon. If the Tide defense could keep him away from the Tiger 44, Dye would be confronted with the tough decision of whether to kick or go for the down. As events transpired, Dye faced a tough decision, but it had nothing to do with a first down.

The Alabama defense, led by John Hand (78), harassed Auburn quarterback Pat Washington all afternoon.

Fullwood took Washington's pitch, followed his blocking, and found himself in the clear. He streaked down the right sideline into the end zone. Auburn was back in the game. Alabama still led, 17–13, but Dye's decision turned out to be whether to go for one or two on the conversion. He chose the latter. Washington lined up in the wishbone for the conversion, rolled left, and pitched the ball to Jackson at just the right moment. Bo crossed the plane of the goal and cut the Bama lead to two, 17–15, with 9:11 left in the game.

Shula took over on his own 20. The Tigers closed all the running lanes and Carruth was contained on two successive plays. On third and nine, Shula dropped back and found Moore in roughly the same place on the same screen that had been almost disastrous for the Tide in the third quarter. This time, Alabama wasn't so lucky. Moore bobbled the reception, knocking the ball up and into the hands of Auburn's Kevin Greene, who returned it to the 17.

Fortune, however, was not yet smiling on Auburn. Jackson slipped for no gain, and Washington lost a yard when he failed to get the ball to Agee. On third and eleven, Bo blasted up the middle to the Bama four-yard line. Auburn had first and goal. Worse news for Tide fans was that Cornelius Bennett had been shaken up on the play.

Fullwood carried the ball on the next play, but a holding call pushed the Tigers back to the eleven. With time becoming a factor now, Washington faked an end around with Jackson and handed off to Fullwood, who progressed only as far as the 10. Washington then pitched out to Fullwood, who was already on the sideline. On third down, Washington faked to Agee and carried the ball himself, but he was kept out of the end zone at the one-yard line. Fourth and one. What followed would come to live forever in the folklore of the state.

Dye pondered the situation for a moment. Offensive coordinator Jack Crowe asked about kicking the field goal. The head coach shook his head and said, "No, no." He chose to go for the touchdown rather than attempt an eighteen-yard kick that could have given the Tigers the lead, 18–17. Crowe sent a play into the Auburn huddle. The play itself became as memorable as the decision.

The Tigers lined up in the wishbone, with Agee at fullback, Fullwood to his left, and Jackson to his right. Washington pitched to Fullwood, who was sweeping right. Jackson broke left, and the two halfbacks nearly collided. Almost everyone at Legion Field had expected Bo to carry the ball. As it turned out, Fullwood was given the pigskin. He went around right end, only to run into two defenders. Fullwood kept his footing and his balance and might have been able to twist into the end zone had it not been for a third defender. Rory Turner, a freshman, met Fullwood head on, driving him out of bounds and ending Auburn's scoring threat.

Jackson had not heard the play call correctly. He, too, was expecting to get the ball, but his assignment was to block for Fullwood. It will forever be debated if Fullwood would have scored had Jackson led the way for him. Unfortunately for Auburn, Alabama now had the ball on its own four-yard line with 3:27 left in the game.

Perkins tried to run the ball out of the shadow of his goalposts. In two plays the Tide moved six yards. Shula's third-down pass fell incomplete, and Bama punted. Auburn fielded the punt at its own 44. With 1:45 to go, the Tigers ran the ball once, were penalized, and then shifted to their passing offense. With 1:20 on the clock, Washington was sacked back to his own 38. On third and long, Washington found Fullwood over the middle, and he moved the ball past the midfield stripe to the Bama 49. It had been a big play for Auburn, but it was still short of the first down. Washington called his last time-out with thirty-three seconds left and facing fourth and three.

All eyes were on Number 34. Sure enough, Washington pitched to Jackson, who carried the ball to the Tide 46. One play later, Washington connected with Trey Gainous, who ran out of bounds at the Bama 25 with fourteen seconds to go.

Dye called for his kicker, McGinty, to try for the potential game-winner from forty-two yards out. Interestingly, Perkins chose not to call a time-out to try to jangle McGinty's nerves. This time there was no problem between snapper and holder. McGinty, however, planted his left foot well ahead of the ball and hooked the kick into a sea of shimmering crimson in the end zone stands. The ball was at least twenty-five feet wide and to the left of the goalpost.

The Alabama sideline went berserk, drawing delay-of-game penalties that placed the ball on the Tide 15, with nine seconds left. Shula took the snap and fell on a knee as the final seconds ticked off the clock, keeping the ball as a souvenir.

Alabama 17, Auburn 15. The Crimson Tide had just executed the biggest upset in the series in at least twelve years and found some therapy for the pain of a losing season. Many of the Tigers, including Jackson, found themselves in a new situation, never having lost to Alabama before. A third successive victory in Legion Field had gone up in smoke painfully, and all that was left for consolation was a trip to Memphis and a date with future conference-mate Arkansas in the Liberty Bowl.

IN THE Auburn dressing room, dead silent except for the raucous noise of the Alabama celebration outside, Dye tried to console his players. "Men, I think we can learn from today's game," he said. "When you win, you win as a team, when you lose, you lose as a team. This is certainly a team effort here today. Offense, defense, kicking, and coaches. We all contributed, every one of us. And it starts with me. It starts with me."

The story of the Game came to be the Call. Dye's decision to go for the greater score rather than the field goal puzzled everyone and fed controversy for the future. In his weekly postgame show, Dye compared the decision to one made by Bear Bryant in the 1982 Iron Bowl. In the third quarter of that game, with the Tide ahead, 19–14, Bryant chose to kick a field goal for an eight-point lead. Auburn came back to win, and the Bear blamed himself for the loss, focusing on that one decision particularly.

In hindsight, he said that the one thing he would change was the play that had been called. The play should have been to Jackson, and everyone in the state of Alabama agreed with him.

In the aftermath of the win, Perkins found that beating Auburn was the key to finding fast relief for the pressures on an Alabama coach. After a year on the hot seat, Perkins could relax, at least for a while.

THE TIGERS licked their wounds in time to subdue Arkansas, 21–15, on an arctic December night in Memphis, on the same tundra where Bear Bryant had made his coaching exit two years earlier. Alabama, of course, was involuntarily home for the holidays after enduring a losing campaign for the first time in more than a quarter century.

Dye's first class of players at Auburn, who closed out their careers with the Liberty Bowl win, could not have foreseen, upon arrival in 1981, what would happen in those four years. They had suffered through a losing freshman season, then enjoyed a sublime run that yielded two wins over the Crimson Tide and a Southeastern Conference championship. To begin their senior year, however, with such high expectations, only to end up losing four games, the most bitter of which came at the hands of their fiercest rival, was anticlimactic, to say the least.

Conversely, Alabama would savor forever its one day in the 1984 sun and wasted no time in making Dye the butt of Crimson ridicule: Know how to get to Memphis? Go to the one-yard line at Legion Field and take a right. Another joke went: Hear about Dye's talk with God after the game? "Lord, why'd you tell me to go for that touchdown instead of the field goal?" "Hmmm, I don't know, Pat," came the holy reply. "Why *did* we tell him to do that, Bear?"

ROLL TIDE

One for Us Lifers

IN THE fall of 1984 it wasn't very easy to be an Alabama fan. Oh, sure, Bo Jackson had tested our mettle when he made it fashionable to pull for Auburn in 1982, but most lifelong Tide supporters pretty much kept the faith. It was basically the fence stragglers, the "I-65" fans, who found themselves wearing orange and blue after big, bad Bo came along.

But in 1984, once Alabama had slipped to 1–4 or 3–6, it seemed that you had a better chance of finding an empty gun rack in a Chambers County pickup truck than you did of finding a vocal, visible Tide loyalist. I found the strength to resist the urge to abandon ship, as did all other *true* Tide fans. Don't think I'm overlooking the obvious. For years Auburn people had to do some holding out of their own while Bear Bryant ruled the state with a petulant drawl and a mighty bottle of Coca-Cola. Auburn people, however, are used to the second-class citizen routine. This sudden role reversal wasn't so natural for us Bama people.

Bear Bryant was gone. In his place as statewide cultural icons were Pat Dye—who Auburn people liked because he reminded them of Bryant—and Bo Jackson, who in 1984 didn't even know everything yet, least of all left from right. After that nightmarish 23–22 nonsense in 1982 and the "whoever's ahead before it starts raining like hell wins it" Game the next year, topped off with a 4–6 Alabama record going into the season finale in 1984, a third straight loss to Auburn would have wiped out any hope of piping down all those born-again Tiger fans and restoring Bama to state dominance.

We Bama fans stuck to our guns. I had a good feeling about the 1984 Auburn game. I was confident the Tide would come out fired up. I anticipated that Paul Carruth and Ricky Moore would close out their careers in style, making someone else's season miserable. I expected Mike Shula would do just enough to keep the Tide in the Game, rather than make a bunch of nervous mistakes. Granted, I was sure that Bo Jackson, health problems and all, would play against Alabama on a gurney if he had to. I was also sure that Auburn's Gregg Carr and Ben Thomas would knock Carruth halfway to Alabaster if he didn't get some blocking.

When Auburn went down the field like a knife through butter to go up 7–0, I sat there unfazed. People had been doing that to Alabama all year long on their first drive. When Bama answered that score to tie things up, it was like the Game was finally starting for real.

When Bama went ahead, 17–7, it was like taking the family car out when you're not old enough to drive—you know you're about to pay the price, so you might as well make the most of it. When the axe finally fell, in this case Fullwood going sixty yards in a hurry to the same end zone he would find impenetrable later, it was time to brace for the worst and hope for the best.

Let me say this much about the whole goal-line fiasco: I think Dye did the right thing in going for the touchdown, but if I'm calling the shots for Auburn there's no way in the name of John Deere that I'd give the ball to anyone but Bo Jackson. Jack Crowe, or whoever drew the longest straw on the sideline and got to call the play, should have been dumped off the top of Red Mountain.

Still, after dodging that large bullet, it wasn't over. Bo would have one more chance. And Fullwood. And Gainous. And all the other Bad Guys. Incredible. Washington moved them right back down the field, setting up McGinty for his momentous miscue, which cost him his scholarship.

I've never been so drained after a football game in all my life. I didn't care that Alabama had no bowl game to go to. In fact, I really didn't even care that Auburn wasn't going to New Orleans (well, actually, I thought it was pretty neat that one of my brothers, who was—and it hurts to admit this—an Auburn student at the time, had taken New Year's in the Big Easy for granted). All I cared about was that it was finally time to shut up all those Auburn fans-for-rent and pray they wouldn't jump the fence again. Bama had won the only real bowl—the Iron Bowl.—S.B.

WAR EAGLE

What the—?

I T WAS a strange year, and it ended with a strange Game. We had *no* intention, or even thoughts, of losing this Game. After watching Alabama's collapse in 1984, Auburn folks aimed for nothing less than rubbing the Tide's face into the AstroTurf for an afternoon of humiliation. It was payback time.

Of course, it didn't work out that way. Not only did Alabama not get humiliated, it didn't even happen in the afternoon. On the Auburn side, everybody seemed to be waiting for something to happen, maybe hoping that Bo would take over, or just waiting for Alabama to roll over and die like a good 4–6 team.

The fact of the matter is that 1984 didn't have to happen the way it did. Auburn played a somnolent game plan, running into the line on more plays than I care to remember. A more open offense could have turned things our way. I heard a lot of theories in the aftermath of this Game, but the one that rings the most true has to do with toughness and intimidation.

I think Pat Dye and Jack Crowe wanted to make an impression on the Alabama team and on Alabama football in general. They wanted to stuff the ball down the Tide's throat. They wanted to beat them into submission. They wanted to whip Alabama in a physical slugfest. They wanted to put the fear of getting hit by Auburn into a generation of Alabama players. This was the same team that had scored forty-two points on Florida State *without* Bo Jackson. With Bo, there should have been no way for the Tigers to lose. *Should* have been.

As far as the play on the goal line, I'm not about to second-guess the decision not to kick; I was one of the thousands in the stands yelling "Go for it!" In retrospect, Auburn probably had a much better shot at the touchdown than the field goal. Of course, I was thinking Bo Over the Top, part 2. Everybody was. It was the one thing that nobody had ever stopped. I have to agree with Dye's postmortem when he said that he should have called a single play instead of an option and gone with Bo for the touchdown.

It happens in football sometimes. You get so caught up in the chess match with the opposition that you outsmart yourself. I can't get angry with Bo for going the wrong way. It was the kind of thing that just happens. It was nobody's fault. Confusion cost Auburn a Game. It's one of the oldest sayings in this sport, but this is a game played with a funny-shaped ball. Sometimes it bounces your way, sometimes it doesn't.

Robert McGinty. What can you say? The guy was a freshman thrust under the hottest spotlight imaginable. He can't be blamed for missing. At the same time, game-winning kicks are the reason skinny kids like McGinty get football scholarships. He was ridiculed after that Game, and I can't blame him for leaving Auburn. I *can*, however, blame him for transferring to Florida!

We had so many high hopes in 1984, so many grand dreams that fell short. We wanted to whip Miami, beat Texas, clobber Alabama, get the Heisman for Bo as a junior. We wanted to take 1983 and do it one better, get that last win and claim a national championship. It didn't happen, but that's the way of the world in college football. Dreams don't always come true, despite our best intentions and efforts.

It's a very old lesson, as old as the game itself. Getting to the top is hard. Staying there is immeasurably harder. Don't believe me? Ask Alabama. And while you're at it, tell 'em that they stole one in 1984.—W.C.

1985

OF HEROES GREAT AND SMALL

RAY PERKINS PROBABLY WOULD have been fired but for his team's stunning upset over Auburn in 1984. Even with the season-ending win, the select group of alumni in control of his employment were getting impatient with Bear Bryant's hand-picked successor and were hardly willing to endure another 5–6 campaign. Further, the 1985 Tide schedule, which included a season-opening trip to Georgia, followed by a date with Texas A&M and battles with all the usual adversaries, had to be even more unsettling for the Tuscaloosa power brokers.

In the previous winter, however, a trend continued that would help steady Perkins's welcome at the Capstone. The coach and his staff always battled to bring in the talent to lift Alabama back into the elite of the Southeastern Conference. Nobody took recruiting more seriously than Ray Perkins, and his 1985 crop of signees included Bobby Humphrey, Derrick Thomas, Gene Jelks, and junior-college transfer receiver Al Bell. There was no question that Pat Dye had whipped the Tide for several years in the game within the game, as recruiting is often called, and only now, after two solid incoming classes, were Perkins and Alabama beginning to even the score.

Dye, for his part, did more in the offseason than thaw out after the trip to Memphis, his third bowl win in as many tries. The Tigers signed Ron

Stallworth, probably the most sought-after defensive recruit in the country, defensive lineman Tracy Rocker, wide receiver Lawyer Tillman, and other blue-chippers to scholarships.

Of course, all these new faces had to blend in with tested veterans to be successful on the field, and once again, in the eyes of the national media, Auburn had a formidable mix of the two. The Tigers, for the second straight year, were the top-ranked team in the country in many polls, and their 1985 roster remains arguably the most impressive collection of talent amassed in recent memory by either state school.

At the top of the list was Bo Jackson, now firmly ensconced as the front-runner for the Heisman Trophy that had been associated with his name for three years. Brent Fullwood, who had stepped in admirably in 1984 following Jackson's shoulder injury, returned, along with rugged fullback Tommie Agee and quarterback Pat Washington. However, Dye's embarrassment of riches would cause him trouble at signal-caller, as sophomore Jeff Burger and freshman Bobby Walden challenged the senior Washington throughout summer practice for the starting job.

Defensively, prodigies Rocker and Stallworth were thrown on a golden pile of linemen that already included Gerald Robinson, Harold Hallman, and Gerald Williams, and linebacker Aundray Bruce. In terms of sheer talent, the 1985 Tiger defensive front line stacks up well with any assembled in college football history.

Behind the line, the personnel were less formidable but solid. Sophomores Edward Phillips and Russ Carreker were establishing themselves at linebacker, and Tom Powell and Kevin Porter shone in the AU secondary. This was a team without an obvious weakness. They looked to be the embodiment of Pat Dye's coaching philosophy: run the ball down their throats and stop 'em cold when they try to return the favor.

Over the summer remarkable news trickled down from the Plains. After four years of faithfully running the wishbone, which Dye had learned under Bear Bryant, the Tigers were switching to the more contemporary two-back I-formation. It wasn't a huge surprise, considering Jackson figured to get the ball more often and that all three contenders for the starting quarterback job were gifted passers who could use the extra receiver in the new set. The wishbone had become part of the Dye aura, but apparently the head man was going against his nature to open up the offense. Of course, with the famously conservative offensive coordinator Jack Crowe at the controls, many questioned the wisdom of abandoning the so-far-effective wishbone for a new attack.

Alabama's overall talent was not as daunting, but a number of players who had survived a baptism of fire as underclassmen in 1984 had shown signs of maturity late in that dreadful season. Mike Shula was now unquestionably the leader of this team, and lettermen Wes Neighbors and Bill Condon anchored a line that would have to get the gutsy quarterback time to come into his own. Another prized signee, Larry Rose, would be pressed into action immediately and ultimately became the first Alabama offensive linemen in history to start every game in his freshman season. In the skill positions, Kerry Goode's rehabilitation from a knee injury suffered in the 1984 opener was going slowly, and with Ricky Moore and Paul Ott Carruth graduated after stellar careers, the freshmen Jelks and Humphrey would be counted on heavily. If neither of the two newcomers panned out, Greg Richardson and the transfer Bell figured to offer an aerial option for the pass-oriented Perkins.

Cornelius Bennett and Jon Hand anchored a defensive unit that was the SEC's best in 1984 and which had lost virtually no one to graduation. Curt Jarvis and Brent Sowell figured to help Hand solidify a front wall that, while not as imposing as its counterpart across the state, was still impressive. The young Derrick Thomas looked to learn from Bennett and Wayne Davis, the Tide's top linebackers, while Freddie Robinson and Ricky Thomas headed a seasoned secondary.

Of all these Tide players, only Jon Hand was entering his final season. If Perkins couldn't replace Bryant in the hearts of the Alabama faithful, he was definitely doing a fine job of replacing the legend's football players. The third-year coach was in the middle of something substantial in Tuscaloosa, but his young team was going to be tested early and often. Talented freshmen notwithstanding, the Tide basically returned the same players who had stumbled through the miseries of 1984.

AUBURN OPENED the year against the Ragin' Cajuns of Southwestern Louisiana, a favorite punching bag of both Iron Bowl participants. The nationally televised game was a showcase for Bo Jackson, and the senior made the most of it with 290 yards as Auburn rolled, 49–7. Then came a 29–18 win over Southern Mississippi to set up a showdown with Tennessee in Knoxville. The Tigers were now ranked number one in the nation but found themselves on the short end of a 24–0 halftime score, the result of the Vols' Tony Robinson's picking apart the Auburn secondary. Meanwhile, Dye alternated between Washington, Burger, and Walden at quarterback, but the Tiger offense never clicked. Auburn settled down to make it respectable in the second half, but it was too little, too late. Jackson, the nation's pre-eminent college football player, took himself out of the game with a bruised knee, and he did not return. Nor would the Tigers return to the top of the polls after suffering an embarrassing 38–20 setback.

After a 41–0 bludgeoning of Ole Miss at home, which was another Jackson touchdown-fest, the Tigers faced a rematch with Bobby Bowden's Florida State Seminoles. It was another big one, but not quite as fast-paced as the 1984 rendition. The game was tied at the half, but Auburn broke loose in the third quarter to pull ahead, 35–17. FSU came back to pull within eight, 35–27, but in the fourth quarter the Tigers exploded for 28 unanswered points and ran away with a huge 59–27 victory.

Following a tough 17–14 win at Grant Field over a fired-up Georgia Tech squad, highlighted by a game-winning 80-yard Jackson dash, Auburn shut down Mississippi State at home, 21–9. Then undefeated Florida came to Auburn and eked out a rare Jordan-Hare win, 14–10. Dye was impressed enough with the Gators' play to go to the opponents' dressing room and congratulate first-year head coach Galen Hall. Jackson was injured just before the half and couldn't finish the game. East Carolina, the school that gave Dye his start as a head coach, was then dispatched, 35–10, for Home-coming. At this point in the season, the Heisman Trophy was a contest between Jackson and Iowa quarterback Chuck Long. Like Pat Sullivan before him, Bo would have to make a major impact at the end of the season to claim the elusive prize.

Against Georgia, Jackson, still not fully recovered from the thigh injury suffered against Florida, did what champions do in tight situations. He rose to the occasion with a bravura performance, dazzling the touted Bulldog defense for a huge game, gaining 121 yards on nineteen carries, 48 yards on two pass receptions, and two explosive touchdowns. The Tiger defense followed Jackson's lead, stuffing the Dawgs as Auburn ran away with a 24–10 win in Athens.

ALABAMA AND Georgia kicked off the 1985 SEC schedule with a Labor Day night game in Athens, the Tide's first visit to Sanford Stadium in nine years. This was Alabama's chance to make an early impression against one of the SEC's most consistent contenders. Al Bell caught an early touchdown pass from Shula, leading the way to a 13–3 advantage after three quarters. Then, after the Dawgs had blocked a punt and recovered it for a touchdown to take a late lead, Shula led Bama in a classic hurry-up drive that culminated with another scoring strike to Bell in the waning seconds, and the Tide won, 20–16.

Next up: Jackie Sherrill's Texas A&M Aggies, at Legion Field. The Aggies played a solid, aggressive game against the Tide but hurt themselves with penalties, and Bama fullback Craig Turner bulled for 114 yards as Alabama cruised over the eventual Southwest Conference champions, 23–10.

Easy victories over Cincinnati (45–10) and Vanderbilt (40–20) followed—both showcases for the freshman Humphrey. The Vandy win helped ease some of the lingering pain of the 1984 Homecoming disaster and pushed Bama to 4–0 heading into a showdown with Penn State in Happy Valley. Both teams had improved considerably in the span of a year, and this battle was up to the standards that had been set for their splendid ten-year series. The Nittany Lions took their second win out of five tries in the set, 19–17, and used the momentum to vault to a national championship match with Oklahoma in the Orange Bowl.

Things got no easier for the Tide, as Johnny Majors's Tennessee Vols, the same squad that had dismantled Auburn and Jackson earlier, traveled to Birmingham. Once more, Tony Robinson shone against an Alabama school, taking the Volunteers to an early lead before leaving with a knee injury that would end his career. Shula again showed some last-second heroics, but Van Tiffin's sixty-yard field goal attempt at the gun fell short, and Tennessee took control of the Sugar Bowl race, winning 16–14.

At 4–2 and on a losing streak, the Tide visited the field to which they had relegated Auburn a year earlier, the Liberty Bowl, to take on Memphis State. The Tigers led early, but Shula's 367 yards and four touchdowns brought on a 28–9 Bama win. Mississippi State witnessed Gene Jelks's coming-out party the next week, as the freshman gained 288 yards in a 44–28 romp for the Tide.

Perkins and turmoil, never far from each other, met again. The Crimson Tide was 6–2, heading to Baton Rouge to play Louisiana State University. The Bengal Tigers had a strong team in 1985 and gave Bama a stiff challenge, leading 14–7 in the fourth quarter. On cue, Shula led another courageous late drive, and when Jelks took a pitch on a trick play and threw back to Shula, who lunged into the end zone, the LSU lead was 14–13 with less than three minutes to play.

After the classic drive, everyone in Tiger Stadium and the national television audience waited for Perkins to go for the two-point conversion and the lead—but he didn't. Perkins sent Tiffin onto the field, and the kicker dutifully split the uprights to tie the game, 14–14. LSU missed a short field goal in the closing seconds, and the game finished deadlocked.

Predictably, fans were apoplectic. Alabama had played to a *tie?* In many ways, the situation was similar to that which Dye had endured in the previous Iron Bowl, going for the greater score on fourth and goal. Perkins justified his decision in much the same way Dye did, saying he felt his defense would give the ball back to the offense with enough time to win. In the eyes of Alabama fans, however, Dye had at least been aggressive. Perkins was simply playing not to lose. Auburn folks, naturally, made the most of the situation, purposely misspelling Alabama's battle cry as "Roll Tied."

A 24–13 HOMECOMING win over Southern Mississippi put Alabama at 7-2-1, heading into the fiftieth rendition of the Iron Bowl. Usually the fort-night between the tenth and eleventh games on the Tide schedule allowed for a bit of relaxation before the biggest battle of the year, but not in 1985. On the Wednesday after the Southern Miss win, ten days before the Auburn game, the *Crimson White*, Alabama's student newspaper, printed an infa-mous ad exclaiming "Jerk the Perk," the rallying cry of those who wanted Perkins removed as the Tide's head coach.

Perkins, naturally, shrugged it off, saying he had more important things on his mind, namely preparing for Auburn. It seemed amazing that the Tide endured such scrutiny during a season where four points separated them from being undefeated. But the potential for a major distraction heading into the Auburn game was still there, and how Perkins and his team han-dled it would go a long way toward determining if they were ready for the Tigers on November 30.

As for Auburn, the resounding Georgia win could not have come at a better time. Jackson's strong showing against a tenacious Bulldog defense reestablished his reputation as the top player in the country, a fact Dye was quick to point out in his Heisman lobbying for Jackson.

There was, however, another side to Jackson's performance against Georgia. Midway through the game he suffered a serious injury: a rib had been cracked and another broken. Some players would be out for the year with such a condition, but this was the Iron Bowl—and Jackson never missed the Iron Bowl. Jackson's long struggle in 1985 with injuries was not going to end on the bench.

Few could argue that Auburn had a substantial edge in depth. Alabama had a handful of impact players, such as Cornelius Bennett and Al Bell, but Auburn was deeper in every position, bigger along the front lines, and still hurt-ing from the 1984 loss. They also had Jackson, and Saturday was his birthday.

The Tide would ride on Shula's arm—he led the nation in passing efficiency—Bennett's shoulders, and hope that one of the freshmen running backs would have a big day. If Auburn built up an early lead, conventional wisdom held, Bama had no chance.

The Tigers headed into Saturday as a four-point favorite, although the Game had not been decided by more than three points since 1981. Rumors abounded the week before the Game that Auburn had already accepted an invitation to play in the Cotton Bowl against the Southwest Conference champion. Alabama was said to be on the way to Hawaii's Aloha Bowl against a Pac-10 team. The only complication could come in Nashville, where Vanderbilt was hosting Tennessee on the Saturday of the Game. An unlikely Vandy win would make Bama eligible for the league title and a trip to the Sugar Bowl. No one in Tuscaloosa, however, was holding their breath.

A MARVELOUS fall afternoon was the backdrop for the fiftieth renewal of the Game. A steady rain had fallen on Birmingham through the night and morning, resulting in a damp and discolored playing surface. To no one's surprise, Tennessee coasted past Vanderbilt early in the day, 30–0, securing the SEC title and ending Alabama's faint hopes for a Sugar Bowl berth.

A special coin, minted to commemorate the silver anniversary of the series, was used for the toss. Auburn kicked off, and aided by a penalty, stuffed Alabama's return very deep at the Tide six-yard line. The Alabama offense proved to have a case of jitters with an illegal procedure call on the first play, but Shula quickly generaled them downfield with short, effective passes that set up the run. On the fifteenth play of the drive, Craig Turner, untouched, jogged into the end zone from the Auburn one, giving the Tide a 7–0 lead. Perkins's confidence in Shula and his receivers was obvious, and his diversified offense moved the ball with relative ease against the talented Auburn defense.

After a good return of the ensuing kickoff, the Tigers were penalized on their first play, setting up first and fifteen at their own 21. Washington was sacked on the next play, fumbling the ball, which was recovered by the Tide at the Auburn 14. Shula was back in business, but the Tigers' defense was prepared this time. Three plays later Van Tiffin entered the game to convert a twenty-six-yard field goal, and the Tide led, 10–0. The quick start was nothing new for Bama in 1985, as it was now outscoring opponents in the first quarter, 69–6.

Brent Fullwood could return the following kick only to the Auburn 11. With Jackson carrying on two of the next three plays, the Tigers still failed to make a first down and had to punt the ball. Although Lewis Colbert was able to back up Greg Richardson to the Tide 25, the shifty junior found a clear lane and returned the punt 62 yards to Auburn's 13. The Alabama fans

Alabama quarterback Mike Shula (11) had to have protection if the Tide was going to have a good afternoon.

were raucous, just as in 1984, surging with the momentum created by this spirited showing from the underdog Tide.

While Alabama was again on the doorstep, again the Tiger defense held firm. After three plays, Tiffin returned to the field for a thirty-two-yarder, which he converted, giving Alabama a 13–0 lead early in the second quarter.

The two teams exchanged punts, setting Auburn up on its own 47. The Tigers immediately went to the air, and Washington connected with a wide-open Freddie Weygand for a forty-four-yard gain to the Tide nine. On second and seven, Jackson, the birthday boy, rocketed through the line for the touchdown, his fifth against Alabama. With the point after, Alabama's lead had been cut to six, 13–7.

Once more the two teams exchanged punts. Alabama then took the ball inside its own 10 and began to march toward the Auburn goal. On a crucial third and thirteen, Shula found Craig Turner with a delay screen, and the burly senior punished the Tigers for nineteen yards up the sideline. The next play Shula discovered Al Bell deep against the Auburn secondary, and he took the ball inside the Tigers' 30-yard line, despite an interference call. After a short gain by Jelks, the drive faltered. Tiffin came on again, hitting a forty-two-yarder and giving Bama a nine-point lead, 16–7, with 1:02 remaining in the first half.

The Bama kicker pooched the kickoff, and Auburn began its last drive of the first half at its 23-yard line. Dye pulled out all the stops to make it into the Tide end zone. Washington was able to get the ball as far as the Bama 33, and the Tigers were content to settle for a field goal attempt. Chris Johnson promptly kicked the longest field goal of his career, a forty-nine-yarder on the last play of the half, cutting the Alabama lead to 16–10.

THE SECOND half started with a fizzle as Auburn stalled out on two series and Alabama on one. The Tide started its second drive of the half at its own 13. Shula was able to mount an eight-play drive to the Auburn 36, but when he failed to make a third-and-fifteen play, Bama had to settle for a Tiffin field goal attempt, a fifty-two-yarder. The junior kicker had plenty of distance on the ball, but it was wide left. The score remained 16–10, with just over four minutes left in the third quarter.

On the last possession of the third quarter, the Tide's Kermit Kendrick intercepted the Tigers deep in his own territory, but the defender was taken down on his own three-yard line. Perkins called a conservative series of plays to try to muscle the ball out from under the shadow of the goalposts.

As the sun slipped behind the old steel mills to the west, the two teams held up the traditional four fingers. Do or die time. For the next fifteen minutes each side would make the most of its promises.

Resuming the offense on the opposite side of the field, Bama tried to power the ball away from its goal line. On third and three, with Auburn blitzing, Shula pitched the ball to the freshman Jelks, and the halfback broke open a thirty-nine-yard run to the Auburn 49. On the next play it looked as if the Tide were going to gain large chunks of yardage regularly as the freshman Humphrey added ten more yards to Bama's offensive statistics. Shula tried to match that gain with a deep pass to Richardson, but it was underthrown and picked off by Kevin Porter in the end zone.

Trailing by six points with 13:25 left, Auburn's offense took over and began to show the form that had made the Tigers the favorite in this Game. Dye had his quarterback hand the ball off throughout the drive, distributing it to Jackson, Ware, and Agee. The Auburn juggernaut ran down the field from its own 20-yard line to the Alabama 17. With the Tide defense battered and expecting another run, Dye switched to his passing offense. On his first attempt, Washington was sacked by Bennett. His second was incomplete. It looked as though the Tide had found the brakes on the Tiger offense. Facing third and nineteen, Alabama blitzed, but Auburn's coach had called the perfect play, a screen to Jackson. The big man was felled inside the Bama five-yard line. With first and goal, Washington predictably fed Bo the football, and Jackson gained two yards. On second down, Washington tried to connect with his tight end, but he rushed the pass and missed his receiver. With three yards to go to score, Washington kept the third-down snap, but he progressed only as far as the one-yard line.

With fourth and goal, Auburn was about to lose five yards for having too many players on the field. Calling for a time-out, Dye brought his entire offensive unit to the sideline. It was exactly like the situation in 1984. With the game on the line, the Tigers faced fourth and goal on the one. This time Dye did what everybody expected him to do. He called on Jackson. The best player in the nation, just as he had done three years earlier, dove over the top of the line. He was met head-on by a Bama defender and stopped for an instant, inches short, but as he fell Bo twisted forward just enough to cross the plane. The side judge quickly ruled it a touchdown. Auburn had tied the game, and all they needed to take the lead was for its place-kicker, Chris Johnson, to convert the point after. The freshman missed—the ball flew wide right.

For a moment, Tide fans were jubilant that the game was tied. Then they saw the yellow flag on the field. Just as Auburn had been flagged earlier, there were twelve Bama defenders on the field. Johnson's second attempt was perfect, and the Tigers had their first lead and the familiar score of 17–16 with 7:03 left in the game. Ironically, Alabama was flagged a second time for too many players on the field for the second kick.

The Auburn drive had been classic Pat Dye football. The Tigers had gone head to head with the Alabama defense and had simply blown them off the line, showing the pedigree of a team that had not been outrushed all season. Auburn had gone eighty yards on sixteen plays and looked like it wanted to keep on going.

As if there hadn't been enough excitement on the last few plays, Bama muffed the kickoff. After the penalty yardage had been assessed, Auburn kicked off from the Alabama 45. Four Tide players collided trying to catch the ball just inside the 10-yard line, and the ball bounced free. The Tigers barely missed corralling the fumble, which rolled out of bounds at the Bama 11-yard line, and the Tide averted disaster by the slimmest of margins.

When the Alabama offense returned to the field, it needed eighty-nine yards with just less than seven minutes to play. Things did not look well on the crimson side of the ball. The Tiger defenders stuffed Jelks on first down, and the heralded runner lost two yards. Shula took to the air on the next play, looking for Bell along the sideline. His pass appeared to be too high for the smallish receiver, but Bell extended his body its full length and made the catch, going out of bounds at the 26 for a critical first down.

The following play was the stuff of which legends are made. With the offense having more room in which to work, Shula pitched the ball again to Jelks, and the freshman broke across the line and toward the middle of the field. His blockers executed their tasks perfectly, and suddenly Jelks was in the open, streaking down the left sideline as Alabama radio commentator Paul Kennedy yelled, "Run for glory! Run for glory!" Jelks raced seventy-four yards untouched to give the Tide a 22–17 lead with 5:57 left to play. Perkins called for a two-point conversion, trying to gain a full touchdown advantage, but Shula's pass to Bobby Humphrey fell incomplete.

Once again, the Tigers stared at the length of the field to regain the lead. With just less than six minutes to go, Auburn took over on its own 30. Jackson carried the ball well, and Washington connected with Weygand for twenty-one yards, taking the ball into Alabama territory. The senior quarterback scrambled for critical yardage on the next crucial third-down play, and Jackson continued to gain positive chunks of yardage as the clock rolled toward four minutes. The Tide defenders were covering Auburn's receivers

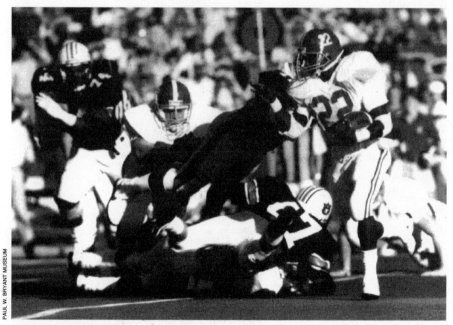

PAUL W. BRYANT MUSEUM

Freshman running back Gene Jelks (22) carried for almost two hundred yards on the afternoon.

well and forced Washington to scramble out of the pocket. On third and a short two, Bo was hit at the line, but spun away from the tackle and went out of bounds at the Alabama 17. Bama, however, was flagged for a late hit on one of the most important plays of the game.

After marking off the penalty, the Tigers had a first and goal on the Tide eight. Agee gained two, then Bo stormed to the one-yard line, very nearly scoring. Dye knew that the Tide was capable of last-minute heroics and wisely let the clock tick off vital seconds. On the third-and-goal play, Reggie Ware plowed into the Alabama end zone.

Dye chose to go for two, but Washington's pass to Jackson was batted down by Cornelius Bennett, and the Tigers' lead was again a familiar score, 23–22. Due partially to the late-hit penalty against Bama, however, the Tide regained possession of the ball with fifty-seven seconds to go.

The situation was remarkably similar to 1982. The score was the same, and Alabama had the same faint opportunity to move the ball into field goal range. On that gray after-noon three years earlier, Walter Lewis had more time to move the ball and a far less-talented Tiger defense facing him. Although the 1985 Tide had not lost a game when it had led going into the fourth quarter and Shula had performed bril-liantly in clutch situations throughout the season, the young man from Miami had less than a minute to work some magic.

Alabama started on its own 20. Shula's first pass was incomplete. He was sacked

Auburn's Reggie Ware (36)
carried the ball into the end
zone for the lead.

AUBURN UNIVERSITY PHOTOGRAPHIC SERVICES

on the next play. With thirty-seven seconds on the clock, he called time-out. The ball rested on the 12-yard line. The situation was bleak. As Bama faced a third and eighteen, the Tigers looked to be in control. Desperate situations, however, bring out the best in some players. Shula connected with Jelks, who took the ball out of bounds at the 26. The play had been good for fourteen yards, but the Tide was still short of the first down and had only twenty-nine seconds on the clock. On fourth and four, Shula pitched to Jelks, who gave the ball on a reverse to Bell. Shula laid a perfect block on the only defender facing his receiver, and Bell sprinted upfield to the Tide 46.

Shula's next pass was incomplete and almost intercepted. With only fifteen seconds to go, Shula stood in the pocket for what seemed like an eternity. He was trying to find Bell on the sideline but had to settle for Richardson in the middle of the field. He took in the pass and was run down by an Auburn defender. Richardson, at 165 pounds and known as "Little Richard" to his teammates, carried his would-be tackler out of bounds at the Auburn 35 for a nineteen-yard gain with six seconds remaining.

Incredibly, the Iron Bowl had come down to a final kick for the second consecutive year. Tiffin trotted onto the field and set up at the Tiger 42. Neither side had any time-outs available. The snap was good, the hold perfect. In a scene that today adorns Crimson living rooms across the state, Tiffin powered a fifty-two-yarder just beyond Kevin Porter's reach and into the Legion Field night. The young man was dead solid perfect. As time expired, "The Kick" split the uprights. The score: Alabama 25, Auburn 23.

Auburn was flagged for being offsides, but Tiffin didn't need a second opportunity. The Tide sideline mobbed the kicker. Perkins was among the hordes surrounding Tiffin. With tears streaming down his normally expressionless face, he threw his arms around his kicker, screaming "Van Tiffin! Van Tiffin! I love ya, Van Tiffin, I love ya!" In a postgame interview, Tiffin said, "I was really lucky it didn't get blocked . . . I saw Kevin Porter dive at my feet as I kicked the ball." Asked if he knew the kick was true, he replied, "Well, I looked up, *then* I knew it was good."

In the Alabama locker room, Perkins lead his team in prayer. Surveying his players with a beaming smile, he said, "I love all of you. But I told you that earlier this week. I started not to bring you up here—I thought some of you might get hurt." Giddy laughter erupted around the locker room as he continued: "I want to thank every person here for reaching down, for giving everything they had today. . . . This feeling is why you came to Alabama. You will remember it for the rest of your life. You remember last year when I told you after the Cincinnati game that we had started a new

Bama's Van Tiffin kicks a fifty-two-yarder as time expires to make this one of the most memorable Iron Bowls in recent history.

era at Alabama, an era that everyone here is a part of? Remember? Well, I just want to make one simple statement, and I'm making it for the last time—Alabama is back!"

AUBURN FOUND some solace the following Saturday, when Bo Jackson was awarded the Heisman Trophy. Jackson was Auburn's second winner in fifteen years.

Alabama rode the momentum of its monumental victory to the shores of Honolulu, where it easily disposed of the USC Trojans, 24–3. Although relatively few Tide supporters made the trip to do the "Hula with Shula," the experience was a pleasant one for the team and coaches, and the sunny weather matched the current condition of the Alabama program, which had weathered its worst period in more than twenty-five years.

Perkins, who had been precariously close to unemployment barely a year earlier, was now the toast of the Alabama world, having upset Auburn in successive years. What's more, his football team was young and would be among the early favorites in the 1986 SEC race.

Auburn made the trip to Dallas for its Cotton Bowl date with Texas A&M. Alabama fans called it the Loser Bowl, having defeated both teams in the regular season. A competitive game got out of hand late as the Aggies pulled away, and Alabama alumnus Jackie Sherrill drew the ire of Tiger supporters with a last-second touchdown when the issue had already been settled, making the final score, 36–16. The Tigers, on top of many preseason polls, finished 8–4 in another season of broken dreams.

Dye and Auburn were at a crossroads. For the second successive season, a supremely talented Tiger team had fallen far short of expectations and had lost to Alabama in excruciating fashion. This, as well as the loss of many key seniors, including Bo Jackson and Pat Washington, meant his program was due for an overhaul. He would not disappoint them.

ROLL TIDE

Three Hours for All Time

FEW THINGS are as near and dear to my heart as Auburn-bashing. As a Bama fan, this is a natural instinct. Nevertheless, there are times when gallantry on both sides of the rivalry demands respect. One of these came on November 30, 1985. In my mind there will never be another college football game like the 1985 Iron Bowl. Truly, this one offered a little bit of everything that draws people to the sport. The underdog roars to an early lead and looks ready for a blowout. No one really expects it to happen, and sure enough, the favorite charges back. The third quarter is the calm before the storm, a prelude to the greatest fifteen minutes in the history of the series.

Of all the glorious Alabama moments I have experienced none will ever top the feeling of watching Van Tiffin's kick sail through the uprights. I had all but given up only moments earlier. Watching Shula get sacked at his own 12-yard line, I sat dreading the thought of another year of gloom. When Bell ran the reverse, I didn't think he had a chance. When Richardson caught the pass over the middle, I didn't think he'd get out of bounds. When Tiffin ran onto the field, I didn't think he'd make it. When the official signaled that he did, I didn't think I'd ever forgive myself for being such a doubter.

I guarantee that if you ask the Tigers who played in this Game about the one low point of their entire football career, most would say "Bama, '85." Strange as it may sound coming from a true believer, no one who played in this game has any reason to regret how he played for sixty minutes. In this, the Game of Games, heroes abounded. Long live Pat Washington. Long live Mike Shula. Long live Bo Jackson and his broken ribs. Long live Van Tiffin. Long live the Game.—S.B.

WAR EAGLE

This One Hurt

OF THE hundreds of Auburn games I've seen over the last two decades, this was by far the worst loss. Getting blown out, you can handle. To lose like this, however, to have it all in your hands and see it vanish in less than a minute, to watch it end with no chance to reply, that is far worse. To this day, I cannot watch Tiffin's kick. When I reviewed the tape of the Game for this book, it ruined my whole day.

Try to imagine what 1985 was like. The season had been an uphill battle for recognition and respect. In the last game of the season, with less than a minute to play, you stand at your lousy visitor's seat in Legion Field and see your team drive toward the possibly winning score. A victory redeems all that has passed in the last ten weeks. Ahead is a year of celebrating. The noise around you is all laughter, cheers, and excitement.

Yet when the opposition gets the ball back, they don't get stuffed. They make a couple of first downs. They cross midfield. Now you're back into the Game, cheering for all you're worth, but you still don't really believe you'll lose. How could you think such a thing when you were feeling so good just a moment ago? Time is running out. They won't have time to score, you tell yourself. They line up for an impossibly long field goal. There's no way they'll make it; it's just desperation.

The kick is good.

The clock runs out.

The Game is lost.

Suddenly, instantly, the cheering around you is cut off. It is swept away by a screaming, raucous roar from the opposite side of the field. You watch, silent, stunned, as the field is swamped by an ugly stain of red and white. Disbelief all around you.

"Was it really good?"

"It didn't look good from here."

Finally, you begin to file out, silently, somberly. The opposing fans are everywhere, even in your section, and they are far from silent. The jam of people backs up for nearly half an hour, and you stand there amid the crumbling concrete and dripping steel of Legion Field, a place you abhor. You try not to listen, but every voice seems amplified, in your ear.

When you finally clear the wretched gates, you walk through the awful neighborhood, past the packs of Alabama campers and motor homes, all blaring out that damn song. Corpulent rednecks who never darkened the door of a college classroom romp around you, all hollering that damn phrase.

You hear it again and again. You hear it while you're stuck in traffic for hours, trying just to get away. You read it as you stare blankly out the windows, shoe-polished on the back of pickups and rusty jalopies, painted with the score you just want to forget.

That night, try as you might to shut them out, all you can hear are snatches of conversation about the Game. You toss and thrash in bed, unable to sleep, seeing the replay in your mind over and over. You watch it in growing dread because your ordeal is just beginning. You know that you'll be seeing it and hearing about it for days, months, even years. You know that *they* are waiting for you at work, at school, and on the street with struts, smug grins, and the inevitable, "So, what did ya think of the Game?"

The first few days are hellish. You keep the television off, especially during the local news. You avoid newspapers. Slowly the rhythms of daily life begin to mute the din. You still see the T-shirts and the bumper stickers (Christmas shopping is even more of a chore), but they get fewer and farther between as the months drag on. It gets easier, but there is still a bitter taste in your mouth that won't go away. On the best day of the next year, your joy is dimmed by the dark memory of the Game. On the worst day of the next year, there will be a reminder of the outcome that makes you feel just that much worse.

Eventually, finally, you find yourself in the stands again. A year has passed and the bitterness and the memories of the last 365 days well up inside you. All you want is for the pain to end, to take your turn in the victor's seat. You will do it all again. You are back here, knowing that you might just have another year in the wilderness ahead of you because you don't even have a choice. It's in your blood, your bones. You will always be back, but that doesn't make the long walk back to the car any easier.

Even so, there is the one shining moment of the 1985 Game, and his name was Bo Jackson. There has never been an athlete quite like Bo. There will probably never be another like him again. His performances in the 1985 season and the 1985 Game are only a small fraction of his magnificent career, but they were enough to earn him the highest individual honor in college football. Despite the grousing of anti-Bo, anti-Auburn elements in the national media, Bo richly deserved the Heisman Trophy.

What did Bo Jackson do for Auburn? As Coach Dye said, "Bo was a talent that gave us a chance to win every game we played." I can't imagine Auburn winning the monumental 1982 Game without Bo, and the 1983 contest, of course, was a virtuoso Jackson performance. As far as the debacle just chronicled, Auburn would have been spared a lot of heartbreak at the end, because the Tigers wouldn't have been close without the quiet courage of Bo Jackson. He, along with his teammates and coaches, put Auburn back on the national map years ahead of schedule. He has excelled ever since.

Vincent Jackson survived a daunting childhood to become an exemplary member of society. With the guidance of his late mother, Florence Bond, and his wife, Dr. Linda Jackson, Bo has become a potent voice for children with disabilities and for education. He is a family man, proud beyond words of his three children. He has never stooped to the fads of braggadocio, trash talking, or touchdown dances. Bo Jackson is an outstanding role model for decent people everywhere.—W.C.

1986

A TREND IS REVERSED

EVEN BEFORE AUBURN'S 1985 season ended in Dallas, Pat Dye decided to make serious changes, both in his program and in his mind-set regarding the Game. Auburn's offensive performance after leaving the wishbone had been a mixed bag. The I-formation, with Jack Crowe calling the plays, wasn't moving the ball with any kind of consistency and showed no more ability to come back against a fast team than did the wishbone. The Auburn faithful blamed Crowe for the two losses to Alabama, particularly in 1984, and he was let go early in 1986, followed by defensive coordinator Frank Orgel. The change paid off handsomely when defensive line coach Wayne Hall was promoted to defensive coordinator and proceeded to build squads that were among the elite of the conference for years to come.

Dye was tired of quarterback problems, so he called on another Heisman great, Pat Sullivan, who was in private business in Birmingham, to join the Auburn staff as quarterbacks coach. It was a calculated risk, as Sullivan had never coached before, but he was one of the most beloved players in Auburn history. If the return of Number 7 to the field didn't add numbers to the win column, he would certainly fire up the Tiger fans by his presence.

Coming off of a New Year's Day bowl with a Heisman Trophy winner in 1985, Dye's job was not in jeopardy, but he was taking a beating in the press. Two consecutive losses to Alabama were not serving to endear him to Auburn alumni. Whatever the complaints, the importance of the Game and the desire to beat Ray Perkins, whom Dye regarded as something of an upstart, were enough to cause Dye to break out in hives the night after the '85 Game. After that experience, Dye resolved to back away from the hype and the tension surrounding Auburn's greatest rivalry. He would do everything in his power to win, but he was going to stop fearing the thought of losing.

Ray Perkins entered his fourth season at Alabama favored to win the SEC, and it was easy to see why. His 1985 team returned seventeen starters, including Cornelius Bennett, Gene Jelks, Mike Shula, and Van Tiffin, the latter two quickly becoming Tide folk heroes. Also, 1986 had been a bountiful recruiting year, as Perkins claimed highly sought-after players such as cornerback John Mangum, linebacker Vantriese Davis, and quarterback Billy Ray. Perkins was confident enough to schedule a twelfth regular-season game against a traditional national power, Ohio State, in the Kickoff Classic. The Alabama schedule also included dates with Notre Dame at home and Penn State on the road. Perkins was obviously looking to move his team back into the national picture in a big way.

In spite of this, Perkins was still having a hard time with his many critics. His often-abrasive style was still rubbing his own camp the wrong way. Perkins knew that to cement himself as a successful heir to Paul Bryant he needed a national championship. He had to beat Auburn to keep his job, but only a significant splash on the national scene would silence the carping.

FOR THE first time in three years, Auburn was considered an SEC follower rather than a leader. With the departure of Bo Jackson, halfback duties fell to senior Brent Fullwood, who was less well known than his predecessor, but still an All-America-quality back. Dye was fond of saying that Jackson was the only player in the nation capable of keeping Fullwood on the bench.

Junior Jeff Burger would start at quarterback, and he brought the passing game back to the Auburn offense with a vengeance, aided by a spectacular sophomore receiver, Lawyer Tillman. The defense looked to be stronger and more mature, led by linebackers Kurt Crain and Aundray Bruce, tackle Tracy Rocker, and cornerback Kevin Porter. After releasing Orgel and Crowe, Dye declined to name a full-time offensive coordinator, relying instead on "offense by committee" with the plays being called by receivers coach Larry Blakeney, running back coach Bud Casey, Pat Sullivan, and Dye himself. It was a convoluted system, but the presence of Sullivan and

Blakeney in the offensive loop assured Auburn of a more aggressive passing game in 1986.

The Tigers had easy opening wins at home against Tennessee-Chattanooga (42–14) and East Carolina (45–0), followed by a showdown with Tennessee, which had been picked by some as the favorite in the conference. After the embarrassing 1985 loss in Knoxville, the AU defense was particularly anxious for revenge, and they ravaged the Vols all day long, allowing only a single touchdown with a two-point conversion. Fullwood had one of his best games ever, with 207 yards, and Auburn showed ABC's cameras a thorough 34–8 whipping.

Auburn had a home-and-home series with Penn State set to begin this season, but the Nittany Lions abruptly decided that two SEC teams a year were too much and pulled out. As a result, Auburn's 1986 out-of-conference schedule was on the weak side. Western Carolina, Vanderbilt, and Georgia Tech followed Tennessee and were all demolished. Mississippi State was having its best season in years, but they were sorely disappointed in Starkville as the Tigers stuffed the run and sacked quarterback Don Smith repeatedly, rolling easily to another blowout, 35–6, in a televised game.

The Tigers flew into Gainesville looking to snap a two-game losing streak to Florida. Auburn led, 17–0, going into the fourth period. Florida's Kerwin Bell was injured and didn't play until the final fifteen minutes. In one of the great comebacks in SEC history, Bell passed and scrambled for a touchdown, then drove far enough for Robert McGinty (who had transferred from Auburn after his 1984 Game debacle) to hit a fifty-one-yard field goal. With only seconds left on the clock, Bell threw for a final touchdown and executed a two-point conversion, and Florida managed the miracle, 18–17.

Cincinnati took their lumps as Homecoming fodder, 52–7, and then it was time to play Georgia for a shot at the Sugar Bowl. Vince Dooley came back to Auburn with a big, tough team and played a game of old-fashioned physical football. Georgia walked away with a classic, 20–16.

Georgia fans, not known for fine sportsmanship after big wins, stormed the field at Jordan-Hare Stadium and began tearing up the turf. It was the first time in memory that an opponent's fans had invaded Auburn's field, and fights broke out on the field and in the stands. The Auburn campus police turned on the stadium's high-powered sprinkler system, spraying down the fans on the field and in the visitors' section. Auburn fans would cheer "H-O-S-E, hose them Dawgs!" for years, and T-shirts reading "If you can't beat 'em, hose 'em," were seen on Georgia fans well into the nineties.

BEFORE ALABAMA could focus on living up to preseason expectations, two tragedies rocked the team. In April, running back George Scruggs was killed in a car accident and defensive back Vernon Wilkinson was seriously injured. Less than a week from the season opener with Ohio State, defensive lineman Willie Ryles collapsed on the practice field and died of a blood clot.

Playing with heavy hearts, the Tide managed a messy 16–10 win over the Buckeyes in the Kickoff Classic, then flew to Columbus, Georgia, for Ryles's funeral. In time, Alabama's concentration returned. Vanderbilt (42–10) and Southern Miss (31–7) were dispatched with ease, followed by an impressive win in a rare matchup with Florida in Gainesville, 21–7.

The Tide then looked to a Birmingham showdown with Notre Dame, seeking to overcome the darkest blot on Bear Bryant's record, namely the Bear's never having beaten the Irish during his long career. The Legion Field crowd was ready for a blowout and was not disappointed. The play of the game came courtesy of Cornelius Bennett. The senior All-American pummeled Irish quarterback Steve Beuerlein for an unforgettable sack, igniting the crowd and team, and Alabama rolled to a 28–10 win in a game that turned a lot of heads in the state and the nation.

After a 37–0 shutout of Memphis State, Alabama traveled north to Knoxville for a date with Tennessee. Bobby Humphrey ran for 217 yards, and the Tide easily ended a four-game losing streak at the hands of the Vols, 56–28. Afterward, Bama was the second-ranked team in the nation, looking for their first real shot at national honors since the 1970s. Those hopes were dashed a week later in Legion Field when Penn State dominated Alabama defensively, pinning a 23–3 loss on Perkins's team and unleashing the old complaints once again. Mississippi State, coming off the loss to Auburn, had Alabama at home next, and it was a case of serious deja vu as the Tide blew out the Bulldogs, 38–3. Humphrey was again superb, gaining a school-record 284 yards on the ground.

Louisiana State was next, rolling into Legion Field for a crucial SEC battle. Alabama played well, solidly outgaining the Tigers, but Shula threw two interceptions and Humphrey fumbled twice, one inside the LSU one-yard line. The Bayou Bengals pulled off a big win in Birmingham, 14–10. Alabama could no longer afford a loss in the conference if they were to have a shot at the Sugar Bowl. Temple was expected to be an easy Homecoming win, but Bama struggled against the Owls, eventually walking away with a 24–14 win. The season was not the unqualified success that some had predicted, but there were many bright spots. The sophomore Humphrey was already a sensation, the first Tide back to rush for more than one thousand yards in a season (in 1942 Auburn's Monk Gafford was the first Tiger to reach that mark).

By all accounts, the pre-Game week in 1986 was particularly intense, featuring some of the toughest language in the history of this always-heated rivalry. In an interview with the *Atlanta Constitution*, Perkins belittled Dye, saying that the Georgia graduate "can't possibly have the same feeling as I have about this game. . . . He's not an Auburn person. I went to Alabama and played there." Then he added insult to injury in a speech to the Montgomery Quarterback Club.

Auburn and Dye had been trying to move the Tigers' home games with Alabama to Jordan-Hare Stadium and met with outraged resistance from Alabama and Birmingham officials. At the Montgomery Quarterback Club, Perkins commented on the proposed move with the words, "It won't happen." In so doing, he unleashed an emotional response from Auburn officials, alumni, students, and fans that would last for years.

This had not been an easy year for Pat Dye. His defense had collapsed twice against teams that it should have been able to put away. Rumblings from fair-weather fans and a small, vocal Auburn minority that had never accepted Dye led to other rumors, including reports that Dye would defect to the University of Texas. In the end, Dye resolved simply to ignore the distractions.

A common thread ran through the editorializing and coffee break conversations before the 1986 Game. There was little question that Auburn again had the edge in overall talent, even considering outstanding individual Alabama players such as Humphrey, Jelks, and Bennett, but there was a sense that the Tide would find a way to win regardless. Auburn led the conference in offense and defense, but its schedule had been relatively light, with the only impressive win coming early against Tennessee. Auburn had failed to live up to expectations for three consecutive seasons, and many thought the success of 1982–83 had been too much, too soon.

Whatever the reasons, Auburn teams with the potential to dominate the conference and challenge the nation had fallen short in opportunity after opportunity. Alabama, on the other hand, had apparently bounced back from the disasters of 1984, and Perkins seemed to be building a strong team for the future. The Tide's only losses had come at the hands of the eventual national (Penn State) and SEC (LSU) champions. Alabama still had a chance to go to the Sugar Bowl if it could beat Auburn and Tulane could upset LSU.

Despite the recent loss to LSU, Alabama was ranked number seven going into the Iron Bowl. Auburn was number fourteen, because of the Florida and Georgia defeats. The state sportswriters, who had followed both sides closely, picked Alabama by a single point, 21–20. The bookies went with the rankings and made the Tide a three-point favorite.

The weather was a concern. For years it seemed that Legion Field required a good wetting before a game could begin, and in 1986 the clouds were leaden at kickoff time. The Alabama mascot, Big Al, brandished an umbrella, not for the rain, but in jest of Auburn's hosing the Georgia fans off the field two weeks prior. In response, the Tigers' mascot, Aubie, carried a garden hose throughout the pre-Game festivities.

Alabama entered the Game with a banged-up offensive line. Larry Rose, a star for the Tide at guard, had orthoscopic knee surgery the Monday before the Game and was out for the season. Center Wes Neighbors had a broken right hand, but he would play well in a heavy cast, snapping the ball with his left hand. Strong tackle Larry Otten was suffering from a pulled hamstring and was unable to participate. Auburn, however, would come onto Legion Field at full strength. Both teams were elated by the announcement of first team All-American honors for Auburn's Fullwood and Tamburello and for Alabama's Bennett.

AUBURN OWNED the ball first, and the new and improved passing offense was able to move the ball as far as midfield before having to relinquish it. Alabama executed only three plays before returning the pigskin. On the Tigers' second possession, Burger came out throwing and then began handing the ball off to his running backs. Slowly Auburn began to move downfield with short gains on the ground punctuated by high-percentage passes that backed the Tide toward its end zone. Burger had the ball first and ten on the Alabama 31 and decided to try for a quick score. Lawyer Tillman was in the end zone, and the defender covering him, Ricky Thomas, was shorter than the receiver and unable to cover the play. So Thomas did the only thing he could to save a touchdown. He rolled into Tillman's legs, earning a fifteen-yard interference call but keeping Auburn off the scoreboard. With the ball on the 16-yard line, the Tiger offense began to run out of steam. A short run by Fullwood, an incomplete pass, and a delay-of-game penalty later, Burger attempted a dangerous pass on third down. The only person near the ball was Alabama's Steve Wilson, who made the interception in the end zone, killing the Auburn drive.

With the ball on his own 20, Alabama's Humphrey had little more success than Auburn's Fullwood—at first. He was wrapped up on his first-down carry, but on the next play he led the Tigers on a spectacular forty-two-yard chase down the sideline. Two plays later, Humphrey again zipped through a hole, this time taking the ball to the Auburn four-yard line. Perkins figured he had a good thing going and called Humphrey's number again. The Bama running back took the ball to the one. He was stopped again on his second attempt. Facing third and goal, Bell replaced Humphrey in the backfield, but Bell was a decoy. Shula connected with his tight end, Angelo Stafford, in the corner of the end zone to score the first points of the afternoon with just over three minutes left in the opening quarter.

Auburn responded on the ground, using its full complement of running backs. Starting at the Tigers 28, Fullwood rose to the Humphrey challenge and ripped through the line on first down, breaking tackles on his way to a thirty-one-yard gain. After a short run by Agee, Burger threw to Fullwood, but he was stopped just short of the first down. Reggie Ware, coming out of the wishbone formation as a fullback, moved the chains. The running game opened up for Auburn as Tim Jesse and Vincent Harris ran a pair of plays for another first down. The quarter ended with Auburn threatening on the Alabama 18. As soon as the two teams switched sides, Fullwood opened the second period by dashing untouched through the line for a touchdown and tying the score at seven apiece.

Alabama failed to do much but exercise Jelks on two runs and a failed pass route and punt the ball back to Auburn. The Tigers' Trey Gainous returned the punt twenty-one yards, giving his team great field position. Almost immediately Auburn was back on Alabama's 10-yard line. Four plays into the drive, Fullwood carried the ball easily into the end zone, but a penalty nullified the score and pushed Auburn back to the 20. Three plays later, the Tigers could advance the ball only to the 10. The field goal was a short attempt and should have been automatic, but the kick sailed wide right. Auburn had failed to score on two out of three opportunities inside the Bama 20.

Bobby Humphrey carried the ball on Alabama's next series, and he picked up a first down after two carries. Perkins then directed Shula to take to the air, misfiring at first on two short routes, but finally completing a pass to Greg Richardson to keep the drive alive. After narrowly avoiding an interception, Shula, who was being forced to throw too soon for his receivers to get open, switched back to the run. Humphrey raced twenty yards to the Auburn 23. Two unsuccessful plays later, he ran a sweep outside to the 12 and a first down. One play later, Doug Allen took the ball to the seven-yard line. Shula went back to the air, to Humphrey in the corner of the end zone, putting Bama back on top, 14–7. The officials, however, hadn't seen Bell

obstructing the defenders closest to Humphrey. The noncall notwithstanding, it had been an excellent drive for Alabama, answering Auburn's mis-
fortune with a Humphrey showcase.

Auburn took over on offense at its 27, needing to get some points to
go with its statistics. They would need to wait for another opportunity as
this drive stalled on a penalty and an inspired Alabama defense. The Tide
lost yardage on the punt reception and through a clipping call, setting its
offense back to the five-yard line.

As deep as Bama was, it took only a simple handoff to Humphrey to
dig themselves out quickly. The big sophomore broke tackles and pounded
the ball out to the 26, but then the offense began to sputter. Facing third and
long, Shula dropped back but had to scramble, dashing madly to the right
side and just past the first-down marker. Humphrey carried the ball twice for
seven tough yards, and Shula found Bell again to move the chains to the
Auburn 49. A short pass to Humphrey yielded only a few yards, but he followed that with a great run to the Auburn 26. With little time left on the
clock before the half, Alabama moved quickly to take advantage of the situation. Shula threw incomplete on the first down. On the next he was looking for Bell in the end zone. This time the Auburn secondary was where it
needed to be. Bell was covered thoroughly, and the pass was picked off by
Kevin Porter. Auburn had averted another Bama score, and the Tigers ran
out the clock to end the half, trailing 14–7.

ALABAMA CAME out running in the second half but had to punt when the
offense failed to make a first down. Auburn took over at its own 24. On the
second play of the possession, Burger overthrew Tillman and was intercepted
by Freddie Robinson at the Auburn 47. The turnover looked like a great
opportunity for the Tide, but the Tigers' defense dug in and forced another
punt, giving the offense the ball on the Auburn 14. The Tigers, however,
fumbled the ball back to the Tide on the following play at the Auburn 16.

The Auburn defense demonstrated why they were the top-ranked unit
in the country by stopping the Tide and forcing a fourth-down situation.
Van Tiffin trotted out for a short attempt, and Alabama extended its lead to
ten points, 17–7.

When the Tigers next had the ball on offense, they were able to make
a first down, but the drive stalled and again their well-exercised punter
returned to the field, avoiding a return and giving Alabama the ball at its
own 20, with 6:47 left in the third period. The Auburn defense managed to
hold Humphrey back on two plays, but he broke free on a third and moved
the down markers. His success was followed immediately by Doug Allen on

an identical play for an identical gain and a first down. The Tide continued to move the ball on the ground, with Humphrey and Allen making nine yards on two carries. Shula called his own number to get the first down in Auburn territory. The drive began to fizzle out after a holding call moved the Tide back to first and twenty at its own 45. Perkins went to the pass again, but a shovel pass barely gained three yards, and the next two were incompletions. Though not quite as worn out as Auburn's punter, Bama's Chris Mohr returned to the field to surrender the ball back to the Tigers.

Trey Gainous muffed the punt but fell on the ball at his own 21 to begin Auburn's next possession. Tim Jessie, running from the tailback position, ran around left end for a much-needed nineteen-yard gain. Harris thundered through the middle for another five, but then Burger lost the snap and fell on the ball, wasting second down. On third and seven, Jessie slipped down in the backfield. Auburn would have lost another possession had Bama not been flagged for a late hit, giving the Tigers new life. Burger immediately rifled a pass between two defenders to Tillman on the sideline for a first down at the Alabama 34-yard line. Another completion was good for eight yards, and the third quarter ended with that play.

The scenario was playing itself out much as it had in 1985, and both groups of fans remembered that the lead had changed four times in the fourth quarter the previous year. Everyone expected fireworks. Alabama was doing very well, with Humphrey playing one of the best games of his career, and Auburn was beginning to play like the conference leader in offense and defense.

Whatever confidence Alabama loyalists were feeling going into the fourth quarter, they couldn't have appreciated the period's first play. Brent Fullwood took the ball and burst through the line like greased lightning and into the end zone. The point after was good, and suddenly this Game was looking as competitive as those of recent memory. Alabama led, 17–14, with almost a full quarter to go. This Game was paralleling the previous year's eerily.

Alabama took the ball at its 25. Keeping the ball on the ground, the Tide began to sweep down the field on the feet of Humphrey, Allen, and Jelks. In five plays the three backs moved the ball to the Auburn three-yard line, much of that coming on a spectacular Jelks run around right end that ended with his tightroping the sideline. A clipping call, however, backed them up to the Auburn 18. Humphrey carried the ball again, but a delay-of-game penalty moved the Tide back another five yards. Shula threw incomplete into the end zone and then had to scramble on the next play, taking the ball out of bounds at the 20. Tiffin came in for what looked to be an easy three points, but he missed, sending the ball wide to the left.

Auburn's following offensive series began with the same kind of miscues that had stalled the previous Alabama drive, starting with an offsides call on first down, backing them up to their own 17. The Tigers' coaching staff called for a run-and-pass mix that quickly moved the ball down the field and past the first-down marker occasionally. Burger was finding his receivers, and Fullwood made crucial third-down yardage when needed. Although the halfback was shaken up on one such play and had to leave the field, he returned to take the ball through the line for the drive's second and third first downs before having to leave the field a second time. Fullwood limped out again, forcing Auburn to go to the air. Burger threw two incompletions before connecting with a leaping Tillman at the Alabama 21. The Tiger faithful almost lost their religion when Tim Jessie fumbled a handoff twice before falling on the ball at the 31 for a ten-yard loss. The rest of the drive was not as graceful. Burger threw to Tillman, who had drawn double coverage in the end zone. The pass was underthrown, and Kermit Kendrick made the interception, killing Auburn's drive on the Alabama four. Burger failed to see an open Fullwood, and Auburn had committed its fourth turnover of the Game, squandering an opportunity to take the lead. The clock showed 7:56 left to play.

Taking the ball over inside its five-yard line, Alabama quickly ran the ball up the middle and beyond the first-down marker to the 18. Humphrey carried on the next three plays but failed to make the down. So Bama returned the ball to Auburn at the Tigers' 33-yard line. As long as Fullwood was in the backfield, Auburn ran the ball. He and Agee carried the ball for a first down—just barely—at the 43. On the next play, Fullwood avoided three defenders in the backfield and ran out of bounds, gaining only a yard. When he went to the sideline for a short rest, Auburn went to the air. Burger connected with his tight end, Reeves, at midfield. On third and three, the quarterback couldn't find an open receiver and scrambled to the line of scrimmage. With 2:18 remaining in the Game, Auburn faced a critical fourth-down situation.

The next play would decide the Game. Auburn's offensive committee had to call a sure thing, and most thought that they would go to Fullwood, counting on their talented senior to get the desperately needed yardage. When Auburn lined up, however, Fullwood wasn't on the playing field. Alabama called a quick time-out to consider its options. It also gave Auburn another opportunity to consider its choice of play. When play resumed, Burger dropped back and threw a pass to the flat. Trey Gainous, with a history of being in the right place at the right time, was the target. The pass was low, and Gainous, who was covered well, dove sideways and pulled the ball in just inches off the AstroTurf. From the stands it was hard to see whether the ball had been trapped or caught. The official nearest the play ruled the pass complete and a first down.

Dye didn't call the next play himself, he simply pointed to the end zone. With Fullwood in the backfield, the ball stayed on the ground. The senior ran the ball through the Alabama linebackers to the Tide 21. Tommie Agee carried the ball next through the middle for another eleven yards. With first and goal and 1:20 left to play, Harris carried to the seven.

As the clock ticked down to double digits, confusion reigned on the Auburn sideline. Dye and Casey were trying to find Scott Bolton to send him onto the field and run a reverse. The offense waited while precious seconds passed. The reverse was signaled in, but the wrong players were on the field. Frantically, Lawyer Tillman signaled for a time-out as he lined up on the right side. He had never run the reverse in a game, only in practice. In the noise and the tumult of seventy-five thousand raucous fans, he went unnoticed by both his quarterback and the officials.

Not realizing that the substitution had not been made, Burger ran the play. He took the ball to the right and tossed back to Tim Jessie, who was heading for the right corner of the end zone. Tillman knew how the play worked, and he was in the right place to take the next handoff from Jessie and turn the left corner. He took the play inside, the blocking was there, and Number 85 sailed nearly untouched across the goal line and into Auburn legend for the biggest touchdown of his life. The Auburn faithful erupted in celebration, making the previous chaos look organized, quieting down just enough to let Chris Knapp kick the extra point and make the score 21–17 with only thirty-two seconds left. It had taken fifty-nine and a half minutes, but Auburn had taken the lead in the Game.

After Humphrey returned the kickoff to the 30, Alabama had twenty-seven seconds to steal Auburn's thunder and pull off yet another Iron Bowl miracle. This time, however, a field goal would not be enough. Had Tiffin converted his earlier attempt following Fullwood's fumble, the task would have been a little easier. It was not up to the little senior from Red Bay to lead the Tide to the promised land. This time, that burden fell on Mike Shula.

Shula's first pass was batted down, incomplete. With twenty-two seconds left, his second pass was too high and deflected. He couldn't find an open receiver on third down, so he scrambled out of bounds just short of the Bama 40-yard line. Six seconds remained on the clock, and it was fourth down. Perkins made the only call he could, a Hail Mary pass. Shula took the ball, dodged a tackler, and hurled his longest, highest pass just as the last second ticked off the clock. The ball came down into a mob of three Alabama and three Auburn players well downfield. It was batted to the turf. There were no flags. There were no last-second heroics for Alabama. The Game had been another classic, and Auburn broke a two-year losing streak to win, 21–17.

Fullwood and Humphrey walked away with well-deserved MVP honors. Cornelius Bennett, not believing that he had lost to Auburn in his last Game, sat disconsolately on the sideline. Fullwood saw his friend and rival and ran toward him, pulling Bennett to his feet. He embraced the other senior in respect and admiration. It was a class act. For those who follow these two teams in daily love and hate, it was a poignant reminder that frequently the players on both sides of the field had grown up together and played ball together; they were more likely to be close friends than bitter enemies.

THIS WIN probably meant more to Pat Dye than any other in his distinguished career. Under virtually constant pressure since the 1984 season from much of the state press and deeply hurt by a year of rumors, Dye had enough

Auburn's Lawyer Tillman (85) scores on an end-around play that he had never run before and enters the Tigers' pantheon of heroes.

to deal with before Perkins's accusations about the meaning of the Game to an "outsider." The Auburn coach was jubilant in victory, seeming more like one of his players, more like an enthusiastic college student than a worldly wise, fortyish football coach. He wasn't shy about revealing his reasons. "With all the talk this week," he said in the aftermath, "this was certainly the sweetest win ever for me." When asked again about Perkins's pre-Game comments, Dye was blunt and to the point. "It's awful hard for me to believe that this game meant more to Ray than it meant to me. I don't believe that he loves his players any more than I love mine."

Lawyer Tillman, who became a household name overnight, called his touchdown "the greatest thrill of my life." Tillman, like Bo Jackson, had been the recipient of some hard words from the Alabama coaching staff during recruiting, and like Jackson, always seemed to bring something extra to the Game.

In the other locker room, Ray Perkins tried to settle his mind about a Game that meant everything to him. "My gut doesn't feel too good right now," he said. "I'm going to hurt from this loss. And the players are, too . . . it would be wrong if it didn't hurt. We'll learn from it."

Bobby Humphrey had delivered a Herculean effort in his first Iron Bowl start, gaining 204 yards against the SEC's top defense, and it hadn't been enough. Alabama would once again have the balm of a Sun Bowl trip to ease the pain of an Iron Bowl loss, and the Tide beat Washington 28–3 on Christmas Day, capping a year of what might have been.

IN HIS post-Game press conference, Ray Perkins blasted a report that he would be leaving Alabama to rejoin the NFL coaching ranks by accepting the head job of the Tampa Bay Buccaneers. In December, however, Perkins found professional football appealing when he was offered and accepted the position with Tampa Bay. The Bear's anointed heir left for warmer climes. Some wondered if he would have gone had Alabama won the Iron Bowl; others said that Perkins had had enough of following a legend.

Following a brief search, Alabama president Joab Thomas selected an old friend of Perkins's, Bill Curry of Georgia Tech, to take up the mantle of Tide head coach. Although the spirit of the Bear was again invoked at the time of Curry's hiring, rumblings from the old guard had begun. It would be a hard road for a Tech man to walk, but Thomas was determined to change Alabama's national reputation as a football factory and move the university's priorities back to academics. He denied Curry the athletic director's office, choosing Steve Sloan in his stead. In Thomas's eyes, Sloan, one of Bear's boys, could mollify the critics, while Curry, a fine coach with a reputation as a strong academic and moral voice, could lead the team to victory without sacrificing the classroom. It was a calculated move, one that would affect Alabama football for many years to come. It was not lost on the Alabama faithful that Curry had never beaten Auburn as a head coach, losing seven consecutive times to the Tigers.

AUBURN TRAVELED to Orlando for the Citrus Bowl on New Year's Day and defeated Southern Cal, 16–7, for the school's five hundredth all-time victory, but not without controversy. First, Dye had accepted the Citrus Bowl bid by telephone, then barely an hour later received an invitation from the Orange Bowl. Dye refused to renege on his commitment, even though it would cost Auburn more than $1 million in bowl revenue. The second and more lasting problem was Dye's allowing Brent Fullwood to play in the bowl, despite the fact that Fullwood had stopped attending classes late in the fall quarter. It was completely within NCAA rules for Fullwood to participate, but Dye was harshly criticized by many for placing football above academics.

Dye didn't see it that way. He felt that Auburn owed Fullwood something for his patience and performance. Fullwood would have been a four-year starter anywhere else, but at Auburn he had been in the shadow of Bo Jackson for three seasons. In Dye's mind, both situations were matters of living up to his personal commitments. The criticism was brutal, but Dye weathered the storm. "Sometimes I get in trouble making decisions [from the heart]," he said later. "But I don't mean to stop doing what I believe to be the right thing so that I can be popular."

ROLL TIDE

Par for the Course

NINETEEN EIGHTY-SIX was supposed to be a banner year for Alabama sports. Ray Perkins's first recruits, now seniors, were going to lead the way to New Orleans. I remember, going into the fall, how bright the prospects looked. The football team looked like a runaway freight train after demolishing Notre Dame and Tennessee. Bobby Humphrey was breaking records, Cornelius Bennett was breaking quarterbacks, and Ray Perkins was actually breaking out an occasional smile or two.

Then something went wrong. Along came the LSU loss. With one obvious exception, that was the worst loss of the season. Winning that one would have meant Bourbon Street, but the Tide found a way to lose. I'll never understand how LSU took four straight on the road from Bama, but they did. As for 1986, it only got worse.

I was at the Auburn game at the invitation of some Auburn friends. Thus I found myself mired in orange-and-blue country, but I didn't care. I was too swept up in the energy of the event to care what some prissy Auburn woman behind us thought about my sweatshirt or my strange cheering. I cheered with everything I had for three hours, just like everyone around me, except I was cheering for the other team.

I have two memories of this Game. The first is seeing Gene Jelks streak down the sideline in the fourth quarter, much as he had the year before. It seemed there was no way Bama would be denied at that point, and I was warmed by the thought of celebrating a third consecutive Iron Bowl title in the midst of the Tiger throng.

The other recollection, which I would willingly discard were it possible, is that of sitting with my head down, utterly dejected, while the Auburn band played "Louie, Louie" about twenty feet away from me. My friends, whom I had determined at this point were not so much gracious as sadistic, danced and yelled to their hearts' content. I stared at the concrete.

This Game was typical of the whole Bama year—high hopes, everything seemingly under control, then heartbreak. It was hard to imagine, watching Humphrey run so effortlessly through Tennessee (and Auburn, for that matter), that this team would go 8–3. From number two in the country to the Sun Bowl.

Making matters worse, Perkins bolted for Tampa. Say what you will about him, Ray Perkins turned Alabama around. The lure of the NFL proved too strong, and I can't blame him for leaving, but it's hard not to wonder how things would have been different if he hadn't left town.

Rather than finding out and looking forward to more trash talk between him and Pat Dye, we were left with the pain of 1986's disappointments. We had made it to the threshold and fallen short.

For Alabama, just like for all of us Tide fans on that November night, it would be a long ride back.—S.B.

WAR EAGLE

This One Was Fun!

THIS GAME wasn't a grand reaffirmation of faith. It wasn't a pivotal moment in the history of the series. It *was* something of a turning point, for both

Auburn and Alabama. What it was, was *fun*. This was the Game that put the greatest party song of all time, "Louie, Louie," permanently in the Auburn band's repertoire. This was the Game that gave us the opportunity to stick it to the living embodiment of Alabama arrogance, Smilin' Ray Perkins—with interest. This one was a blast.

I loved this one. We gave 'em seventeen and then stuck it to 'em in the fourth quarter. We dangled the prize in front of 'em for fifty-nine minutes, then snatched it away.

We even gave Van Tiffin a chance to do it again. But he missed it. If he hadn't, Shula would only have had to get close with a minute left. After hearing Van Tiffin's name all year, this was too sweet to be true.

Perkins's expression alone was worth the price of admission. He had done everything short of insulting Sue Dye's flower garden, and he couldn't back it up. He made a fool of himself with the silly comments about Pat Dye's motivation and added insult to injury by saying Auburn didn't have the clout to take control of the Game site. Sorry, Ray. He blew it and ran away to the pros a loser.

Lawyer Tillman. What a guy. Without a doubt, the best college receiver I ever saw. He may have only caught two in this one, but he made the most famous improvisation in the history of the Game (Connie Frederick notwithstanding). Jeff Burger went through a lot of garbage while he was at Auburn, but all he did was win. Kurt Crain was (and is) nothing but a champion, an Auburn man to the core. Brent Fullwood. Ben Tamburello. Tommie Agee, one of my all-time favorite players. I can't quit without mentioning Chip Powell. Powell was a walk-on. He'd been told that he was too small and too slow. He had no chance of starting in college. Dye tried to talk him into becoming a manager and learning to be a coach instead of getting his brains beaten out on the scout team. Powell stuck it out for five years, and all he did was lead the SEC in interceptions in 1986, running on nothing but heart and desire and guts.

Pat Dye? The guy who didn't understand the Game? The one who was too old-fashioned to beat a newfangled pro coach like Perkins? He blew Tampa Bay Ray off the field. Instead of building the Game up to his players and the fans, he played it cool, keeping the team relaxed and loose and the fans upbeat and confident. His Game plan was great, maybe a couple of breaks away from being a blowout. It broke a streak of luck for Bama and started Auburn on a sublime run. Did I mention that it was fun?—W.C.

1987–88

CHAMPIONSHIPS AND GROWING PAINS

THE SEASONS AND GAMES of 1987 and 1988 were bookends. Auburn was building to its peak as the SEC's flagship team of the 1980s, and Alabama struggled while working toward its own future in the next decade. It was a time of great triumphs and great turmoils, and, sadly, it was not a time of particularly exciting Auburn-Alabama Games.

1987

IN THE summer of 1987, Auburn quarterback Jeff Burger was embroiled in a dispute with his psychology professor, who accused Burger of plagiarism on a report, flunked the senior for the course, and reported him to Auburn's academic honesty committee for punishment. The committee, heavily weighted with faculty from the college of liberal arts, suspended Burger for the 1987–88 school year. Burger appealed to the university administration, which overruled the faculty council and reinstated Burger for the fall. This fracas did little to stem the ongoing hostility between Pat Dye and the anti-athletics factions of the Auburn faculty or to slow down criticism of Dye as the overseer of a "football factory."

After a ten-win season the previous year, Auburn was unlikely to sneak up on any opponents in 1987, and the Tigers were the preseason favorites to win the conference. The team was deep and talented, lacking only experience at running back. The schedule was challenging and began with a big rematch in Auburn. The Texas Longhorns, shorn of Fred Akers and inaugurating the regime of David McWilliams, came to town looking to use Auburn as a catapult back to national prominence. The upper deck on the east side of Jordan-Hare stadium had been completed in the offseason, raising Auburn's home field capacity to 85,214 fans. It was a sign of the times as Auburn demolished Texas, 31–3. Some observers list this game among the events leading to the decline and dissolution of the Southwest Conference.

Auburn was less fortunate in Knoxville. Neyland Stadium is historically unfriendly to the Tigers, but Auburn had the upper hand for most of the contest. Late in the game, the Vols pulled to within a point after a long drive. Faced with the possibility of a conference loss early in the season, Tennessee head coach Johnny Majors chose to kick the extra point, making the final score 20–20. Majors was generally lauded for smart strategy in going for the tie, a fact that would not be lost on Pat Dye in the months and years to come. The rest of the early 1987 season was more successful for Auburn, including tough 20–10 road victories over ACC foes North Carolina and Georgia Tech.

It looked like smooth sailing for Auburn until Burger's name showed up in the headlines again. This time Burger and junior tackle Jim Thompson had ridden in a private airplane for a hunting trip early in the season. Although the pilot and owner of the aircraft was an Alabama booster, there was a possibility that the NCAA would see the trip as an illegal benefit for the players. Dye held both players out of the Mississippi State game while Auburn awaited a ruling. Untested sophomore Reggie Slack stepped into Burger's shoes for the game and came through with flying colors as the Tigers won, 38–7. Finally, the NCAA determined that the hunting trip had indeed been an innocent violation, and Burger and Thompson were reinstated for the Florida game.

Auburn's 1987 schedule ended with a killer foursome. Florida came first, entering Jordan-Hare on a wild Halloween night before a national television audience and a raucous sellout Auburn crowd. The Tigers had not beaten the Gators in three years, and they paid off Galen Hall and his new superstar, Emmitt Smith, in spades. Florida fell hard, 29–6. Auburn was drained emotionally and physically when it faced Florida State the next week, and Bobby Bowden's dominant Seminole team avenged years of frustration by demolishing Auburn, 34–6, knocking the Tigers out of contention for the national title. Auburn recovered enough to whip Georgia in Athens, 27–11, beginning several years of sending the Bulldog faithful to the parking lot early. The tie with Tennessee put Auburn in position to win the SEC outright, as all the other teams in the conference had at least one loss, but the Tigers would have to beat Alabama first.

THE HIRING of Bill Curry, who had never played or coached at Alabama and was not one of "Bear's Boys," caused a major uproar throughout the state. Public opinion held that President Thomas had gone too far in his efforts to enhance the university's reputation as a leading academic institution and that Curry's selection was as much a commitment to creating choirboys as it was to building football powerhouses. Regardless of Thomas's motives, it was an unnerving time for Curry. Alabama fans were already calling for the heads of Curry, Thomas, and Sloan before the Tide played a game in 1987.

In contrast to Ray Perkins, who inherited a precariously thin cupboard of quality young players from Bryant, Curry found a solid supply of talent awaiting him in Tuscaloosa, thanks to Perkins's knack for recruiting. Bobby Humphrey and Gene Jelks returned as juniors to the Tide backfield. With two tremendous athletes vying for time at halfback, the coach decided that one should be moved to another position in order to have more impact on the field. With Humphrey's historic 1986 season in mind, Curry named him as the starting tailback. Though Jelks made no effort to hide his displeasure, he accepted a move to defense, playing cornerback.

The next of Curry's innumerable problems was replacing the graduated Mike Shula, a three-year starter, at quarterback. The choices included junior Vince Sutton (who had arrived in Tuscaloosa in 1984 to great expectations but had found little success on the field and was redshirted in 1986) and junior David Smith, who was, like Shula, a steady left-hander capable of, solid, if unspectacular play. A pair of freshmen, Jeff Dunn and the highly touted Billy Ray, also contended for the position.

Defensively, the loss of Cornelius Bennett, who was a principal in an NFL megatrade that would send him to Buffalo and four Super Bowls, can scarcely be overstated. Junior Derrick Thomas was now expected to be a leader, as were linebacker Randy Rockwell, safety Kermit Kendrick, and new cornerback Gene Jelks.

Curry made his debut on Labor Day weekend in Legion Field against Southern Miss (the construction of an upper deck at Bryant-Denny Stadium forced Alabama to play all of its 1987 home games in Birmingham). Jelks made Curry's position switch look like a stroke of genius when he intercepted a pass in the first quarter and set up Bama's first score. David Smith, who had been selected as the starting quarterback, performed well, throwing for two scores, as the Tide dusted USM, 38–6.

In spite of the impressive opening-day win, few people gave Alabama a chance the next week when the team traveled to Happy Valley to meet eleventh-ranked Penn State. The Tide, however, created havoc for the defending national champions, and Alabama rolled, 24–13, in a game that wasn't as close as the score indicates.

A week later, a national television audience watched what was supposed to be a Heisman duel between Humphrey and Florida quarterback Kerwin Bell. The day, however, belonged to a smallish Gator freshman from Pensacola, tailback Emmitt Smith. Florida claimed its first win over Alabama since 1963, 23–14. The next week, quarterback David Smith suffered a broken collarbone early in the fourth quarter against Vanderbilt, and the Commodores tied the game late. Humphrey, however, saved the day with a late touchdown, securing a 30–23 win.

Alabama smoked Southwestern Louisiana, 38–10, and with the Tide at 4–1, most of Curry's critics were silent. Few faulted him inordinately for the Florida loss. Nevertheless, the true challenges, namely Tennessee and Auburn, lay ahead, with only a seemingly simple trip to Memphis coming before the Vols. Perhaps they just didn't take Memphis State seriously, because Tide mistakes of all varieties allowed the Tigers to claim a huge 13–10 upset.

Needless to say, Curry's critics reached a new level of outrage with the humiliating loss in Memphis. With undefeated and eighth-ranked Tennessee coming into Birmingham for a Saturday night matchup, the Tide faced a huge test of pride and power. It passed on both counts, blasting the Vols, 41–22, in a game that was over by halftime. After a week off, Bama hosted Mississippi State in Legion Field, beating the Bulldogs, 21–18. At 6–2 overall and 4–1 in the SEC, the Tide faced an undefeated and fifth-ranked LSU. Derrick Thomas, on his way to earning All-America honors in 1987, summed up Bama's 22–10 victory in a jubilant Alabama locker room: "The Tide don't lose in Baton Rouge."

The high point of the previous Bama season had been the rollicking 28–10 win over Notre Dame in Birmingham. Unfortunately for Alabama, Lou Holtz's Irish monster was a year bigger and better in 1987, as a visit to South Bend revealed. With some help from eventual Heisman winner Tim Brown and in the daunting shadow of Touchdown Jesus, the Irish won a blowout, 37–6. It was the Tide's worst regular season loss in thirty years. Curry changed his quarterback four times during the game. At 7–3, with a team that didn't know what to think of itself, Curry would lead the Crimson Tide into the Iron Bowl for the first time.

THE 1987 Game was the last of its kind in that Auburn and Alabama had agreed to end the old fifty-fifty ticket split for a home-and-home arrangement, albeit both "homes" were to be Legion Field, at least from Alabama's point of view. Auburn had never accepted the split as an accurate representation of the fans in the stands—virtually all of the stadium workers and most of the more than five thousand Legion Field bond holders with free tickets were Bama fans. The Tigers were still pushing for a true home-and-home series, and Alabama was fighting just as hard to keep the Game at the Tide's second home field.

Alabama president Joab Thomas had even asked the Southeastern Conference to change the Game to a rotating, rather than annual schedule. It was a surprising request: Alabama athletics were deeply in debt and needed the guaranteed season ticket sellout that came with a home Game. Also, nobody in the conference relished giving up a comfortable whipping of a "weak sister" for a slugfest with the Tide or Tigers. The other league presidents told Thomas that he could either work out his problems and continue to play Auburn on an annual basis or get out of the conference. When the 1987 Game kicked off, the controversy over the site of future Games was still unsettled.

GOING INTO the Game, questions centered around whether or not Alabama's rushing attack could move the ball against Auburn's nation-leading defense. No running back had gained a hundred yards against Auburn in 1987. The Tide had an All-American linebacker in Derrick Thomas, but Alabama cornerbacks Jelks and Mangum were dwarfed by Auburn's Tillman and would be forced into man-to-man coverage inevitably. The Tigers' running game had been suspect early in the season, but freshmen Harry Mose and Stacey Danley were beginning to perform well. Most observers figured that Auburn would win or lose based on the play of Burger and Tillman.

The Game was one of great tension and great momentum shifts, but not of great offense. Alabama moved the ball fairly well in the first half, but big runs from Humphrey never materialized. The Tide only threatened to get into the end zone once, and not because of its offense. After Phillip Doyle missed a fifty-three-yard field goal attempt early in the second period, Auburn took over and looked miserable as a three-man sack leveled Burger on first down. The running game went nowhere, and the Tigers tried to punt. Derrick Thomas blocked the punt and pursued the ball out of bounds at the Auburn 10.

It was a great opportunity for Alabama, but three running plays ended just short of the end zone. On fourth down, instead of going to

Humphrey from the one-yard line, Curry elected for a play-action pass. Dunn's throw sailed out of the back of the end zone, and Auburn took over at the goal line.

Things looked grim for the Tigers until Burger hit Danley on third down, getting out to the 12-yard line. Two plays later, Auburn was on the verge of the play that would be the difference in the Game. Burger dropped back to pass and found Tillman racing down the sideline past the 50. Jelks was covering Tillman man-to-man, and Burger threw the ball high. The lanky Auburn receiver was behind Jelks and leaped for the ball. Jelks caught Tillman coming down and made a touchdown-saving tackle. When Tillman put the ball down after the play, Jelks kicked it in frustration, earning a fifteen-yard penalty on top of the long pass.

It looked as if Auburn's drive would end there as Derrick Thomas sacked Burger, but Alabama drew another penalty after the tackle for piling on. Stacey Danley broke through on the next play and raced to the Alabama five-yard line. Finally, freshman Harry Mose came out of the wishbone and sailed around left end for a touchdown. Mose was a huge talent and could have gone on to be one of Auburn's all-time greats, but his career ended in the 1987–88 offseason when a dangerous congenital spinal column defect was detected. Mose, though, will always be remembered as the only player to get a touchdown in the 1987 Iron Bowl.

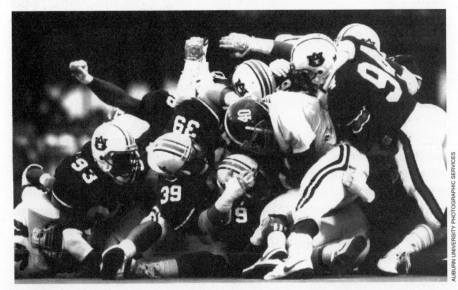

Alabama's Doug Allen (40) is stacked up. In 1987, the Tigers' defense shut out the Tide for the first time in thirty years.

The second half was an Auburn showcase. Danley came into his own as a power runner when the passing game gave way to Dye's beloved ball-control offense. The Tigers scored only once in the final half, a Win Lyle field goal to clinch the win late in the Game, but Auburn had held on to the football for twenty-three minutes in the second half. Alabama had only seventeen offensive plays in the last two quarters, compared to Auburn's thirty-eight. The Game ended 10–0, Auburn's first Iron Bowl shutout since 1957.

The win propelled the Tigers to the Sugar Bowl as the undisputed SEC champion for the second time in five years. Alabama fell to 7–4, a more than respectable record virtually anywhere, but it wasn't nearly enough for Alabama fans.

ALABAMA FOLLOWED the Auburn loss with a holiday trip to Tampa (just as Ray Perkins had a year earlier) for the Hall of Fame Bowl and a match with Michigan. The Wolverines built a 21–3 third-quarter advantage before Humphrey led a charge to push Bama ahead, 24–21. Michigan drove sixty-two yards in the final minutes, ending the game with a dramatic fourth-down twenty-yard touchdown pass to win the game, 28–24.

The game was a mirror of Curry's first year in Tuscaloosa. There were embarrassments, stirring comebacks, and late collapses all along the rocky road Bama traveled in 1987. Huge victories over Penn State, Tennessee, and LSU helped to endear the rookie coach to the Alabama faithful, but ending the season with three losses, particularly the Iron Bowl, sustained the protests of those who had objected to Curry's setting foot in Tuscaloosa.

IRONICALLY, THE conference championship and Sugar Bowl berth led to nothing but controversy for Auburn. Syracuse, the Tigers' opponent, was undefeated going into the bowls and a national media darling. Auburn started out looking dominant, forcing the Orangemen to quick-kick twice in the first quarter. Syracuse came back to make a game of it, and led, 16–13, as Auburn tried to answer in the last minute. With seconds left on the clock, the Tigers faced fourth and ten from the Syracuse 20-yard line, and Dye called for the field goal. The kick was good and the game ended with a 16–16 tie. Syracuse coach Dick MacPherson went ballistic, feeling correctly that Dye had robbed his team of a claim for the national title.

Most of the national media agreed, renaming the Auburn coach "Pat Tie" and castigating Dye for committing the cardinal sin of denying a northeastern team a shot at the brass ring. Dye took it all in good humor, going as far as to autograph and sell (for Auburn's scholarship fund) hundreds of ties sent to his office by a Syracuse radio station. Auburn fans reciprocated with a huge crate of sour grapes shipped third class to MacPherson. The Syracuse coach continued to bad-mouth Dye in the press for nearly a month and only shut up when Dye offered a ten-year home-and-home contract to settle the whole thing. For some reason, McPherson declined the offer.

1988

IN 1988, the most significant event in the rivalry occurred, not on a playing field in the fall, but in administrative offices in the spring. Auburn's push to bring the Game home to Jordan-Hare Stadium was finally resolved with an agreement between Auburn, Alabama, and the city of Birmingham, which had come into the controversy late with a lawsuit. The significant area of dispute by this time wasn't whether or not the Game would be played in Auburn, but when. Alabama forces had tacitly admitted that Auburn did indeed have the right to determine where it played its own home games, but they insisted that Auburn continue the series in Birmingham. The Auburn fans and administration were having none of it. They were still incensed by Ray Perkins's suggestion that Auburn didn't have the power to bring the Game home, and they had always rejected the idea of Legion Field, situated in the heart of Tide-stronghold Birmingham, as a "neutral site." Alabama reluctantly agreed that the mutual contract with Legion Field was about to expire, and Dye and Auburn president James Martin insisted that the 1989 Game be played in Auburn.

Taking note of the huge influx of cash accompanying the Game, Birmingham mayor Richard Arrington weighed in on January 8 with a lawsuit seeking to compel Auburn to continue playing in Legion Field. The Birmingham media were universally opposed to the change. Other state sportswriters were divided along team and regional lines. The Montgomery papers, predictably, were all in favor. Many thought the dispute would be settled in the state legislature. That body has done a great many stupid things in its time, but few legislators were foolish enough to infuriate half of their constituents, and they refused to touch the issue.

The dispute was finally settled by lawyers for the city of Birmingham and the boards of trustees of the two universities. Auburn compromised and agreed to play in Legion Field as the home team one last time, in 1991. They insisted on playing in Auburn for the first time ever on December 2, 1989. In the words of one Auburn official, "We gave up a year and got forever." For Alabama fans and alumni, who had always thought in their heart of hearts that Auburn could not overcome their legendary clout, it was a bitter pill to swallow. The long dispute was finally settled. Auburn had won the right to play its home games at home, and Alabama had lost a major psychological edge in the ongoing feud.

IN THE summer of 1988, the newspapers exploded with accusations that had the potential to bring down the Dye regime at Auburn. Charley Dare, a freshman Alabama lineman, accused Dye of offering to fix Dare's ACT scores during the recruiting process so that he would be eligible to play his freshman year, if Dare would come to Auburn. According to Dare, Dye had arranged for him to take the test at a high school in Florida where the brother-in-law of Auburn assistant Bud Casey was a teacher. Supposedly, this individual was to fix the test to get Dare past the NCAA-mandated minimum score of 18.

At first, Dye laughed off Dare's accusations. He had not seriously pursued Charley as a recruit, and he certainly would not have been willing to jeopardize his career for the lineman. As the SEC and the NCAA began to ask tough questions, Dye hurriedly marshaled his forces, getting support from the Auburn administration after a stormy meeting, and hired the best lawyer he could find. Legal representation alone would cost Auburn $350,000 over two years.

The investigations revealed that no Auburn player had ever taken the ACT at the Lake Wales high school where Casey's brother-in-law taught. Plus, Dye's office and telephone records refuted the times and dates that Dare said the alleged offer was made. Just before the final report from the NCAA was issued, Charley claimed that Auburn had also offered him $70,000. In the words of NCAA investigator Ed Lupomech, "Did it hurt their credibility? I guess I'd better not comment." By the middle of the 1989 football season, the SEC and NCAA gave Dye and Auburn a clean bill of health.

Why this whole controversy ever happened is still an open question. Whatever the reasons, the Dare case caused no small amount of bad feelings on both sides, most particularly between Curry and Dye.

AUBURN WAS again the favorite to win the SEC in 1988, despite the fact that the Tigers were replacing a two-year starter at quarterback. Reggie Slack, however, was extremely popular on the Auburn campus and had proved himself on the field, subbing for Burger in the 1987 Mississippi State game. The running back position would be a question mark, as sophomore James Joseph returned from a year off due to knee surgery, to be joined by Stacey Danley. The offensive line looked solid, led by Jim Thompson, Rodney Garner, and Rob Selby. Aundray Bruce departed from the defense, becoming the first pick in the NFL draft. Still, Wayne Hall's defense looked to be just as tough without him, returning a devastating front three of Tracy Rocker, Ron Stallworth, and Benji Roland and linebackers Craig Ogletree and Quentin Riggins.

The Tigers came out winning big, with four straight shellackings—Kentucky, Kansas, Tennessee, and North Carolina. The biggest of the four was at home against Tennessee. Auburn mauled the Vols, avenging the 1987 tie with a 38–7 blowout.

The 1988 Tigers stumbled only once in the regular season, at LSU. Auburn dominated the game, moving the ball at will and shutting down the Bengal Tiger offense for fifty-eight minutes. Auburn, however, was plagued by careless penalties, accumulating 220 yards in total penalty yardage for the game, and couldn't get the ball into the end zone, managing only two field goals. In one of the most famous comeback drives in SEC history, LSU quarterback Tommy Hodson led his team down the field as time was running out. With only seconds on the clock, he found an open receiver for the winning touchdown. The win sparked a reaction from the famously noisy LSU stands that registered on a seismograph many miles away. It also knocked a great Auburn team out of the running for a national championship.

Auburn responded with three straight shutouts over Akron, Mississippi State, and Florida. The victory over the Gators was certainly the biggest, as Auburn had not won in Gainesville since 1972, and it was Florida's Homecoming. It was a 16–0 Auburn win, and the nation began to take notice of the Tigers again. Southern Miss and Georgia were dispatched without incident, and with a 9–1 record, Auburn had a chance to capture a share of the SEC title and return to New Orleans once again.

AFTER FAILING to score against Auburn in 1987, Curry shook up his offensive staff with the addition of Homer Smith as offensive coordinator and Tommy Bowden as quarterbacks coach. Smith was considered by many to be the top offensive mind in college football and a pioneer of the shotgun formation. His intricate offensive schemes, however, would take time to implement, time that Curry didn't necessarily have. Critics who had previously lambasted the Alabama coach for being too conservative and one-dimensional now flip-flopped and griped about how Smith's offense was too complicated for the Alabama players. Sometimes, as Curry came to know well, you can't win for losing.

A long, hot summer enveloped the Alabama football program before the 1988 season arrived. Bobby Humphrey, a leading candidate for the Heisman Trophy and the top rusher in the university's history, was attacked in the parking lot of a Tuscaloosa night club early one July morning. The assailant broke Humphrey's jaw with a crowbar and was never apprehended. Even worse, Joe King, a veteran Tide lineman, was wounded in an inner-city Birmingham neighborhood known as a drug haven, and Curry kicked him off the Bama roster.

Mercifully, the football season began, and the Tide opened with a trip to Philadelphia to take on Temple. Gene Jelks returned the second-half kickoff for a touchdown, negating a slow Bama start, and the Tide toyed with the Owls, 37–0.

Another infamous incident occurred the next weekend. With Hurricane Gilbert bearing down on the Texas coast, Curry decided not to risk disaster and postponed a scheduled game with Texas A&M until after the Iron Bowl. As it turned out, the storm came no closer than five hundred miles to College Station, and Aggie coach Jackie Sherrill was incensed. Curry's decision was lampooned nationally, and a new dish called Chicken Curry replaced chicken-fried steak as the College Station entrée of choice. Nonetheless, the Tide had an unplanned week off.

Newly renovated Bryant-Denny Stadium was the scene as Vanderbilt visited the Alabama campus. The Tide's showing was as impressive as the new look of the stadium, and the Commodores were thrashed, 44–10. The win, however, was a costly one for Bama: Humphrey and Jelks, seniors who were assuming legendary status on the field, both suffered season-ending injuries in the game. The effect would be profound on the 1988 Tide.

A rare trip to Lexington was next on the schedule, as Kentucky waited to ambush wounded Alabama. The Wildcats were pumped up and struck early, but the Tide avoided a major upset, winning 31–27. Homecoming brought Ole Miss to Tuscaloosa, where the Rebels were winless in fourteen visits. The worm turned as Ole Miss beat Alabama, 22–12. The debacle easily marked Curry's lowest ebb as coach of the Tide. A brick was hurled through his office window after the game which, according to a mirthful quote from an anonymous member of the Tide staff, could not have been thrown by a Bama quarterback, as none were that accurate.

No one could dispute that Curry was on the hot seat in Tuscaloosa. At the same time, in Knoxville, Johnny Majors was probably afraid to sit down at all. His Volunteers were 0–5 heading into a home stand against the Tide, and Vol fans were showing that mutiny is not an art confined to west Alabama. Majors had come to realize that in the eyes of supporters, coaches are only as good as their last game, and a defeat at the hands of Bama would guarantee a losing season. That is exactly what happened, as the Tide prevailed, 28–21.

The eighth game of the ten-year set with Penn State was next in Birmingham. The Bama defense was spectacular, holding the Lions to eight first downs and 170 total yards. Bama won, 8–3, behind the stellar play of Derrick Thomas, among others.

After such a classic defensive struggle, Alabama turned things around with a wild offensive assault against Mississippi State for Homecoming. The teams combined for nine hundred yards of offense, and Bama's David Castieal scored four touchdowns in a 53–34 romp.

Once again, Alabama and LSU would play a game with Sugar Bowl implications, this time in Tuscaloosa. The Tide charged out to a 15–0 lead before the Tigers responded with sixteen unanswered points to claim a fourth-quarter lead. Philip Doyle put Bama back on top with a field goal. LSU's Tommy Hodson, just as he had done against Auburn, led the Bayou Bengals down the field in the closing minutes. With twenty-eight seconds left, a field goal gave LSU a 19–18 victory. The loss effectively knocked Alabama out of the SEC championship race. The Tide then sleepwalked through a 17–0 stuffing of Southwestern Louisiana in Birmingham and turned all thoughts to preventing a third straight loss to Auburn.

FOR THE first time since the series resumed in 1948, Legion Field was not technically split fifty-fifty in the stands. Alabama had claimed the lion's share of the 78,000 seats, with Auburn only receiving 10,900 tickets. Despite the overwhelming Tide advantage in numbers, the Auburn folks made up for it with disproportionate crowd noise from their end-zone seats. Going into the Game, Auburn was a touchdown favorite by virtue of its having the best defense in the nation. Conventional wisdom held that Alabama would need to keep Auburn's stellar front line away from David Smith and that Derrick Thomas had to have a huge game for the Tide to spoil Auburn's Sugar Bowl party. Pressure from CBS moved the Game up to the Friday after Thanksgiving.

The Game started badly for the Tide, when Tracy Rocker sacked Smith on the first play. After a Bama punt, Stacey Danley led the Tigers on their first possession to the Bama eight-yard line before the drive stalled. Win Lyle knocked in an easy field goal to give the Tigers a 3–0 lead. Alabama responded with its best offensive drive of the day, key plays coming on a Smith screen to Robert Stewart for twenty-five yards and another pass to Greg Payne for twenty-four more. On third and goal from the Auburn three, a scrambling Smith was stopped for a loss, and Phillip Doyle tied the Game, 3–3, ending Alabama's five-quarter scoring drought against the Tigers.

A long pass to Lawyer Tillman set up a quick Tiger opportunity, but Auburn fumbled the ball away deep in Alabama territory. Facing third and three from his own six, Alabama's Smith went back into his own end zone to pass. Auburn tackle Ron Stallworth dragged the senior quarterback down for an Auburn safety. Trailing 5–3, the safety set up good field position for the Tigers. Despite an effective passing attack, penalties bedeviled Auburn and stopped the drive. Lyle added another field goal to extend the lead to 8–3. Alabama threatened to score midway through the second quarter, but Smith was intercepted at the goal line to kill a promising drive.

Early in the third quarter, an Auburn drive died when Reggie Slack was inexplicably called out of bounds three yards away from the sidelines before completing a pass to James Joseph. Alabama's lone sack of the day stopped the Tigers on the next play and forced a punt. Neither team was able to move the ball for several series. Effective punting by the Tide's Chris Mohr kept Auburn buried deep through most of the quarter. On a third and nineteen play, however, Lawyer Tillman handed down judgment on Alabama for a third consecutive year.

On the decisive play of the Game, Auburn's Slack threw long from his own 14-yard line. It was the same play that had broken the Game open in 1987—517–X Takeoff. Tillman zipped down the right sideline, covered by Alabama's Lee Ozmint. In a virtual replay of the play against Jelks, Tillman pulled in the ball, giving Auburn a fifty-three-yard gain, a badly needed momentum boost, and a first down in scoring position. Danley, who had been knocked unconscious by Bama's Spencer Hammond late in the second period, returned to hammer the ball closer to the goal line. Slack threw the ball to Freddie Weygand at the one-yard line. While the replays suggest that Weygand was out of bounds, the officials ruled the pass complete. The lone Auburn touchdown of the Game was scored by Vincent Harris, a fullback who had spent most of his career in Coach Dye's doghouse but who had a stellar effort in blocking and running against the Tide. His run gave the Tigers a twelve-point lead late in the third period.

Alabama came back late with a nice drive. Smith hit Lamonde Russell in the flat for a thirty-six-yard gain. Smith found Russell again for nineteen more to the Auburn 12-yard line, then scrambled out and threw to a wide-open Greg Payne in the end zone. With 3:23 left to play Alabama had closed the gap to 15–10. An onside kick attempt flew into the hands of Auburn's James Joseph, and the Tigers ground out the clock for their third consecutive victory over the Tide. With that, Auburn had claimed a share of its second straight SEC championship.

There were many great performances in this Game. Alabama's Derrick Thomas recorded a sack and thirteen tackles. Keith McCants had a hand in seventeen stops. Chris Mohr punted for an average of 43.3 yards, including two kicks for 51 and 58 yards. David Smith played a gutsy Game, coming back time and again despite being sacked six times for 39 yards. When he left the field for the last time, the Auburn fans saluted his heart and courage with a standing ovation. The Tigers' defense played a dominant Game, holding Alabama to only 12 yards rushing. Tracy Rocker went on to claim the Outland and Lombardi Trophies as the unanimous top defender in the nation in 1988, but in the Game, Rocker was eclipsed by Ron Stallworth's seven tackles, four sacks, and the safety. The Auburn offense had been hampered by an astounding 112 yards in penalties, but its best performances came from Slack, Joseph, Danley, and the senior hero Tillman.

ALABAMA HAD little time to deal with the dejection of losing again to the Tigers. The Hurricane Bowl, as the rescheduled game with Texas A&M was

Auburn senior Lawyer Tillman hauls in a long bomb during the 1988 Game.

being called, was just six days away, moved up to Thursday, December 1, to accommodate ESPN.

Rumors abounded in the days leading up to the Aggie game that an influential group of Alabama alumni had raised $2 million to buy out the remaining three years of Curry's contract. Acting university president Roger Sayers arranged a news conference in College Station the day of the game to refute the innuendoes and give Curry a vote of confidence: "Bill Curry is our football coach next week, next year and at least for the next three years and beyond. We will honor Coach Curry's contract . . . because we are pleased with his leadership."

With that settled (for this year) Curry was able to focus on the final game of the regular season. A&M was favored by as much as a touchdown and would go on to represent the Southwest Conference again in the Cotton Bowl. Alabama, however, put together its most inspired performance of the year, and the Aggies were simply overmatched. Bama closed the regular season in style, winning 30–10 and silencing Sherrill's carping. Derrick Thomas summed up the night best when he said, "The only hurricane that blew in tonight was Alabama."

The Crimson Tide made its third trip to El Paso in six years (some Alabama fans were moved to wonder if Bill Curry knew Marty Robbins was dead) to face Army in the Sun Bowl on Christmas Eve. The Cadets quickly proved they were worthy competition, holding a 14–13 advantage at halftime. The lead switched back and forth throughout the second half, before Bama scored twice to lead by a point. Army's last chance was snuffed out when freshman Charles Gardner intercepted a pass in the end zone, and Alabama survived a surprising challenge, 29–28. With the win, the Tide finished 1988 with a 9–3 record, topping the previous year's mark by two games. Curry, however, still had not beaten Auburn.

ON PAPER, Auburn's Sugar Bowl opponent, Florida State, lined up better against the Tigers than any other team in the country, including eventual national champion Notre Dame. The Sugar Bowl was an exciting affair, even though it was low-scoring. The game came down to a thrilling drive and a heartbreaking finish for the Tigers. Trailing 13–7, Slack directed the Auburn offense downfield with less than two minutes remaining in the game. He converted on fourth down an amazing four times. With time running out, Slack found Tillman running along the goal line, shadowed by FSU's flamboyant Deion Sanders. At the last moment, Sanders leaped up on Tillman's back and shoved the Auburn senior out of the way, intercepting the ball. Deion returned the ball ten yards, then high-stepped along the

Auburn sideline in celebration. Despite the obvious and blatant pass interference on the play, no flags were thrown, and Auburn fell to 10-2. The
Tigers would enter the 1989 season as the two-time defending SEC champions, and the Tigers knew what awaited them in December. For the first time
ever, Auburn would host the Game.

1989

HISTORY ON
THE PLAINS

Sweet Auburn! loveliest village of the plain, . . .
Where crouching tigers wait their hapless prey.

Oliver Goldsmith

THE TALK BEGAN MINUTES after the end of the 1988 Game. "Oh, hell," Alabama folks said. "Now we've got to go down *there*." The site change was going to be *the* story of 1989.

After a competitive recruiting season, in which Auburn claimed the state's top running back, Darrel "Lectron" Williams, and quarterback Stan White, and Alabama landed the defensive trio of Antonio London, Eric Curry, and John Copeland, the preseason pundits picked Auburn to swing a Threepeat and claim the SEC championship. Tracy Rocker had moved on to the NFL, but his younger brother, David, stepped into his shoes and anchored yet another strong Auburn defensive line. Quentin Riggins and Craig Ogletree were being lauded as two of the best linebackers in the conference. Reggie Slack returned for his senior season at quarterback, accompanied in the backfield by halfback Stacey Danley and now-fullback James Joseph. The vacancy created by the loss of Lawyer Tillman was filled by lightning-fast Alexander "Ace" Wright, Shane Wasden, and Greg Taylor.

137

Alabama looked to be strong on defense in 1989, returning standout linebacker Keith McCants, roverback Lee Ozmint, nose guard Willie Wyatt, and cornerbacks John Mangum and Efrum Thomas. The offense, however, was still questionable. Homer Smith's radical schemes would become more familiar to the Alabama backfield and receivers, but the man running the offense on the field was something of an unknown himself. With the departure of David Smith, Jeff Dunn became the presumptive starter, but many had misgivings about Dunn's skills and performance under pressure. The offensive line, led by center Roger Shultz, was sound, and Marco Battle would team with Craig Sanderson as the top recruiting threats. Junior-college transfer Siran Stacy figured to boost the struggling Bama running game.

Even with the considerable talent that had been assembled in Tuscaloosa over the past three years, Bill Curry still lacked anything close to job security. Before the 1988 season, Joab Thomas had retired as university president, by many accounts under pressure from the alums. Incoming president Roger Sayers forced out athletic director Steve Sloan. Sloan, who had refused to fire Curry for anything other than a losing season and had presided over the Game site change, found his Bryant credentials weren't enough to keep him at the top of Alabama athletics.

He was replaced by Cecil "Hootie" Ingram, another old-time Alabama alumnus. Ingram left the AD's office at Florida State to take the job, and many speculated that he had been hired to woo Bobby Bowden into the Tide head coach's office. While all this was going on, Curry was trying to marshal his forces for the 1989 campaign. Despite Curry's record, which was better than either of his two predecessors in their first two years, the conventional wisdom was that he needed to (preferably) beat Auburn or at least produce a conference champion to remain as Alabama's head coach in 1990. Lacking the support of the president and the athletic director who had hired him, Curry saw that his back was against the wall.

AUBURN OPENED the season against one of the weakest of the weak sisters in Division I-A, West Coast subpower Pacific. It was a 255-yard Slack-to-Wright showcase as the Tigers romped, 55–0. Southern Miss had ruined Bobby Bowden's 1989 national championship dreams by upsetting the Seminoles on opening day in Jacksonville. Two weeks later, they looked to be a formidable opponent for Auburn, but the Tigers coasted to an easy 24–3 win. Ranked third in the nation, the Tigers went to Knoxville, where they ran into a thunderstorm and a revitalized Tennessee team. The game wasn't as close as the 21–14 final score, but Auburn's undefeated dreams were suspended for another year.

The Tigers regrouped for a second consecutive road game, this time at Kentucky, and handed retiring head coach Jerry Claiborne yet another defeat, 24–12. Dye's troops then came home for a match with LSU. Neither offense could get anything going, but the Auburn defense kept Tommy Hodson in check as the eastern Tigers pulled out a must-have 10–6 victory. Grumblings about the Auburn offense grew steadily louder after the team traveled to Tallahassee to face Florida State. Many predicted a Seminole blowout, and the Bowden offense, led by quarterback Peter Tom Willis, showed why with a turf-blistering assault. Auburn stayed with FSU for the duration, but it ended as a 22–14 road loss, and Auburn seemed directionless at 4–2, with the toughest part of the SEC season still before them.

In an effort to regain control of the sputtering offense, Dye took his team to the woodshed. Eschewing the pass for the more traditional "four yards and a cloud of dust" running game, Dye's methods led to a tough, physical 14–0 win over Mississippi State, reinstating the duo of Joseph and Danley at the heart of the Tiger offense. To some it was a dull, monotonous game, but for the Auburn team it was a turning point.

As turning points go, Auburn versus MSU didn't hold a candle to Auburn versus Florida. Galen Hall had been forced out as the Gators' head coach early in the season because of NCAA violations and had been replaced with interim coach Gary Darnell. Thanks to a tough, talented defense and the running of junior Emmitt Smith, the Gators had not lost a game since Hall's departure. As Florida alums prepared to draft favorite son Steve Spurrier, Darnell knew that he needed to keep winning to have a prayer of keeping his job. The game was a tough, emotional battle. If the rivalry between the two schools wasn't fierce enough, both teams needed this win.

The defenses shone, with both offensive squads kept in check for virtually the duration. A Reggie Slack fumble on the Auburn five-yard line led immediately to an Emmitt Smith touchdown, but the junior Heisman candidate was otherwise contained. Finally, trailing 7–3 with three minutes left, Slack led the Tigers on a desperation drive. On a fourth-down play with less than thirty seconds on the clock, Slack connected with Shane Wasden for the winning score. The noise in Jordan-Hare Stadium, already louder than anybody could remember, caused the goalposts to resonate like massive tuning forks.

The Gators last drive ended with a desperation pass into the end zone that was batted down, and Auburn had tamed the Gators for the third straight year, 10–7. A few Florida players sat disconsolate on the visitors' bench long after the game. Emmitt Smith had never gained one hundred yards on Auburn, and his team had never beaten the Tigers during his career as a Gator. The Auburn faithful, however, were less than kind to Smith at the moment, chanting his name mockingly until the running back was escorted off the field by a teammate. For one Florida assistant coach the frustration was unbearable. He brawled with an Auburn student and was arrested. The Auburn-Florida rivalry is a lot of things, but it's rarely dull.

For the Auburn football team the come-from-behind win was a much-needed emotional tonic. Finally, after a season of almosts and maybes, this team had a chance to live up to its potential and win a third SEC championship.

Louisiana Tech fell quickly at Homecoming, and a trip to Athens yielded a 31–3 victory that was never even close. Then it was time for the Game—a *home* Game.

THE ALABAMA season began in Birmingham with a chance for Bill Curry to avenge one of his darkest moments as a head coach. The 1987 loss to Memphis State had irked the Alabama faithful almost as much as losing three straight to Auburn. New acquisition Siran Stacy started his Alabama career with an impressive 160 yards, leading the Tide to a 35–7 revenge win. Keith McCants showed why he had been selected as a preseason All-American the next week against Kentucky, but Jeff Dunn went down halfway through the game with a knee injury. He was replaced by a former walk-on named Gary Hollingsworth, a player who had grown up an Auburn fan. The offense managed enough production to win, 15–3, in Tuscaloosa, but the fans were grumbling again about Smith's offense.

Hollingsworth looked better the next week, building a 17–0 halftime lead against Vanderbilt, but the Commodores nearly pulled off the upset. Although the Tide won, 20–14, the natives were more than restless. The next week, Curry had another chance at redemption, playing against Ole Miss, and his offense finally came into its own. After falling behind, 21–0, Bama exploded to blow out Ole Miss, 62–27. The Tide was nearly caught at Homecoming against Southwestern Louisiana the following week and had to come back in the fourth quarter for an ugly 24–17 win.

On the Third Saturday in October, many pundits picked Tennessee to topple Bama in Birmingham. The Big Orange had embarrassed Auburn, the preseason favorite, and the Tide had struggled against two weak sisters early. Judging by the game's outcome, somebody forgot to tell Alabama. The Tide came out roaring and played a brilliant game. When it was over, the Tide was a 47–30 winner, the offense was hitting on all cylinders, and Alabama was clearly the SEC's strongest team at the season's midpoint.

A trip to Happy Valley followed, and Alabama's perfect record came close to ruination. The Tide led, 19–17, late in the fourth quarter, but Penn State running back Blair Thomas executed a virtual one-man drive on the ground and as a receiver. With seconds on the clock, Thomas was stopped just short of the goal line. Joe Paterno, one of the greatest living legends in 1-A football, went for a sure field goal rather than give the ball to Thomas one more time. The kick, however, was not as automatic as it looked. In one of the most memorable moments in Alabama history, Thomas Rayam bolted through the Nittany Lion blockers and blocked the kick. People immediately began to talk about the Tide going undefeated in 1989.

Mississippi State and LSU were efficiently dismantled, and Alabama was 10–0 and bound for Auburn for the first time ever. When Miami defeated top-ranked Notre Dame the following weekend, the Tide swelled to number two in the polls, most likely bound for the Sugar Bowl to battle the Hurricanes. Alabama clinched at least a share of its first SEC title in eight years with the win over LSU, but Auburn lay squarely between the Tide and an undisputed conference championship.

THE 1989 Game was the most hyped ever. The top news item in the state two weeks before it was played, the Game and the rivalry hit the national headlines on November 21, when Alabama players Siran Stacy and Charley Dare received death threats and Curry asked the FBI to investigate.

During a press conference, Curry suggested that ticketless Alabama fans should surround the stadium and listen to the Game on the radio, much as they had done earlier in Baton Rouge for the LSU game. The idea did not go over well with Auburn officials, particularly in light of stories about a run on red spray paint in Birmingham and Tuscaloosa. Auburn ticket manager Bill Beckwith, a prime mover in the drive to bring the Game to the Plains, didn't mince words: "The place for Auburn people, if they don't have a ticket, is at home watching the game on television. And that's the place for Alabama people, too. [Curry] seems like he's trying to incite a riot. We don't need riffraff surrounding our stadium."

Dye, concerned about the emotional tinderbox of Game day, sent representatives to most of Auburn's student groups, urging AU students to come to the Game, be loud, treat Alabama fans politely, and leave peacefully.

Unlike Curry, who forbade his players to talk to the press the week before the Game, Dye maintained his normal, open access. He talked about Alabama in tones that were complimentary but not fawning. "I have total respect for that program and the University of Alabama, but at the same time, I ain't afraid to talk about 'em. I ain't afraid to play 'em. I ain't afraid to lose to 'em, and I ain't afraid to win."

Dye was clearly miffed by the predictions of the state sportswriters, who overwhelmingly chose Alabama as the favorite, but he conceded that in light of the teams' respective records, he couldn't blame them.

If there was any doubt about the Game's outcome in Alabama hearts, it was well hidden. Two weeks *before* the Game was played, bumper stickers circulated in Birmingham and Tuscaloosa reading "We Beat Your Ass On Your Grass" (the natural grass–AstroTurf debate had been a heated sidebar to the decades-old site dispute). Fans who months earlier had been ready to tar-and-feather Curry would have voted for him as governor, if not president, for getting an undefeated season. The thought of embarrassing Auburn in the first ever Game on the Plains was high on the list of goals for Tide fans in 1989. Of course, some were still fuming at even having to go to Auburn.

Tiger fans were doing a slow burn in the face of Alabama's early celebrating. It was hard for Auburn people to imagine losing this Game, this long-sought goal, but staring at an undefeated Alabama, imagine they did. It wasn't pleasant to visualize crimson-clad fans exiting Jordan-Hare Stadium in triumph, but that was the drumbeat that Auburn fans heard day in and day out leading up to the "first time ever."

The Game was widely publicized, far more than a number-two-versus-number-eleven clash at the end of a season normally would be. The First Time Ever was covered by *USA Today*, the *New York Times*, the *Los Angeles Times*, and the *Washington Post* and was front-sports-page news nationwide. CBS would televise the contest.

THE CARS, campers, and motor homes began trickling into Auburn on Wednesday. On Thursday the trickle became a deluge, then a flood. For the Tide's bus ride from Tuscaloosa, Alabama fans lined the interstate overpasses, just as they had for the funeral of Paul Bryant, but this time to cheer.

On Friday, the Alabama varsity worked out in Jordan-Hare Stadium for the first time in history. During the drills, Curry stood on the sidelines talking to reporters, and he was clearly moved both by the importance of the next day's Game and by the surroundings. "This is the biggest game I've ever been a part of," the veteran of two Super Bowls said. He surveyed the almost quiet stadium. The white concrete risers and ramps shone brilliantly in the lights, the grass was thick and dark, the hedges and ornamental landscaping perfect. Curry, whose employers had fought tooth and nail to keep him from standing on that field, said, "This is a beautiful place, isn't it?"

Auburn students held a parade through town, then filed into Plainsman Park, Auburn's baseball stadium, over ten thousand strong, for the largest pep rally in the school's history. Dye and the starters gave the students a new hand signal for the Game, four fingers raised high, not for the fourth quarter, but for a fourth consecutive win over Alabama. After the rally, Dye took his team out of the wild carnival atmosphere and bussed them thirty miles to a hotel in Columbus, Georgia, so they could get some sleep. It was the ultimate irony. The Game at Auburn had gotten so big, not even Auburn could stay at home the night before.

GAME DAY dawned. This would be the largest crowd ever in Jordan-Hare Stadium, 85,314 people, and the largest to see a football game in state history. Auburn had sold even the lowest row of the stands, usually held back as undesirable seating. A statue of the War Eagle was unveiled early in the day at Memorial Coliseum, across the street from the stadium.

Outside the stadium, Auburn fans were massed along Donahue Drive, waiting for the team. The Tiger Walk is an Auburn tradition wherein the football team, dressed in their Sunday best, walk the three hundred yards from the Sewell Hall athletic dorm to the stadium, led by the Auburn cheerleaders. This time, the Tiger Walk was surrounded by a throng of thirty thousand people. Later, Dye compared the Tiger Walk to another monumental event in the fall of 1989. "To see the look in the eyes and the faces of those fans," he said, "it must have resembled what happened the night the Wall came down in Berlin. It was as if they had been freed and come out of bondage." Some national reporters scoffed at this as overwrought, but to Auburn fans who felt the electric emotion that morning on Donahue Drive, Dye may have understated the matter. The players were moved by the fans' show of faith. Running back James Joseph was so pumped up by the reception that he began hyperventilating in the dressing room and had to be given oxygen.

The stands were more than full by kickoff. The north corner of the end zone was crimson and white, and a professionally printed banner reading "Roll Tide" was erected in front of the Alabama band. A few Alabama partisans were scattered around the stadium, having gone to the extreme of buying Auburn season tickets to ensure a seat at the Game.

Auburn came out throwing, and Slack completed his first two passes for twenty yards. After a short run by Stacey Danley, Slack executed one of the most important plays of the Game. He connected with Alexander Wright for a spectacular over-the-shoulder catch and a forty-four-yard gain. With the ball inside the Bama 10-yard line, Slack threw incomplete into the end zone and then turned to his running backs to power the ball across the goal. Danley fell just inches short on the first try, but James Joseph went over the top and in for Auburn's first score. The officials failed to notice, however, that the Tigers had twelve men on the field.

Alabama converted its first series of plays into a first down on the arm of Hollingsworth. He found tight end Lamonde Russell for a fifteen-yard completion, but it was the last useful play of the drive for the Tide and they returned the ball to the Tigers.

Three plays later, Auburn's Lectron Williams lost the handoff, and Alabama's George Thornton recovered the fumble. The Tide's offense sputtered, though, and Curry's team could only convert the turnover into three points.

Auburn played a balanced offense, throwing often and effectively. The Tiger air attack was far more potent than Tide supporters had expected. Slack was able to move the ball out to the midfield stripe, but there the drive stalled and the Tigers had to punt.

Alabama, however, kept the ball on the ground and mostly rode on the legs of Stacy. Hollingsworth occasionally passed, but his throws were mostly high-percentage, short dinks to his running backs. The Tide moved the ball out from the hole in which Auburn punter Richie Nell had placed them. The Tigers' defense applied the brakes to the Alabama runners after they had converted two first downs. Forcing Hollingsworth into a passing situation, the Bama quarterback connected with Lamonde Russell for a large gain to the Auburn 35. After a short run, Hollingsworth again threw a perfect pass to Russell, who went out of bounds at the Auburn eight-yard line. A penalty moved the ball closer, setting the Tide up at the four. The Tigers covered the run well, and Hollingsworth's second- and third-down passes went incomplete. Alabama tried to execute a fake field goal attempt, but the Auburn defenders reacted quickly and thwarted the attempted touchdown pass. Alabama had traveled the length of the field and come up short. Had the play worked, it would have shifted the momentum of the Game to the Tide. As it was, the second-guessing of Curry began immediately, and the first quarter ended with Auburn pumped up, in possession of the ball, and leading 7-3.

The Tigers had to work the ball out from their own four-yard line. They ran twice and threw once to make a first down, but on the following third and ten, an open Wright failed to bring in the ball and the Tigers had to relinquish possession. Although the Tide went on offense near the midfield stripe, the Tigers forced them to punt after three plays, two of which were sacks.

Auburn's Alexander Wright makes a spectacular over-the-shoulder reception on the Tigers' opening drive.

Below, James Joseph (10) draws first blood, scoring on the Tigers' initial possession.

Auburn began its next drive at its own 25-yard line. Keeping the ball on the ground, the Tigers moved the chains repeatedly until reaching midfield. Slack's second-down pass was deflected at the line of scrimmage and came down in the hands of McCants for the Alabama defender's first interception of the year.

The Tide offense took over on its own 37, and Curry gave his backs a workout. They used all three downs to get a first near midfield. A reverse on first down fooled no one, losing four yards. A screen pass to Kevin Turner picked up ten. On third and four Hollingsworth carried a bootleg around left end for ten yards and a first down. A penalty on the next play negated half of Hollingsworth's gain, and the Alabama quarterback threw incomplete. Stacy carried the ball up the middle and fumbled, but Alabama recovered to bring up third and ten. Derrick Lassic picked up a screen pass and the conversion, and the Tide was ready to go from the Auburn 26. After a couple of four-yard runs, Hollingsworth found Marco Battle open just past the line of scrimmage. Battle held on to the ball and followed his blockers into the end zone for an eighteen-yard touchdown, only the second passing touchdown scored against the Auburn defense in 1989. With 1:49 left in the first half, Alabama had taken the lead, 10–7.

Auburn managed only one first down and had to return the ball to Alabama with thirteen seconds left to play. The Tide ran out the clock and the half was over.

Outside of Auburn's mammoth first possession and Alabama's impressive drive for the first field goal, this had been a game of defense. After the initial shock of Slack-to-Wright, the Alabama defense had seen some success at slowing down the Auburn passing game, holding the Tigers to two yards through the air in the second quarter. At the same time, the Tigers, particularly Stacey Danley, were running the ball far better than expected. Bama's Siran Stacy was running well, too, but the routes in Homer Smith's shotgun-option offense weren't opening up regularly. Alabama fans were heartened by the halftime lead, but the Game was still close and the history of this contest was filled with improbable outcomes.

AUBURN KICKED off to start the second half, and Gene Jelks took the return to the Alabama 33, where he was wrestled down by a second-string Auburn defender named Eric Ramsey. After an initial run by Stacy went nowhere on the first play of the second half, Smith, Hollingsworth, and Alabama went to the air and a no-huddle offense to prevent Auburn's making large-scale defensive substitutions. A pass to Marco Battle yielded fourteen yards. Another pass in the flat found Battle at the Auburn 39, and still the Tide ran the hurry-up offense. Amazingly, in the deafening, hostile din of Jordan-Hare, Hollingsworth called every play from the line of scrimmage, using hand signals to communicate with his receivers. After an incompletion, Stacy barreled outside but just short of a first down at the Auburn 30. Following another incompletion on third down, Phillip Doyle was sent in to attempt a forty-eight-yard field goal. The kick was short, and the score remained 10–7.

On Auburn's first play, Slack threw a dangerously short pass that was almost intercepted. On the next play, however, he found Shane Wasden near the 50-yard line. Wasden's race to the goal line was frustrated by Keith McCants, who caught the speedy receiver from behind with a spectacular shoestring tackle, tripping him up at the Alabama 12-yard line. The catch and run had netted fifty-nine yards. James Joseph went nowhere on the third play of the drive. Then Slack hit the junior running back with a perfect throw. Joseph carried it as far as the one-foot line before being stopped. Two plays later, Joseph scored his second over-the-top touchdown of the Game, giving the lead back to Auburn, 14–10.

After the ensuing kickoff, Alabama began at its 23. On the second play from scrimmage, Hollingsworth passed to Russell for a first down at the 40-yard line. It was a different set of downs, but the Tide ran the same plays, repeating them as if each had been scripted for the individual downs. Stacy gained a few yards up the middle. Hollingsworth threw incomplete and then found Russell at the Auburn 43. Alabama was moving the ball impressively when Hollingsworth connected with Kevin Turner over the middle. The junior fullback was able to gain another ten yards, but the football was stripped away by Auburn linebacker Quentin Riggins. Safety Dennis Wallace recovered the ball, and Auburn took over at its own 21.

Knowing the value of hitting an opponent hard after a turnover, Auburn's Larry Blakeney and Pat Sullivan pulled out the Slack-to-Wright takeoff play again. This time, the Alabama defense knew it was coming, but knowing something is not the same as stopping it. Efrum Thomas, not wanting to be burned by Wright again, pushed the Auburn speedster out of bounds as Slack launched the ball long down the sideline. Wright recovered, ran back onto the field, and caught the ball, gaining sixty yards on the play. After Joseph and Danley carried twice for a total gain of eight yards, Slack was chased out of the pocket. He was dragged down a yard short of the first down at the Alabama five-yard line. The field goal unit came on the field, and Lyle converted the short attempt, extending Auburn's lead in the Game, 17–10.

The Tide, hampered by a poor kickoff return and a penalty, couldn't answer and punted. The Tigers took over on their own 20. On the first play of the possession, Danley bolted through the right side of the line for a fast nine yards. Alabama was forced to respect the pass now, and running avenues opened. Slack missed Danley with a second-down pass, but on third down Danley moved the chains. A penalty cost Auburn five yards, and Danley then barely gained a yard. Facing second and fourteen, Slack threw a precise strike to Herbert Casey on the sideline for a first down at the Auburn 45. The Tigers kept the Tide honest with a Lectron Williams run for a yard gain on first down. They followed this with yet another Slack-to-Wright reception that placed the ball at the Alabama 45, just short of the first-down marker. With seconds left in the third quarter, Joseph powered through the line for another Auburn first down. On the final play of the quarter, Williams was caught in the backfield for a three-yard loss.

As the squads raised the traditional four fingers in the air and changed sides, there was a growing confidence on the Auburn sidelines and a greater sense of urgency for Alabama. The Tigers had dominated the third quarter after sleepwalking through the second. Alabama knew that Auburn had to be stopped here or this Game might be long over before the final seconds ticked off the clock.

Slack began the final period with a strike to Wright that placed the ball on the Tide 33. On the next play, Danley tore through the line and ran through the entire Alabama linebacking corps for a twenty-yard gain. Joseph was stopped for a yard gain on the following first-down play. Then Williams carried the ball, dodging left and right and into the secondary before the defense could react. Charging through a would-be tackler, the freshman dove into the end zone for a twelve-yard score. The extra point gave Auburn a two-touchdown lead, 24–10.

For Alabama, if anything was going to happen, it needed to happen now, with the offense taking over at its own 25. The next play was one of the Game's big plays—but Bama partisans didn't much care for it. Hollingsworth tried to get the ball to Kevin Turner over the middle. Auburn's Darrel Crawford darted across the path of the ball to claim a bobbling interception. The Tide defense relinquished five more yards to Auburn on an offsides penalty on the next play, giving Auburn first and five from the Alabama 30.

With a comfortable lead on the scoreboard, the Tigers kept the ball on the ground. Danley carried inside for three, then carried again to the 21 for a new set of downs. Williams dove across the line to the 17. On second down, he took the ball outside for a short gain. Danley was stopped short of the first down, and Lyle came on the field for the field goal attempt. With the ball positioned on the crest of the field, Lyle converted the thirty-one-yarder, making the score 27–10 with 9:36 left in the Game. At this point, it looked as if the Tide would not get back into the Game. Nevertheless, Alabama was intent on demonstrating why it had won eleven consecutive games since losing to Auburn in the 1988 Iron Bowl.

The drive began at Bama's 26. Hollingsworth almost gave up another gift interception on the first play, but Auburn's Elton Billingslea could not hold on to the ball. Turner took a screen pass outside for a short gain, then slipped underneath the coverage on the next play to pick up the crucial first down. Running without a huddle, Hollingsworth found his high school teammate Craig Sanderson downfield at the Auburn 34. A facemask penalty gave Alabama an extra five yards, and the Tide was still in business at the 29. Hollingsworth had to scramble out of bounds at the 25. Still calling audibles in the din, Hollingsworth fired a strike to Russell at the 15 for another first down. On the next play, Battle raced for the right corner of the end zone, covered by Auburn's Eric Ramsey. Hollingsworth pumped his arm, causing Ramsey to hesitate, then lobbed the football perfectly to Battle for an Alabama touchdown. The point after cut the Auburn lead to ten, 27–17. It had been a face-saving drive for a quick score.

Auburn converted one first down before having to punt. For the first time in the second half, the Alabama defense had stopped an Auburn drive. Hollingsworth returned to the field with the ball on the Alabama 31 and needed another score quickly.

The no-huddle offense had worked previously, and the Tide came out throwing. A short pass to Turner went to the 38. Hollingsworth next threw to Sanderson near midfield. A third pass was batted away from Russell. Then Hollingsworth faked to Stacy and ran a bootleg to the Auburn 40. A finger-tip reception by Battle was just shy of the necessary yardage for the first. On second down, Hollingsworth found Stacy at the 25 to move the chains. Battle took another reception on the sideline to the 16. Inside the 20, Alabama chose to keep the ball on the ground and the Auburn defense stiffened. Turner carried for no gain, creating a third-and-short situation. From the shotgun formation, Hollingsworth threw to John Cassimus just shy of the goal line. Auburn's Dominko Anderson was covering and timed his hit on Cassimus just as the ball reached the receiver. Cassimus couldn't hold on. Facing fourth and a foot with 2:40 left, Curry decided to go for the first down. At first, Martin Houston looked to have been trapped in the backfield, but he bounced off his would-be tacklers and took the ball outside for the desperately needed yard. With first and goal from the nine, Hollingsworth again tried for Battle in the corner of the end zone, but his receiver couldn't make the catch. Houston took the second-down handoff to the five. On third and goal with less than two minutes left in the Game, Hollingsworth found his receivers triple-covered and threw the ball away. Needing two scores, Curry sent in his kicker, and Doyle made the field goal, bringing the Tide within a touchdown, 27–20.

Curry had no choice but to try an onside kick. The two head coaches huddled with their kicking teams. Get the ball, Dye said, and we'll win this Game. Get the ball, Curry said, and we'll get it downfield and win the SEC championship and beat these guys once and for all. The Sugar Bowl Committee was watching the Game and meeting via a conference call, ready to take a vote after the final gun.

Alabama's Alan Ward lined up to kick the football, which the Tide made no pretense of kicking deep. Eight Alabama players lined up in a tight formation on the left side, and they raced toward Ward's bouncing kick. The ball did what it was supposed to do on an onside attempt, bouncing high into the air. Alabama's Antonio London dove at it, but he was blocked out of the way, and the ball fell into the sure hands of Frank Macintosh, a redshirt junior and Auburn's backup quarterback. In the biggest Game of his life, Macintosh may have been the player who saved the day for the Auburn Tigers.

Alabama still had three time-outs, but with 1:48 left, they needed to hold Auburn without a first down. The Tigers helped the Tide's cause by jumping offsides for a five-yard loss. From just behind midfield, Danley carried for a ten-yard gain. On second and five, Danley made the needed yardage, barreling through the middle for a first down. Alabama stopped the clock, but Danley got the call again, breaking tackles, bouncing off defenders, and running with rugged abandon for another first down to the Alabama 20. The Tide had to spend their second time-out. With 1:29 remaining, Danley was stopped on his next carry for no gain. Alabama stopped the clock for the third and last time. The reality of the Game was beginning to sink in on the Tide sidelines. They were running out of ways to win and running out of time as Danley carried for another three yards and the clock ran unimpeded. On third down, Slack and Dye shocked the crowd with a pass that was batted down and nearly intercepted. Lyle appeared for a thirty-four-yard attempt that would clinch the victory. His kick was accurate, and Auburn led, 30–20.

Hollingsworth returned to the field with thirty seconds on the clock. His receivers were covered well, and he had to throw the ball out of bounds twice to preserve as much time as he could. With fifteen seconds left, Hollingsworth threw the ball as far as he could toward Craig Sanderson at the Auburn 20-yard line. The pass was intercepted. Auburn ran out the last few seconds, and this Game was over. Auburn had won its first truly home Game, 30–20, and Curry had gone from 10–0 against the world to 0–10 against the Tigers.

For Tiger fans, this win in the biggest football game ever in Auburn really did feel like coming out of bondage. All the long years of having to play in an alien stadium, all the times that Bryant and Perkins had scoffed about "never" playing in Auburn, and, maybe just as importantly, all the days and weeks of hearing from Tide fans and the press that Auburn's inaugural Game would be an Alabama showcase, all had come to an end in three triumphant hours. Jim Fyffe closed his play-by-play with a jubilant flourish, speaking for all of them. "All you people that said Alabama was gonna beat us," Fyffe said, "*where are you now?*"

Alabama fans were somewhat shell-shocked in the Game's aftermath. Few, if any, had expected to lose this Game. They did not believe that the undefeated Tide could fall to a twice-beaten Auburn. Many had looked beyond the Game to the Sugar Bowl. Their grand dreams for 1989 had come to a crashing halt, and their beloved team had fallen for four straight years to the hated Tigers. Some, including a few with deep pockets, had decided that enough was enough.

The Tide's highly quotable junior center Roger Shultz was almost at a loss for words. For him the season's other accomplishments weren't enough. "I'd trade those ten wins we have for a win over Auburn," he said. "I'd trade the Sugar Bowl for a win over Auburn. I'd do anything for a win over Auburn."

Pat Dye's 1989 post-Game speech is a favorite of Auburn fans: "I wouldn't swap this year for any year that I've been at Auburn. I wouldn't swap it, men, because I've watched you struggle, and I've watched you wrestle with them angels. But I've watched you grow up and become men." The fifty-year-old coach stopped, his voice breaking with emotion. "I've watched you become men," he managed, his expression that of a proud parent. The players surrounding Dye embraced him.

Despite Alabama's loss, the Sugar Bowl committee extended its official bid to the Tide at the end of the Game. Auburn would play in the Hall of Fame Bowl in Tampa, and Tennessee would face Texas A&M in the Cotton Bowl, forming the first tri-championship of the Southeastern Conference in fifty years.

Auburn played Ohio State in Tampa, destroying the Buckeyes 31–14. As of this writing, no Auburn team has ever lost to a Big Ten opponent. The 1989 Tigers finished the season at 10–2 and ranked sixth in the nation. The 1986–89 senior class became the winningest in Auburn history with thirty-nine victories in four years. At the time, it seemed that Auburn had nowhere to go but up.

Alabama went to New Orleans for the Tide's first appearance in the Sugar Bowl in a decade. Although clearly outmanned, Bama put up a fight. In the end, Miami walked away with a 33–25 win and the Hurricanes' third national championship in seven years. Curry's preparation for the bowl was complete and intense, but he just didn't have the horses to run with Dennis Erickson's team.

Curry also didn't budge in his commitment to discipline and class in the face of Miami's infamous showboating and taunting. When Alabama's Prince Wimbley mimicked a Miami celebration after a relatively unimportant run, Curry called Wimbley to the sidelines and gave him a dressing-down on national television. When Wimbley tried to look away, Curry grabbed the young man's facemask and jerked him around to meet his coach's blazing eyes. Curry is probably best known and best respected nationally today for that action. In an era of touchdown dances and trash talking, Curry had the character to buck the trend and stand by his principles. Even Auburn fans found new respect for the intense man from College Park, Georgia.

MAYBE RESPECT was what Curry was looking for in the dawning days of 1990. The two losses at the end of the season had destroyed most of the goodwill that he had so painfully built up over the last three years. Hootie Ingram offered Curry, not an extension, but a new contract with no raise, which stripped Curry of the power to hire and fire assistants and gave the athletic director the power to fire Curry at any time, for any reason. Many fans and sportswriters excoriated Curry for blowing the shot at the national championship and, of course, for not beating Auburn. It was this lack of respect and lack of recognition that moved him to do the unthinkable.

Kentucky athletic director C. M. Newton approached Curry about becoming the head coach at the University of Kentucky. It was, of course, a ridiculous proposal. Kentucky was considered a steppingstone for a head coach, the kind of place from which you moved up. For a coach to leave Tuscaloosa after an SEC championship season and go to Kentucky . . . why, that kind of thing just didn't happen. But it did happen. Curry and his wife, Carolyn, visited Lexington and liked what they saw: the atmosphere, the campus, and the lack of daily scrutiny and pressure on the football program. Curry saw it as an opportunity, a chance to take one of the conference "weak sisters" and turn it into a powerhouse. He accepted the offer and ended the Curry era at Tuscaloosa.

Many rank-and-file Alabama fans were outraged by the way Curry had been treated and said so loudly. It was the old guard, however, who Ingram and Alabama president Roger Sayers looked to appease during their hasty search for a new coach. An interview with Florida State's Bobby Bowden was handled badly, and Bowden walked out on the committee. He signed a lifetime contract with FSU a few days later. Finally, Alabama settled on former Texas A&M and NFL Phoenix Cardinals head coach Gene Stallings. A heavy contingent of ex-Bryant players, none of whom had been outspoken supporters of Curry, flanked Stallings at his press conference.

Stallings even resembled Bryant, all the way down to the craggy features and deep drawl. Stallings, however, had a losing record as a coach and had been fired from every head coaching job he'd ever held. Although well respected in the coaching community, he would have to prove himself to Alabama. There would be no free ride, no matter how much he looked like the Bear.

ROLL TIDE

Out to Pasture

WHENEVER HARD-LINE Auburn fans talk about the 1989 Game, their focus is more on the site of this Game rather than the outcome. Why not crow about the SEC co-championship? Why not tout four straight Iron Bowl wins? The answer has something to do with image.

When it comes to football, Auburn will always be Alabama's little brother. This is not intended as an arrogant proclamation, but a simple statement of fact. They can do whatever they want, be it moving the Game, producing a Heisman winner, or even—and I throw this in just for laughs— claiming a national title, but the family tree won't budge. The state's national sports image will always revolve around the Crimson Tide, and no one, whether in Gadsden, Eufaula, or Elk City, Oklahoma, dares pretend otherwise. Just as Pat Dye, despite his greatest efforts, never became Bear Bryant Jr., Auburn will never be Alabama.

Auburn people know this, and it drives them nuts. It got to them so badly that they, literally, took their ball and went home. This shouldn't be an issue of bitterness and jealousy but a simple matter of success evidenced on scoreboards through the years. Auburn will never match Alabama's history on the field. The problem is, too many Tiger fans can't accept that. They've been knocked around by Big Brother so long that they'll do whatever is necessary to see him take a fall. They like to visualize all Alabama supporters as snide and arrogant, perennial riders on a pretentious band-wagon. This premise, of course, is laughable. There is no entrance exam involved in supporting a school.

To suggest that there is a fundamental difference in the makeup of Alabama and Auburn people is silly and divisive. We live together, work together, play together. Hell, we even hate Steve Spurrier together.

Auburn folks like to think that because they've taken a lot more whippings over the years than Alabama, they've somehow *earned* their status as fans. Anybody can pull for a winner, they reason; it takes guts to get behind a traditional also-ran. This also leads to resentment of the Tide and its followers. Consequently, Dye knew he could use the "We'll show them Bama snobs" line to charge up the Auburn faithful to move the Game. It was a smart move, because it hid an important motive: money. Stadium upper decks and first-class practice facilities don't exactly pay for themselves, particularly when Samford and Pacific come to town. What better way to ensure a steady cash flow than to bring in Alabama every other year and force fans to buy a whole season's worth of tickets just for one Game? Even the most pathetic nonconference oppo-nent will be good for a sellout, regardless of how many people actually show up.

No one can deny that a football team has the right to play its home games wherever it chooses. But that's not the heart of the matter here; Auburn's perpetual insecurity is. The Tigers have never been able to escape that big red shadow, and putting up such a fuss about where to play the Game only emphasizes the point.

In the end, the worst part of the whole site debate was that it marked the passing of a unique era. Through 1987, the atmosphere of the Game was incredible. The two student sections faced one another directly, and the sound of either half of the stadium trying to outdo the other was something to behold. Ever since, the rivalry has lost a bit of its luster. But hey, some-times Little Brother gets his way. And that's a shame. Farm livin' ain't the life for me.—S.B.

WAR EAGLE
Walking the Walk

P AT DYE called this Game "the final brick," the last step in the rebuilding of Auburn to annual national power. Sports information director and future athletic director David Housel said, "There will never be another day like it. You can only go to Mecca once." For Auburn, it was nothing short of magical.

For all the long years of struggle, for all the days spent gritting our teeth in the ramshackle confines of Legion Field, this was the payoff. It was Auburn's time to shine, Auburn's time to prove all the doubters wrong. And it all came true.

There was more on the line on that day than a football game. This was the time for Auburn to put up or shut up. If the Tigers had collapsed, it would have opened a wound that would never close. The team and the coaches knew it. None of them wanted to be remembered as the guys who lost to Alabama on the occasion of the First Time Ever.

And they did it. What's more, they did it with style. It was as perfect as a day of football could possibly be. Auburn put up. Alabama, its old arrogance stripped away, shut up. The pre-Game braggadocio from the UAT riffraff was amazing. Alabama students boasted about winning the Game and trashing the place afterward. After the Game they just wanted to get out of town.

I'd have given a lot to see what Ray Perkins looked like when this one was over. The only thing that would have made this win better would have been to have him coaching Alabama that day. Well, OK, Bryant would be better still, but that would require an act of God.

It was a day to remember, a day that will go down as one of the greatest in Auburn history. A hundred years from now, people will still talk about the day Alabama came to Auburn for the first time ever, undefeated, and got their crimson clocks cleaned.

You know, this Game was for a lot of people. It was for the team, who came through adversity and doubt to become champions. It was for the fans, who longed and worked for that day for years. It was for the Auburn staff, which arguably did the best coaching job of the Pat Dye era. To me, it was really for a quiet southern gentleman from Selma. Like him, this Game was all of Auburn wrapped up in one package, all the perseverance, all the class, all the tradition, all the emotion and the history. In my mind, and I'll bet a few others, this was one gentleman's revenge over a loudmouth rival, the long-overdue realization of the fondest dreams of the greatest of all Auburn men.

In the aftermath of this Game, an Auburn old-timer outside the stadium said, "Somewhere, Shug's smilin' down, and Bear's scowlin' up." Without passing judgment on the final rewards of those departed coaches, I think it's safe to say that he was right about one thing. Somewhere out there, Ralph Jordan was definitely smiling on December 2, 1989.

Shug, this one was for you.—W.C.

1990-91

WINDS OF CHANGE

T HE 1990 AND 1991 GAMES are not showcased here because, like their counterparts of 1987 and 1988, they were not as dramatic as the ten featured in this book. Nevertheless, the years 1990 and 1991 will not be forgotten by supporters of either Alabama or Auburn for a multitude of reasons. The Crimson Tide took the long road back to the elite of the Southeastern Conference. The Tigers, meanwhile, fell from the heights of the 1980s and became the prey of a former player and his charges of illegal benefits. By the end of the 1991 season, Gene Stallings had returned Bama to its perch as the state's premier program, while Pat Dye and Auburn were enduring the glare of the predatory media's spotlight and the pain and shock of a demoralizing year.

1990

I T WAS clear from early on that the division among Bama fans that had plagued Bill Curry would not hinder Gene Stallings. In contrast to the reception given to his two predecessors, Curry and Ray Perkins, the entire old-line Alabama camp was in his corner. Some objected to his lack of success as a head coach, but most seemed relieved that a likable man with ties to Bear Bryant was finally in charge. Stallings said all the right things at his introductory press conference, confirming a genuine passion for beating Auburn, while making an effort to abate the growing Tide fear of coaches leaving Tuscaloosa on a whim. "I started my career here, and I'm going to end my career here," he promised.

The Alabama old guard warmly greeted the down-home Stallings, whose demeanor was dramatically different from the formal Curry and the icy Perkins. In fact, when Stallings arrived at the news conference, Paul Bryant Jr. sought him out, telling him, "This is what Papa wanted." His prompt hiring helped steady the Tide program, as reflected in his first recruiting class, considered a solid group by the "experts." United, at least for a while, the Tide camp had solved one of its two major problems. The other one dealt with a four-game losing streak.

The source of this second dilemma, the Auburn Tigers, entered the 1990s as the undisputed king of the SEC. Shares of three successive league championships, as well as the successful effort to bring Alabama to Jordan-Hare Stadium, fixed Pat Dye firmly at the fore of the conference and of the state.

A drop-off for the Tigers in 1990 was not anticipated, as Auburn headed into the season ranked third in the country by the Associated Press. At quarterback, two-year starter Reggie Slack was gone. Dye was faced with three potential successors: redshirt freshman Stan White, sophomore Corey Lewis, and senior Frank Macintosh. Remembering the troubles of 1985, Dye announced that White was his choice before the start of the season, averting a controversy and placing full confidence in the talented newcomer. Rugged runners Stacey Danley and James Joseph were back for one more year, and Ed King and Rob Selby anchored a line described by Dye as his best ever at Auburn. Without Alexander Wright, the deep threat was gone, but Greg Taylor returned, and the hotly recruited Pedro Cherry was a talent who seemed destined for greatness. Victor Hall and Fred Baxter continued the long line of durable Tiger tight ends.

Lamar Rogers and David Rocker, a candidate for national lineman awards, headed a defensive line that met the standards set by earlier Auburn teams, while Darrel Crawford and freshman James Willis stood out as linebackers. Dennis Wallace and John Wiley were veterans in the secondary, capping off an imposing defense.

After assessing Alabama's personnel for 1990, most observers concluded that the Tide's best chance for success hinged on winning shootouts, utilizing the SEC's top offense of a year earlier. The defense, which had been suspect to begin with in 1989, was losing linebacker extraordinaire Keith

McCants a year early to the NFL draft, while Vantriese Davis, John Mangum, and Willie Wyatt had all graduated after distinguished careers.

Young, unproven players such as linebackers Derrick Oden and John Sullins had to fill the gaps. The loss of nose guard Wyatt seemed particularly damaging, but Robert Stewart, who played as a linebacker in 1987 and as a fullback in 1988 before being suspended by Curry in 1989, was moved to the middle of the line as a replacement. End George Thornton returned as one of the few proven impact players Stallings had to work with defensively, while Eric Curry, forced to sit out 1989 as a Proposition 48 casualty, was penciled in on the other side. Linebackers Steve Webb and Antonio London also returned, but taking the place of Keith McCants was a task beyond the capacity of any Tide defender. True freshman Antonio Langham would replace Mangum, while Efrum Thomas and George Teague headed the rest of the Alabama secondary, coached by Bill "Brother" Oliver, who had begun his coaching career as a protégé of Auburn's Shug Jordan.

Although the Tide defense appeared unproven, the offense seemed loaded. Quarterback Gary Hollingsworth, who had already rewritten many Bama passing records, was back, along with tailback Siran Stacy, mentioned by many as a Heisman Trophy candidate. The line that protected Hollingsworth in 1989 remained largely intact, led by Shultz and Terrill Chatman. Tight end Lamonde Russell, who played a large role in Hollingsworth's success, teamed with split end Craig Sanderson and freshman sprinter Kevin Lee to give the Tide a formidable passing game. Another key offensive contributor, whose significance could not be fully appreciated at the time, was kicker Philip Doyle, a preseason All-American.

Stallings did not believe in naming coordinators for his offense or defense, but Mal Moore, an old hand who had served Bear Bryant for nearly twenty years, was brought back by Stallings and given charge of offensive play-calling. Similarly, Oliver, the secondary coach, was essentially the top man defensively, having been the head coach at Tennessee-Chattanooga and an assistant at Auburn and Alabama. His task was an unenviable one— to mold a young group into a squad capable of handling the high-powered attacks of the SEC, such as Florida and Tennessee, both of which lurked on the Tide schedule.

PAT DYE began his tenth year at Auburn hosting Cal State Fullerton. Stan White connected on four touchdown passes, and the Tigers coasted, 38–17. At halftime of the game, freshman running back Otis Mounds, who was being redshirted and was watching in the stands, was paged to the Auburn locker room. Because of a lack of healthy backs, Dye was forced to make

Mounds dress for the second half, and he would carry the ball six times in the game. Mounds was something of a project for Dye and had been a source of some controversy during recruiting. As a teenager, he had been convicted of a drug offense and served nine months in a juvenile correctional institution. Most college coaches wouldn't touch him, but Dye was convinced that Mounds had turned his life around and gave the young man from Dillard High in Fort Lauderdale, Florida, a scholarship and a chance. The leap of faith would pay off handsomely in the years to come, as several of Mounds's Dillard teammates would swell the Tiger ranks, all saying that they were heavily influenced by Dye's trust in Otis Mounds.

A road trip to stifling hot Jackson, Mississippi, followed against the Ole Miss Rebels, who did not fall easily. Only with under a minute to play could the Tigers relax, escaping with a 24–10 win.

Following a week off, Auburn entertained Tennessee in a wild SEC battle and escaped with a tie, 26–26. The Vols had led, 26–9, going into the fourth quarter, before White brought the Tigers back to tie. Auburn celebrated the game as if it had been a win. Tennessee mourned as if it had been a loss. All involved, however, called it one of the greatest football games they'd ever seen. Johnny Majors said, "I don't think I've ever seen both teams give such a furious effort." This time, Coach Dye was generally lauded for going for the tie, and the Tigers were alive and well in the SEC and national races.

After such an emotional roller-coaster ride, the Tigers seemed flat the next week, hosting a Louisiana Tech team that had no intentions of lying down. A major upset was avoided when White directed a last-minute drive that set up a Jim Von Wyl field goal that gave the Tigers a 16–14 victory.

The following week Vanderbilt visited Jordan-Hare, and the 56–6 slaughter quickly showed why the balance of football power in the state of Tennessee is tilted radically toward Knoxville.

Florida State was next, matching "Bobby's Babies," a young, once-beaten FSU squad against the Tigers. Auburn was ranked fifth, the Seminoles seventh, and the hype surrounding the matchup turned out to be well warranted. The Auburn home crowd was pumped for the showdown, drowning out the infamous Seminole chant even before the kickoff.

Lectron Williams broke loose for a long run in the third, leading to a Von Wyl field goal. After two Auburn turnovers in the fourth quarter, FSU looked ready to pull away. Aiming for a knockout punch, Bowden tried his infamous fumblerooski, but AU nose guard Walter Tate was ready for it and recovered the ball near midfield. Led by White and Casey, Auburn drove fifty-seven yards to tie the game, 17–17, with 3:47 left. With plenty of time left, Dye called for the PAT rather than the two-point conversion. It was a safe and winning decision. Florida State's subsequent drive brought the Seminoles to Auburn's 37-yard line, where they faced a fourth-down situation. Bowden chose to go for it, but his quarterback was sacked for a huge loss to the FSU 41. Three plays later, White connected with Casey again, moving the ball to the Seminole 18. With two seconds remaining in the game, Von Wyl hit the field goal and Auburn managed a huge 20–17 win, denying Bobby Bowden his two hundredth career victory.

The Auburn coaches, players, and fans erupted in a memorable celebration. After three years of leaving stadiums with the razzing Seminole chant ringing in their ears, Auburn folks returned the favor, singing out louder and louder versions of the chant for twenty minutes after the final bell. The elusive national title was obviously on Dye's mind when he concluded his postgame remarks with, "What you've done tonight, men, is you've set the stage for what you want to do."

Dye and the Tigers traveled to Starkville to face Mississippi State the following week. The Bulldogs hung tough, and with just over two minutes to go, scored a touchdown, needing only the extra point to tie the game. Tiger Darrel Crawford, however, blocked the kick, and AU again escaped by the narrowest of margins, holding on to win, 17–16. After the game, running back Stacey Danley commented, "I think this game will be our last gift from God." His assessment turned out to be highly accurate.

Auburn traveled to Gainesville the next week to face 7–1 Florida, which was in the familiar position of being on probation and thus ineligible for the SEC title. It looked going in like a golden opportunity for Auburn, as all three teams ranked ahead of the Tigers had either lost or tied their afternoon games. A win would surely vault Auburn to number one in Monday's poll.

With the game tied, 7–7, going into the second quarter, Florida exploded, scoring twenty-seven points in the period to lead, 34–7, at halftime. The 48–7 final score was the worst loss in Dye's career. The pounding in Florida Field dropped Auburn to 6–1–1, and the Tigers plunged to fifteenth in the national rankings. It would only get worse as Southern Miss, at 7–3, came to town and won, 13–12, over the demoralized Tigers.

A young Georgia team supplied a desperately needed tonic for the Auburn ills next, stumbling into town and limping away with a 33–10 loss. At the very least, the win stopped the bleeding for Dye.

September 8 marked the beginning of the Gene Stallings era at Alabama, as the Tide hosted Southern Mississippi at Legion Field. The Bama offense seemed to pick up where it had left off in 1989, cruising down the field for

Gene Stallings took over the
head coaching position at
Alabama in 1990.

a touchdown on its first possession. After that, however, Stallings's debut became a nightmare that allowed the Golden Eagles to claim a shocking 27–24 upset. For the coup de grâce, the Crimson Tide lost Heisman hopeful Stacy for the year with a knee injury.

Florida was up next, making a rare trip to Tuscaloosa. Bama took a 10–0 lead midway through the third quarter before Shane Matthews caught fire and pulled the Gators ahead for a 17–13 win.

Having lost on both of its home fields, the Tide tried its luck on the road, visiting the Georgia Bulldogs in Athens. Georgia coach Ray Goff was hardly in better shape than Stallings, having begun the season with a loss to Ole Miss and was still, in his second year, trying to fill the considerable shoes of Vince Dooley. Alabama dominated most of the day, leading, 16–6, early in the fourth quarter, but the Bulldogs rallied and Alabama was 0–3 after falling 17–16. Unbelievably, another key offensive contributor, flanker Prince Wimbley, was lost for the season with a knee injury suffered on the last play of the game.

The attitude among Tide partisans after this horrendous start points out just how heavily the influence of Bear Bryant still weighs upon

Tuscaloosa. Naturally, some supporters were calling for Stallings's head. The coach's detractors noted the rash of injuries and criticized the conditioning program. The radio talk shows were alive with invective. Auburn fans snapped up bumper stickers reading "Honk If You've Coached at Bama."

The alumni and Hootie Ingram, however, were patient. Had Curry started 0–3 in 1987, he probably would have been tied behind the next bus headed to Atlanta. Stallings was one of Bear's Boys, and the consensus around the state was that sooner or later the Tide would return. After all, Vanderbilt was next.

The Commodores supplied exactly what was needed the following week, giving Bama a 59–28 Tuscaloosa breezer. For the first time in recent memory, a win over Vanderbilt was savored.

A strange road trip, negotiated by Perkins years earlier, put Bama in Lafayette, Louisiana, the next week, facing the Southwest Louisiana Ragin' Cajuns. An embarrassing loss here might have been suicidal, but the Tide coasted to a 25–6 win. There wasn't much to be proud of, but at least Bama fans were now complaining about wins, rather than losses.

After a week off, Stallings made his first visit to Knoxville as Bama head coach. Tennessee had come full circle over the last two years, having lost only two games, both to Alabama. Furthermore, the Vols had just applied a 45–3 pasting to Florida and came into the Bama game undefeated and ranked third, despite earlier ties to Colorado and Auburn. Alabama, at 2–3, was installed as an eleven-point underdog, its largest such point-spread deficit in nearly twenty years.

It seemed to be just a matter of time before Tennessee's high-octane offense would ignite and blow the Tide off the field. But the young defense was playing well, and when it was over, Alabama had beaten Tennessee for the fifth consecutive time, 9–6. The Vols had suffered their third loss in twenty-five games—all to the Tide.

After such a monumental victory over its second biggest rival, Bama seemed to be going in the right direction. A 3–3 record sounded a lot better than 0–3, and the Tide defense was playing on a level that had not been matched in Tuscaloosa since the late 1970s. Homecoming weekend was next on the schedule, and with it came Penn State, marking the last in a memorable collection of matchups between the Crimson Tide and the Nittany Lions.

Only a defensive purist could have appreciated that late Saturday afternoon in Bryant-Denny Stadium. Penn State was held to 201 yards of offense, while the Lions held Alabama's backs to 6 yards on the ground, a school record for rushing futility. Again, Bama mistakes proved fatal, and even another fantastic effort by the Tide defense could not stop a 9–0 defeat.

Nonetheless, for the next game, a trip to Mississippi State, Bama coasted to a 22–0 win. Next, when LSU came to Tuscaloosa, Bama dominated the Bayou Bengals all afternoon, winning 24–3. Obviously, the defense was becoming a story in itself. For the first time, Stallings was a winning coach at Alabama, at 5–4. A bowl berth was clearly in range, with only Cincinnati standing in the way of a winning season. The Bearcats put up little resistance in Legion Field the following Saturday as Bama rolled, 45–7. The Tide secured a bowl bid, and like their counterparts, built up a head of steam heading into the Iron Bowl.

AS DECEMBER 1 approached, it was clear that the 1990 Game would have a New Year's Day bowl bid on the line. It wasn't the Sugar Bowl (unless Auburn won and Tennessee somehow lost to Vanderbilt), but rather the Fiesta Bowl in Phoenix, which had become the subject of great attention. Voters in Arizona, in an election held a month earlier, had rejected a bill creating a state holiday in honor of Martin Luther King Jr. The vote created a furor of activity by civil rights activists, and the Fiesta Bowl was a logical target. Back in Alabama, the backlash was particularly feverish, as the Fiesta had reached a preliminary agreement with Bama and Auburn to match the winner with Louisville on January 1.

The situation was a powder keg. Representatives from numerous groups pressured Alabama president Roger Sayers and Auburn president James Martin to turn down the potential invitation. Alabama's faculty senate, in fact, drew up a resolution recommending that Sayers decline the trip, for fear of showing insensitivity to minorities. Sayers left the decision to the Tide players, who voted in favor of playing in the Fiesta.

Money was another factor. A bid in the Fiesta would be worth about $2.6 million for either Alabama or Auburn, and this fact was not lost on either program. After both schools promised to use the game as an opportunity to step up recruitment of black faculty and students and to honor the accomplishments of the slain civil rights leader, groups such as the Southern Christian Leadership Conference endorsed the idea of the Iron Bowl winner heading west. Subsequently, a deal was reached with the Peach Bowl, in Atlanta, to take the loser of the Game.

For the first time in several years, there was a noticeable change in the atmosphere leading up to the Iron Bowl. Over the previous few seasons, there was little doubt that Auburn had firepower superior to Alabama. Now, with Dye's squad having dropped two of its last three games and Alabama's defense taking over games, most observers saw the matchup as a potential classic, at least in terms of parity. It seemed that a physical, grinding Game was in store, likely to be settled by turnovers and the kicking game. Fans only half-jokingly predicted a 3–0 final score, maybe even 2–0.

The shape of the Game was obviously changing. The athletes on the defensive side of the ball were beginning to outrun and overpower those on offense. Alabama's defense, of course, was drawing national attention, but Auburn's was also a formidable unit and had performed admirably all year, with the obvious exception of the Florida debacle. Either defense had the capacity to win the game for its side, and Stallings was quoted as saying that seventeen points would be sufficient for the Tide to win. Nonetheless, if one team was capable of opening things up offensively, it was Auburn, as long as the freshman White kept the composure that had served him so well early in the season. On the other side, Bama realized that its best offensive strategy would be to run the clock with sustained, conservative drives, letting its defense decide the outcome, as it had in Knoxville.

With Alabama partisans feeling a new surge of confidence, and with the realization that they would have the majority of seats in Legion Field for the Game, the buildup seemed particularly intense for the 1990 Game. Bama T-shirts announced the "Return to Civilization" of the battle, a reference to the 1989 game in Auburn, while Tiger supporters trumpeted the "Drive for Five," as Dye was going for his fifth straight victory over the Tide.

AS GAME day broke, Auburn fans halfheartedly listened to updates coming from Nashville, where Vandy was having early luck against Tennessee. The Volunteers' firepower, however, would prove too much in the second half, sending Johnny Majors to the Sugar Bowl for the last time. Officially, the Game was then a battle for the Fiesta Bowl.

That day the Game was just that, a game, as war in the Persian Gulf was imminent. The Alabama band played "The Star-Spangled Banner" to a thunderous response, and a surge of nervous energy, extraordinary even for the Iron Bowl, enveloped the crowd.

Auburn was the first to go on offense, and it began with a sack. Two plays later, White was intercepted as he tried to float the ball to Joseph. Alabama took possession on the Auburn five-yard line. Three plays later, Jones, the Tide's short-yardage man, bulled straight up the middle for a Bama touchdown. For the first time in four years, the Tide had claimed first blood in the contest, leading Auburn, 7–0.

Both teams then blew first-quarter scoring chances, but Auburn had an opportunity in the second quarter, as tailback Alex Smith carried the ball to the Tide 13. Penalized after the play, the Tigers were given the ball on the

Bama 28. The Tide contained the Auburn offense, blitzing on third down and knocking the Tigers out of field goal range.

Late in the half, White threw from his own 22 for Fred Baxter, but the high pass ricocheted off his tight end's hands and into those of reserve Bama defensive back Brian Stutson, who returned the interception twenty yards to the Auburn 24, the third Tiger miscue of the day. Dye's defense held firm, however, and Stallings was forced to go for a field goal from thirty-one yards out. The conversion gave Alabama a 10–0 lead, with 2:14 left before the break.

With the Tide trying to run out the clock in the closing moments of the half, Hollingsworth and Kevin Turner mishandled a handoff, and Tiger Lamar Rogers recovered the ball at the Bama 38 with forty-nine seconds to play. On a third-down play, White hit Joseph on a screen, and the senior bolted down to the Tide eight-yard line with thirteen seconds left in the half. Two plays later, White lobbed a pass into the end zone toward three receivers who were surrounded by six Tide defenders. Fred Baxter was able to make the catch, and Auburn was back in the game, 10–7, at the break.

Auburn kicked off to begin the second half. The ball was taken at the goal line by Kevin Lee. In what Stallings later called the biggest play of the game, Lee streaked up the right sideline and took the ball to the Auburn 38. The Tiger defense responded and forced the Tide to punt. Still, Lee's return had given Bama a huge edge in field position, which would become more important as the Game went on. The third quarter became a punting contest between Alabama's Tank Williamson and Auburn's Richie Nell, as the two combined for eight kicks in just over twelve minutes. Sophomore Junior Sewell finally broke the monotony, bursting through the Tiger defense for three big runs that put Bama's Doyle back in range. The All-American delivered once again, drilling a forty-yarder to extend the Tide lead to 13–7, with twenty-eight seconds left in the third quarter.

Early in the fourth period, with the Tide backed up at its own 20, Hollingsworth again had trouble with a handoff, this time intended for Sewell. Rogers claimed his second fumble recovery of the Game at the Bama 17, and Auburn was primed to take the lead.

A screen pass to Joseph gained eight yards to the Tide nine-yard line. The Tigers gained only one on second down, setting up a crucial third and one. White faked a handoff to Joseph, then pitched the ball on an end around to Baxter, who never took control of the pigskin. In a mad pileup, Bama's Byron Holdbrooks came up with the ball at the Alabama 12, the Tigers' fourth turnover of the Game.

On Auburn's next possession, facing third and short, Danley took a pitch around left end and was forced out of bounds at the Auburn 40-yard line. With 8:16 left to play, he was short of the marker, setting up fourth and one and the Game's first true drama. Dye appeared to be going for it, lining up his offense in a short-yardage, goal-line set. White stood under center, barking out his signals, as the play clock rolled. The Tigers, though, had no intention of putting the ball in play, and the Tide defense quickly divined the situation. The Tigers were penalized for delay of game. Dye, a champion of smash-mouth football, had had his bluff called. He had too much respect for the Tide defense and too little confidence in his own offense to take the gamble of a fourth-down conversion.

Auburn punted, and the Tide took over on its own 29, with 7:35 to go. Another penalty moved the ball near midfield. On third down, Alabama failed to convert, and it was Stallings's turn to play the gambler. The Tide head coach, however, had faith in his offensive line and, more importantly, his defense, and decided to go for the first down. Alabama set up the play just as Auburn had moments earlier in their fourth-down alignment, but

Auburn's Lamar Rogers (91) recovers a fumble for the Tigers. Turnovers plagued both sides in 1990.

Hollingsworth made no attempt to draw the Tigers offsides. Rather, he gave the ball to fullback Martin Houston, who gained three yards and the crucial first down.

The irony of the two fourth-down plays was unmistakable. Auburn had embarrassed and run over the Tide four straight years, proving its superiority in just this sort of situation. This time, they didn't try. Alabama did, however, and made it work. Now the Game was theirs to win.

After two Sewell carries gave Bama a first down at the Auburn 30, Houston rumbled through the middle of the Tiger defense to the 22-yard line. He was short of the first down, but as long as the Tide held on to the ball and Doyle was at the ready on the sideline, it hardly mattered. On third and short, the Auburn defense rose to the occasion and prevented the first down. Doyle faced another forty-yard attempt, this one to slam the door.

This was the moment Crimson Tide faithful had been waiting for since 1985, a chance to put the Tigers away. Doyle's kick, just as Van Tiffin's had

Auburn freshman quarterback Stan White (11) led the team in his first Game in 1990, but he threw three interceptions on the day.

five years earlier, split the uprights. Alabama was on top, 16–7, with 2:15 left in the Game.

Auburn took over on its own 34, desperate. This time the Tigers had to go for it on fourth and short. White gambled by going deep, but he over-threw his receiver. The Tide forced the Tigers to use their final time-outs. Stallings was still wearing his poker face, fearful of something going wrong in this, his shining moment as a first-year coach. With twenty-six seconds left, Williamson punted the ball one last time, which for good measure rolled out of the back of the end zone.

Auburn took over on its 20, with White going deep again. His day ended as it had begun, with an interception by Efrum Thomas on the Bama 39, with four seconds left. The Game, Auburn's streak, and Alabama's pain were over, 16–7.

As beautiful as the outcome seemed to those in crimson, the 1990 Game was not a pretty sight. Auburn finished the game with five turnovers, three of them interceptions by White, and eight penalties. Alabama had lost two fumbles, both recovered by Auburn, and was penalized six times.

After the Game, when asked about his fourth-quarter decision not to run a play on fourth and short, Dye replied, "I sure wasn't worried about Alabama driving down the field on us, and there was plenty of time left." The coach could not be blamed if he had lost faith in his offense. Indeed, with White at the controls, Auburn could manage only eighty-one offensive yards and three first downs in the entire second half.

The performance of the 1990 Bama defense was stunning. Even Bill Oliver, its chief architect, bristled when asked if he thought that they would perform throughout the year as they did. "Hell, no. . . . We felt we'd be OK, but never did we expect them to do something like this."

Bama, of course, had not done much better with the ball than had Auburn and had gained only 194 yards all day to the Tigers' 237. They were, however, able to move well enough to put Doyle in position for his final kick, which established an SEC record for most field goals in a career (seventy-eight), as well as sealing the Game.

Alabama accepted the invitation to play in the Fiesta Bowl, just as everyone had expected. The Tide, flat after the Iron Bowl, was humiliated on national television by Louisville, 34–7, coached by another one of "Bear's Boys," Howard Schnellenberger.

Auburn made the short trip up I-85 to Atlanta for the Peach Bowl and played a sloppy game in a foggy, rainy Fulton County Stadium against Indiana. The Tigers prevailed in the end, 27–23, on a gutsy, fourth-down naked bootleg by White for the winning touchdown. White was named the bowl

MVP, and all involved saw Auburn recovering from 1990's disappointments to challenge the SEC again.

IN MID-1991 Dye faced a challenge, not to his job or his prestige, but to his life. For years he had suffered from stomach pains that had been written off as indigestion, but in May, he was diagnosed with hemochromatosis, a rare blood disorder. At the time, Dye dismissed his condition as "this little thing," but it was far more serious than the Auburn coach let on. For the first time in his life, Dye was sick. Even after successful surgery, he would never be totally free of the illness again. Dye spent several weeks recuperating. Despite his public statements to the contrary, his competitors quickly added health concerns to their recruiting pitches.

1991

THE TIDE opened 1991 against Temple in Birmingham. Under the direction of senior quarterback Danny Woodson, Bama coasted, 41–3. The game was significant in that it marked the returns of Siran Stacy and Prince Wimbley.

The next week was not so successful, as Bama visited Florida in Gainesville. The talented Gators, who would go undefeated in 1991 against SEC competition, smelled blood and blew the game open, claiming their first-ever home victory against Alabama in a 35–0 thrashing.

A badly needed but unimpressive 10–0 Tuscaloosa win over Georgia followed; then came a 48–17 win in Nashville over Vanderbilt. It marked the coming of age of David Palmer, nicknamed "the Deuce," for his jersey number—2.

Annihilations of Tennessee-Chattanooga (53–7) and Tulane (62–0) put Bama at 5–1 and fourteenth in the polls, as eighth-ranked Tennessee rolled into Legion Field. The Tide suffered two blows during the game because of injury, as Palmer was lost in the first quarter with an ankle sprain and Woodson in the third quarter with a pulled hamstring. Nevertheless, the defense still displayed its 1990 form, as it had virtually all year. With the Vols falling, 24–19, it was a great win for the Tide, which claimed its sixth straight decision over the frustrated Volunteers and gained at least a measure of national respect by finally beating a quality opponent.

After a week off, Bama, now ranked seventh, entertained Mississippi State under new head coach Jackie Sherrill. The Tide escaped with a harrowing 13–7 win. Another near-miss happened the next week in Baton Rouge when Alabama improved to 8–1 with a 20–17 squeaker. The Tide flirted with disaster yet again the following Saturday against Memphis State. Returning to the Liberty Bowl, the site of the embarrassing 1987 loss to the Tigers, Bama built an early lead and held on for a tight 10–7 win.

The narrow escape in Memphis put the Tide at 9–1 for the year, but a lackluster season was failing to attract the attention of the major bowls. Thus the Tide accepted a bid to play in the second annual Blockbuster Bowl, against a Big Eight team to be determined by the Oklahoma-Nebraska game, scheduled one day before the Iron Bowl. Florida, which benefited from playing both Alabama and Tennessee at home in 1991, had already earned its first berth in the Sugar Bowl, to play Notre Dame.

The cold shoulder presented by the New Year's Day bowls was representative of the national feeling about the 1991 Crimson Tide. Observers called Bama "the worst 9–1 team in the country." Stallings had a little fun with one of those detractors, ESPN commentator and former football coach Lee Corso. Stallings said, "I guess Lee ought to know a bad team when he sees one—all of his teams were pretty awful."

AUBURN ENTERED 1991 ranked eighteenth in the country, seeking to begin Pat Dye's second decade on the Plains by eliminating the complacency that seemed to have enveloped the program over the past year. With the departure of running backs Stacey Danley and James Joseph, the passing game looked to be featured more prominently, while the defense, despite losing David Rocker and Lamar Rogers, still rated among the SEC's best. The Tigers also enjoyed a solid recruiting season of their own, reeling in Thomas Bailey, Chris Shelling, and Fred Smith, all of whom would make immediate contributions, and two of Otis Mounds's teammates from Dillard High, running back James Bostic and receiver Frank Sanders.

At the end of the 1990 season, Auburn receivers coach Larry Blakeney left to become the head coach at Troy State. In the wake of Blakeney's departure, Dye decided to end "offense by committee" and appoint a fulltime offensive coordinator. Pat Sullivan was the fan favorite to take the job, but Dye was looking for new blood. Since Dye considered the schemes of former Alabama offensive coordinator Homer Smith to be the most difficult he'd ever had to defend against, the Auburn coach phoned Smith, who was then calling the plays for UCLA. Smith declined to return to the SEC but recommended one of his former colleagues, Tommy Bowden, who had gone with Bill Curry to Kentucky as quarterbacks coach. Dye, who disagreed with but respected the offensive philosophies of Bowden's father, Bobby, decided to hire Tommy. Auburn fans supported the choice and started talking about a new, high-powered "Tommy Gun" attack.

Perennial Division I-AA power Georgia Southern brought its wish-bone attack into Jordan-Hare to kick off the season and promptly built a 17–0 halftime lead in front of a stunned Auburn crowd. The Tigers' depth, however, took effect late in the game, and Auburn won, 32–17, avoiding a major embarrassment. Ole Miss was next and was expected to mount a serious challenge to the Tigers. Two freshmen, Bailey and tail-back Joe Frazier, kept the Rebels at bay, and Auburn won relatively easily, 23–13.

The Tigers returned to Austin, Texas, the next weekend, taking on the Longhorns. Texas had entered 1991 with high hopes but had fallen to Mississippi State a week earlier. The Tigers returned one interception for a score and claimed two other interceptions to take a 14–10 win that put them at 3–0 heading into a huge battle at Tennessee.

The game with the fifth-ranked Volunteers figured to produce the main challenger to Florida for the SEC crown. It was another pivotal clash between the Big Orange and the Orange and Blue, and the Tigers were seeking to win in Knoxville for the first time since 1983.

Just one day before the Tennessee game, in the Friday edition of the *Montgomery Advertiser*, former Tiger defensive back Eric Ramsey made front-page news. Three months earlier, Ramsey had made waves when the *Advertiser* published part of an essay he wrote in a sociology class that accused Auburn coaches of being "condescending" toward black athletes and likened college football to slavery. In a news story just after his essay was made public, Ramsey had threatened further revelations and revealed his own delusions of grandeur. "If I have to be the Martin Luther King of this generation, I will be," he warned.

Now Ramsey claimed that Tiger coaches had provided him with illegal benefits during his playing career, from 1987 to 1990. More significantly, he claimed to have a collection of more than seventy audiotapes containing conversations with various coaches and boosters to prove his accusations. His claims were supported by former fullback Alex Strong, who said that he received "a couple of thousand a year" from coach Frank Young, who had retired after the 1990 season.

Ramsey charged specifically that Auburn booster Bill "Corky" Frost had paid at least two of Ramsey's monthly car payments and supplied him with steaks to help him gain weight. Ramsey, who was married and had a young son, also claimed that Young had paid him three hundred dollars per month more than was allowed by the NCAA for a married student-athlete. Further, he claimed to have taped a conversation with Dye, in which he asked the coach, then a member of Colonial Bank's board of directors, for influence in obtaining an unsecured loan, which he ultimately received, for more than nine thousand dollars.

Asked about his motives in making the accusations, Ramsey replied that there needed to be "a changing of the guard" at Auburn. Several former Auburn players, including Bo Jackson, Frank Thomas, and Ramsey's brother-in-law, Aundray Bruce, publicly contested Ramsey's allegations and spoke out in support of Dye and the Auburn program.

The *Birmingham Post-Herald* reported that Ramsey and his wife, Twillita, had tried to sell the story to *Sports Illustrated* for $25,000. College football editor Steve Robinson referred them to freelance writer Tom Junod, who was in the process of writing a feature article on Pat Dye. The Ramseys, however, refused to tell Junod specifically what was on the tapes. When Junod met with the couple, Mrs. Ramsey tried to deceive him into thinking that she was "Dawn Webb," Ramsey's agent (Twillita's maiden name was Webb). The ruse, which was revealed during a heated exchange between Twillita and Junod, might have been intended to discourage the writer from negotiating a lower price for the story. Junod declined the offer, though, and *SI* later formally stated that its editorial policies prohibited paying for stories.

When the Ramsey story broke, Dye was in Boston presenting findings to the NCAA from Auburn's internal investigation into alleged wrongdoing by the school's tennis and basketball programs, both of which were ultimately placed on probation. He flew to Knoxville Friday night, and his team prepared for battle with Tennessee.

The game with the Volunteers was tight, but in the end the Tigers couldn't stop the Tennessee offense. The Vols pulled away with a 30–21 win. It was a tough setback for the Tigers in the last regular season meeting between the two schools until 1998.

The day after the loss, Auburn president James Martin announced that the school was going to conduct its own investigation of Ramsey's claims. Dye would not comment publicly on the accusations, saying he would speak only "through the proper channels," namely, his attorneys. Dye's contract with Auburn contained a clause that called for his dismissal if he was found to have any knowledge of rules violations, so his silence was understandable.

NCAA investigators quickly met with university officials about the charges. In the meantime, Donald Watkins, Ramsey's attorney, declined to cooperate with Auburn's internal investigation. Alex Strong, after meeting with Dye, recanted his former claims and support of Ramsey, saying, "I want out of the whole thing."

Back on the field, Southern Miss paid a visit to the Plains. The Golden Eagles had managed stunning upsets of both Auburn and Alabama the year before, and they held on for another huge upset, 10–9, despite being solidly outplayed.

Another former player came forward the next day with allegations. In an interview with the *Birmingham News*, fullback Vincent Harris, who played from 1986 to 1988 but was now calling Auburn a "hell hole," claimed to have received payments from assistant coaches. Unlike Ramsey, however, Harris had no evidence to back his claims. The *News* also contacted several other former players, including Jeff Burger, James Joseph, and Stacey Danley, all of whom denied ever receiving illegal payments or having knowledge of others being paid.

The Tigers traveled to Nashville next to play Vanderbilt. The Commodores were 1–4 and seemed to offer Auburn a chance to take out some frustrations on the field. The Tigers, however, had to fight for their lives, winning 22–21. The 1991 Tigers narrowly escaped becoming the first Dye team in ten years to drop three games in a row.

Attorney Watkins, after reviewing the tapes, claimed that Ramsey had a "tremendous amount of credibility." Prior to this case, Watkins was best known as the lead attorney for the scandal-ridden administration of Birmingham mayor Richard Arrington, where Watkins had collected millions in taxpayer-funded legal fees. Auburn supporters immediately surmised that Arrington was behind the Ramsey controversy in an attempt to punish Dye for robbing Birmingham of the annual Iron Bowl riches. In Birmingham, Watkins decided to release some of the incriminating tapes to the media rather than to the NCAA. CNN offered to have the tapes authenticated by the FBI, with Watkins and an NCAA representative present, but Watkins refused to cooperate.

On October 17, nine days before Auburn was to play Mississippi State, Watkins played six tapes for *Birmingham News* reporters. They were recordings of phone conversations between Ramsey and Bill "Corky" Frost, an Auburn alumnus from Lilburn, Georgia. In the exchanges, Frost promised to make payments on Ramsey's car and talked of giving the Ramsey family Christmas cash and paying for Ramsey's car insurance. Frost also acknowledged making "bonus" payments, which Ramsey claimed included five hundred dollars for touchdowns and two hundred dollars for interceptions, as well as beef steaks. The tapes portrayed Frost as an avid Auburn fan and close friend of Dye, although the coach was quick to distance himself from Frost: "Sure, I know Corky Frost. But I also know about fifty thousand other Auburn alumni."

Frost's attorney, Dudley Perry of Montgomery, released a statement, saying: "Mr. Frost is shocked and dismayed that Eric Ramsey, who appealed to him for humanitarian help, would be plotting to hurt Auburn University. . . . Mr. Frost in no way acted as a representative of Auburn University. . . . Mr. Frost's only connection is as an alumnus and supporter of Auburn athletics."

As the controversy deepened, rumors swirled about the future of Auburn and the future of Pat Dye. At his weekly news conference the following Tuesday, Dye made it clear that neither he nor his players were going to comment on the Ramsey affair. He said: "I'm tired of it, myself. I hope that's a good enough answer. If it ain't, I really don't care, as long as I've got control of this team and I think I still do. I apologize for doing it and I wish the circumstances were different. Some of you get in there and twist it and turn it and it comes out like you want it and not like it was intended to be said. . . . One of your compadres [Birmingham radio personality Herb Winches] had me resigning last week. I can assure you it didn't come from here. When you come out with something about me resigning, go ahead and say Coach Dye is getting fired. That's what it's going to take to get me out of here." He also cast doubt about the authenticity of the tapes, then turned his attention to the Homecoming battle with Mississippi State.

Nevertheless, the Tigers again fell short on the playing field, and the Bulldogs claimed a 24–17 win, their first over Auburn since 1981. The loss dropped the Tigers to 4–3 and out of the SEC title hunt.

The next week, with powerhouse Florida coming to town, Ramsey and Watkins journeyed to Washington, D.C., to meet with a House subcommittee investigating collegiate athletic abuses. Watkins announced that he intended to release another batch of tapes, which he claimed were recordings of conversations between Ramsey and Auburn assistant coaches. At this point, it became clear that Watkins was saving his trump card, alleged recordings of conversations between Ramsey and Dye, until the end.

By this time the burning questions in Auburn were Who the hell is Eric Ramsey? and Why is he carrying such a grudge? Ramsey grew up in the poverty-stricken west side of Birmingham. When he reached the eighth grade, he moved in with his grandmother in Homewood, one of the higher-income areas of the city, to attend that district's schools. As a senior at Homewood High, Ramsey became one of the state's top recruits. He had a difficult time making the transition from prized signee to practice field "dog." Ramsey did not like the coaching staff's rigid training approach nor the decision to redshirt him in 1986. The coaches also recommended against his getting married in 1987.

It was during this time that Ramsey says he began to see the football program for what he felt it was. He sensed that coaches were more interested in developing him and other black athletes as players than as people: "So much emphasis is placed on winning and making money that people get away from what's good for the individuals. As long as they're out there playing football, that's fine. But once football is over with, they don't care."

By his sophomore season, Ramsey, his wife, Twillita, and his son were living in a two-bedroom trailer, unable to pay their living expenses because of stringent NCAA regulations. Their dire straits were made more maddening by events within the family. Twillita's sister and her husband, Aundray Bruce, were living the good life in Atlanta, thanks to the signing riches of an NFL first draft pick. Ramsey's desperate search for money led him to Frost, a wealthy former track team member at Auburn, and to some members of the Tiger coaching staff. He had become a starter in the Auburn secondary by 1990 and was drafted in the tenth round of the 1991 NFL draft by the Kansas City Chiefs. He was subsequently cut from the team, which contributed to his bitterness toward Dye and his regime. Astonishingly, Ramsey said that he never would have gone public if he had made it into the NFL. He also claimed higher goals: "What I really want to happen is to have a whole new program, not only at Auburn but in the whole college system. . . . The main thing is I think college athletes should be paid."

Tiger supporters, of course, found this apparent hypocrisy maddening. If Ramsey really felt he should be helped financially, why was he making the accusations in the first place? If he had no vendetta with Auburn, why were he and Watkins releasing the tapes only a few at the time? Some observers darkly suggested a hidden agenda that the Ramseys, as well as Donald Watkins, were following. Were there other elements at play? Many wondered how the supposedly indigent Ramseys were paying for their stylish clothes, comfortable apartment, and new Lexus luxury sedans.

The timing of the release of the tapes gave credence to speculation of Tide involvement. Ramsey had waited to make his accusations until the day before the Tennessee game, easily the toughest road game on the Tigers' schedule. Then Watkins played the Frost tapes over the Auburn open date, to whet the public's appetite and keep the story in the papers. Now, with sixth-ranked Florida on the way, Watkins played another batch of tapes for the *Birmingham News*.

The Gators rolled into Auburn and lived up to their national ranking, although the Tigers made it interesting for a while. The 31–10 decision marked the first time an Auburn team coached by Dye had lost three straight at home.

Dye used the Florida game to speak openly, for the first time, about the Ramsey controversy. In an interview with ABC, he said that Ramsey had asked him, as well as several of Dye's assistants, for money during his playing days but that he was unaware if Ramsey's efforts had been successful: "I don't know of any money changing hands. . . . I don't know of anybody giving him a dime." The next day, on his weekly postgame television show, the coach was sounding ominous about his future: "I may be in coaching or I may not be in coaching when this thing is over."

Before the smallest Jordan-Hare crowd in five years, the Tigers the next Saturday trounced Southwestern Louisiana, 50–7, improving to 5–4 on the year and boosting team morale slightly. Hopes of a winning season and a bowl invitation were still alive, although wins over Georgia and Alabama would be required.

The upcoming battle with the Bulldogs in Athens took on even more meaning for Auburn than it would have otherwise, and Attorney Watkins was ready. On the Thursday before the game, he hinted that he was about to release the tapes allegedly containing conversations between Ramsey and Dye. A tape was played for a *Montgomery Advertiser* reporter. The barely audible tape had been recorded in the spring of 1990, before his senior year, according to Ramsey. In it he told Dye that Young was "helping me out," but the meaning of the phrase was not clear. Another topic on the tape was Ramsey's request for a bank loan. Dye was heard to say that Ramsey would possibly be eligible after the end of the upcoming football season (athletes are allowed to receive loans based on their potential as professional players). In an interview with the *Advertiser*, Ramsey claimed that Dye met with him subsequently about the loan and told him that he "took care of that" and to "go over there and see them tomorrow." Ramsey, claiming that the exchange took place on the practice field, did not have these remarks of Dye on tape.

According to the story, Ramsey then went to the bank the next day and received an unsecured loan for $9,209.99, well before his final season began. Watkins was able to prove that Ramsey did indeed receive the loan on April 24, 1990, but he refused to disclose the loan agreement, saying that he would do so only when he decided to release his alleged Dye tapes.

Between the hedges, Georgia struck early and often against the Tigers, claiming only its second victory, 37–27, over the Tigers in nine years. As Dye made his way to the locker room, he was heckled by Bulldog fans. The defeat eliminated any possibility of a bowl game for Auburn, now at 5–5. And a loss at the hands of Alabama would give the Tigers their first losing season since 1981, Dye's initial year. Even worse, Dye had to face an NCAA representative upon returning from Athens, to discuss what was now commonly being referred to as Ramseygate.

ALABAMA, HOWEVER, was not immune from controversy. As the 1991 Iron Bowl approached, a story in the *Columbus (Georgia) Ledger-Enquirer* reported that David Palmer, Alabama's freshman extraordinaire, had allowed someone else to take his ACT college entrance exams, to keep Palmer from possibly becoming a Proposition 48 casualty. Further, the newspaper claimed that officials at Auburn had already reported the indiscretion to the SEC. Dye and Auburn president James Martin, as well as Gene Stallings and Bama athletic director Hootie Ingram, denied the claims.

Auburn supporters couldn't help but respond with glee to the reports. For months, Tide fans had looked on with delight as Ramsey and Watkins dragged Auburn and Dye through the mud. Although the Palmer story was certainly not as potentially damaging to Alabama as Ramsey's tapes were to Auburn, it at least gave the Tiger faithful a chance to enjoy a turnabout and to warn the Crimson Tide that its own day of reckoning might not be far off.

The 1991 Game was unique in a number of ways. Most significantly, it was the Game that Auburn had given up in order to move all subsequent odd-year meetings with the Tide to Jordan-Hare. Thus for the first (and only) time in the history of the series, the Tigers held the vast majority of Legion Field tickets, at least sixty-five thousand, for a clash with Bama in the newly renovated stadium, which now seated just over eighty-three thousand. Indeed, the sight of the Tigers' logo, the interlocked A and U sprawled across the midfield turf, seemed strangely out of place in the arena, long considered to be an Alabama bastion. Many Auburn fans dubbed this Game "the Sandbox Bowl," in reference to Dye's comment three years previously regarding the compromise of putting the 1991 Game in Birmingham: "We had to throw them a bone and agree to play in their sandbox one last time."

Also there was the pall that the Ramsey controversy had cast over the entire Auburn season. Rather than looking to improve their positioning for a major bowl berth, the Tigers were ending 1991 on this overcast November Saturday. There was no denying that Ramsey and Watkins were major contributors to this, and the only solace available for Auburn was the chance to beat the six-point favorite Crimson Tide.

Something was missing. It is hard to say how tempered the Tiger crowd was by the Ramsey controversy, but there is no doubt that their noise level on the day never approximated that which was reached in the 1989 first-ever Jordan-Hare Game. Also, for the first time in eleven years, the Game lacked major television network coverage. Instead, ESPN was sup-

A peculiar sight greeted fans as they entered Legion Field for the 1991 Game—the field's AstroTurf was painted in Auburn's colors for the only time in the history of the Iron Bowl.

plying the broadcast, giving many the impression that this year's rendition was second-rate.

The fired-up Auburn defense held Alabama to three plays and forced a punt. The Tigers moved downfield and attempted a field goal, but the kick went wide to the left, squandering Auburn's first opportunity. Late in the first quarter, George Teague picked off a Stan White pass and returned it to the Auburn 39. The Tide capitalized on the turnover with a thirty-eight-yard field goal from Matt Wethington. The Tigers responded quickly, turning to their most valuable weapons that day, their tight ends. White found Fred Baxter for a thirty-two-yard gain, then hit Victor Hall for twenty-one more. Von Wyl connected from twenty-six yards away to tie the Game, 3–3.

Auburn had Alabama backed up on its next possession, thanks in part to a penalty. On third down, however, Jay Barker, scrambling for his life, dumped the ball to Kevin Turner. The senior fullback lumbered sixty-eight yards down the sideline to the Auburn 12. Two plays later, Palmer, playing at quarterback, took the snap and rolled right. The freshman carried the ball into the end zone from eleven yards out for the Game's only touchdown. The score gave Alabama a 10–3 lead, with ten minutes left in the half.

White again utilized his tight ends when Auburn regained possession. The Tigers drove the ball into Tide territory but failed to convert a fourth-

and-two situation at the Bama 30. Bama had a chance to score just before the break, as Barker found Kevin Lee at the Auburn 10. On the next play, the Bama quarterback threw to freshman Curtis Brown in the corner of the end zone, but the back judge ruled that Brown did not have control of the ball as he went out of bounds. Another close call occurred in the end zone between Palmer and Corey Barlow, resulting in another incompletion and no penalty for either side. Wethington then hit the right upright with a twenty-seven-yard field goal attempt in the closing seconds, wasting the scoring opportunity. The three questionable plays in succession brought a rare display of anger from Stallings, who harassed the officials until his team was penalized fifteen yards for unsportsmanlike conduct.

Early in the third quarter, the Tigers were gaining momentum, containing the Bama offense deep in its own territory, but Tank Williamson boomed a seventy-one-yard punt to get the Tide out of serious trouble. White found Baxter for another large gain of thirty-seven yards to the Bama 29. The Tide defense, however, continued to shut down the Tiger running game, and after failing to convert the down, Von Wyl misfired on another attempt, this one from forty-four yards out, with 7:06 to play in the third.

Palmer struck again for Bama turning a play into a forty-six-yard gain to the Auburn 26. Wethington then hit a thirty-nine-yarder to give the Tide a 13–3 edge late in the third quarter. On Bama's next possession, the Deuce was loose again, taking a reverse and streaking thirty-two yards to the Auburn 32. The Tide went to the game-breaking freshman once too often, however, as a Siran Stacy halfback pass to Palmer in the end zone was picked off.

Early in the fourth quarter, White again connected with Hall for thirty-two yards to the Bama 27. Frazier then bounced off two defenders and dashed for the end zone, but he was knocked out of bounds at the one-yard line. White bobbled the first-down snap, falling on it for a short loss, then Frazier was trapped behind the line of scrimmage for another loss. White's third-down pass to Baxter was deflected by Langham on another close call in the end zone. Von Wyl converted the twenty-three-yard field goal to cut the deficit to 13–6, with 10:50 left to play.

Alabama responded with a sustained drive, as Stacy, Lassic, and Chris Anderson carried the ball for solid yardage. A third-down pass to Palmer at the goal line fell incomplete, bringing in Wethington for another field goal, but Auburn blocked the twenty-eight-yard attempt, keeping hope alive, with 5:38 left in the Game.

The Tigers' offense, however, seemed to only move backward on this possession, with a holding penalty bringing up a third-and-twenty-five situation. White narrowly avoided being sacked in the end zone, and Auburn had to return the ball to the Tide. Bama then ran the clock further down, and Williamson pinned the Tigers at their own 16-yard line, with 2:30 left.

The Tide defense held for three plays, then Dye decided to go for it. The fourth-down pass, however, was incomplete, giving Bama the ball back with 1:45 to play. Auburn had one last chance for a miracle, with four seconds left, only for White's Hail Mary to fall incomplete. Alabama's defense had carried Stallings through another tight one, winning 13–6.

For the second straight year, Auburn had outgained the Tide, this time 345 yards to 286, but the Tigers fell short on the scoreboard. Collectively, the Auburn tight ends, Baxter and Hall, caught seven passes for 173 yards, almost exactly half the team's offensive production. Nine penalties and three turnovers were too much for the Tigers to overcome.

Aside from Auburn mistakes, the difference in this Game was David Palmer. In addition to scoring the only touchdown, the diminutive Birmingham native, named the state's "Mr. Football" just a year earlier while playing most of his high-school games on the same field, finished with 119 all-purpose yards. He showed considerable toughness for an eighteen-year-old, disregarding the negative newspaper stories and making his Game debut a smashing success.

The pain of losing to Alabama also brought out some toughness in Coach Dye. He was heckled again as he walked to the Auburn dressing room, and this time he had no desire to turn the other cheek. Dye bolted for the stands in pursuit of his detractor, and the patrolmen whose job is supposed to be to protect the coach protected the fan, restraining Dye and ushering him off the field.

Asked about his future at Auburn, Dye laughed and said, "Nobody has told me I'm gonna get fired, except in the news media, and that hasn't exactly been substantiated." Then, after being asked if he planned to quit, Dye laughed again and said, "No, I owe too much money to quit."

Alabama, now 10–1 and still without much national respect, went on to the Blockbuster Bowl and beat Colorado, 30–25, in an exciting game that Palmer again dominated, earning MVP honors in the process. The future was bright in Tuscaloosa. With two straight Iron Bowl triumphs and Auburn in disarray, state supremacy was no longer an all-consuming objective. The quest for championships on a bigger scale was now being openly discussed, as fans wondered how much longer the Tide could extend its ten-game winning streak.

Meanwhile, Dye's program at Auburn was truly at a crossroads. Most people felt that Dye would relinquish his position as athletic director but

AUBURN UNIVERSITY PHOTOGRAPHIC SERVICES

Auburn's Ricky Sutton (92) blocks a Michael Proctor field goal
attempt in the second half of the 1991 game.

remain head coach, and in a few months they were proven right. Dye, who
had never enjoyed administration, seemed happy to be rid of the extra
responsibilities. Newly appointed Auburn president William Muse
announced the hiring of Mike Lude, the former athletic director at the University of Washington and then president of the Blockbuster Bowl, to
assume the athletic director's role on the Plains. At the time of Lude's
hiring, it was widely speculated that his close connections to the NCAA
would help Auburn in the ongoing investigation, but many Tiger voices
were quietly saying that an Auburn man—preferably sports information
director David Housel—should have gotten the job.

     With the media waiting for his demise and with two new bosses, Dye
sought to keep the Auburn family together, accepting the recent past and
looking warily into the future.

1992

DRAMA AND DESTINY
PART 1

LEADING UP TO THE 1992 season, two topics dominated the state's sports pages and fans' conversations. One was the precipitous decline of the Auburn program, which had gone from the heights of December 2, 1989, to a losing season, coupled with the ignominy of waiting for the slow NCAA shoe to drop. The other dealt with the new look of the Southeastern Conference, whose two newest members, Arkansas and South Carolina, were about to participate for the first time. The addition of the Razorbacks and Gamecocks helped bring about a restructuring of the league, agreed upon by representatives of the twelve conference schools in 1991.

The conference was split into two divisions, East and West, each consisting of six schools. Alabama and Auburn were both in the West, while the other traditional league powers, Florida, Georgia, and Tennessee, headed the East. The realignment brought an end to a few traditional rivalries, such as that between Auburn and Tennessee, which would now play only twice every eight years. It also made the SEC the first conference in Division 1-A history to stage an official league championship game, scheduled just after the end of the regular season. The top team in the East and its counterpart in the West would meet in early December to decide the conference representative in the Sugar Bowl.

The new plan was as potentially lucrative as it was innovative, promising huge television revenues and an economic boon to the host city of the title game. After considering Memphis, Atlanta, and Orlando, SEC executives decided to hold the game in Birmingham, which met with statewide acclaim in Alabama. Since both Bama and Auburn were in the SEC West and thus could not meet in the game, either team would have a distinct home-field advantage in Birmingham against the East champion. There was more than a little irony in seeing the Tigers celebrating the choice of Legion Field as a potential site for them to play.

The consensus among SEC followers was that Florida and Alabama would meet in the first championship game. The Gators were ranked fifth in the preseason polls and, despite an embarrassing loss to Notre Dame in the Sugar Bowl, seemed to be the class of the East division. Alabama had recovered from the beating applied by the Gators in 1991 to close out the season with ten straight victories. They did this with a relatively young team. Thus the heart of the Tide was returning, and for the first time since 1986, Bama was ranked in the Associated Press's preseason Top Ten at number nine.

It was impossible for any state fan to dwell on the upcoming season and overlook the off-the-field problems Pat Dye was facing in Auburn. The NCAA investigators looking into Eric Ramsey's allegations were hard at work, and the next major event in the ongoing debacle would be formal notification by the governing body of evidence of violations, due at some point in the fall. The scandal had been made even more embarrassing to Auburn when CBS's 60 *Minutes* aired a segment in January 1992 devoted to Ramsey and his attorney, Watkins. The program gave the former player a national stage to repeat his claims, even though the NCAA had requested that all parties refrain from speaking to the press. Auburn officials honored the request, so no university defense was presented on the broadcast. Dye adhered to the NCAA's wishes but continued to defiantly rebuke those who suggested his job was in jeopardy. Nevertheless, speculation was rampant that his days in Auburn were numbered.

Dye still had a solid supply of talent on the Plains. Stan White, now a junior, was a seasoned veteran at quarterback, and at tailback, a position where no one had stood out since the departure of James Joseph, sophomore James Bostic was making his presence felt. Tony Richardson and Reid McMilion would platoon at fullback once again, and record-breaking kick returner Thomas Bailey teamed with Orlando Parker as receivers to give the Tigers a deep threat. To the delight of Alabama fans, tight end Victor Hall was gone, but Fred Baxter, who had caused the Tide considerable grief over the past few years, was back for his senior season. Wayne Gandy and Chris

Gray anchored the offensive line, and Scott Etheridge, a walk-on junior, replaced Jim Von Wyl as place-kicker. Observers who predicted a miserable recruiting year for the Tigers were stunned when Auburn signed South Carolina running back Stephen Davis, considered by many to be the top prospect in the country. Davis had a combination of speed and power reminiscent of Bo Jackson, but he did not qualify on his ACT exam and sat out 1992 under Proposition 48.

Defensively, James Willis was receiving All-American attention at linebacker, playing alongside Karekin Cunningham. Willie Whitehead and Damon Primus headed the front line, while Chris Shelling and Fred Smith stood out in the secondary. The Auburn defense had not received nearly as much attention as its counterpart in Tuscaloosa over the past few years, but it was a solid group capable of keeping the Tigers in games.

After the 1991 season ended, Auburn quarterbacks coach and Heisman Trophy winner Pat Sullivan left the Plains to take the head coaching position at Texas Christian University in Fort Worth. The loss of Sullivan was painful for Dye and particularly difficult for Stan White, who was considered to be the protégé of Auburn's greatest signal caller. Dye called on his own favorite quarterback, Randy Campbell, to fill the vacant position, hoping to instill some of his never-say-die doggedness and dead-on field-general instincts in the struggling White. Tommy Bowden returned as offensive coordinator, under heavy pressure to improve the play calling from the previous year.

THERE WAS plenty of reason to pick Alabama as the preseason favorite in the SEC West. Jay Barker, who as a starter in 1991 was nothing but a winner, returned for his sophomore season, as Bama looked to enjoy a rare year free of quarterback controversy. Derrick Lassic and Sherman Williams were reliable runners with distinctly different styles, while steady Martin Houston provided power at fullback. David Palmer, of course, was a threat at any position and hoped to avoid a sophomore slump. Flanker Curtis Brown, as well as Prince Wimbley, whose knee was still a question mark, kept secondaries from focusing completely on Palmer.

Any follower of the Tide, however, knew that Stallings and Mal Moore's conservative leanings meant that the heart of the offensive attack would come on the ground, and thus the veteran Bama line would have to deliver. Center Tobie Shiels would be counted on to anchor the group, along with George Wilson and Matt Hammond. Freshman kicker Michael Proctor was expected to fill the void still present after Philip Doyle's graduation in 1990, a stern task for anyone, particularly a first-year player.

The Bama defense was losing a few key pieces from 1991, including John Sullins and Robert Stewart, but expectations were still very high. Eric Curry had been mentioned as an NFL first-rounder since his arrival in Tuscaloosa and would team with John Copeland to become possibly the most dominant pair of defensive ends in the history of the SEC.

Derrick Oden and Antonio London were the heart of a deep, tenacious linebacking corps, while George Teague and Antonio Langham patrolled a secondary that had the luxury of playing five men, because of the effectiveness of the three-man front line that coordinator Bill Oliver espoused.

As ever, a great deal was expected from Alabama in 1992. But in June, before summer practice began, the first of three highway incidents involving Tide players during the course of the season unfolded. The first was in Shelby County. David Palmer, already touted as a major Heisman Trophy candidate, rear-ended a pickup truck and was subsequently arrested for driving under the influence of alcohol. He was granted youthful offender status by the court and thus would be available for all of the football season. Palmer refused to pay for any damages, and the other driver, who claimed to have had a potential professional baseball career ruined by the accident, eventually won a judgment for $168,000, after Palmer entered the ranks of the NFL.

Around the state, fans waited to see how Gene Stallings would respond to Palmer's misconduct. He told Palmer privately that he would suspend him for the first game, against Vanderbilt, but he did not tell the press or any other players. Stallings's silence drew cries of outrage. Would he have been a bit more eager to publicly suspend, or even kick off the team, a reserve lineman? Was Palmer's status as the SEC's most explosive player enough to keep him on the roster? The situation was a rare bit of controversy in Stallings's tranquil time at Alabama, and it would ultimately get worse.

Meanwhile, at Auburn, Pat Dye, who was entering his twelfth season, had no hope of escaping the dark cloud cast over his program. When the Tigers' first game of 1992 finally arrived, a visit to Ole Miss, they had to be wondering how things could get any worse. An inept running game, which totaled minus sixteen yards on the day, as well as a ninety-one-yard fumble return and a fifty-four-yard interception return, let Ole Miss break a 21–21 tie and romp to an easy 45–21 win.

After a 55–0 whitewashing of I-AA Samford, coached by Terry Bowden, the Tigers entertained LSU in Jordan-Hare. The matchup was a shadow of its former self, with both teams now in decline after having been atop the SEC for years. What the game lacked in importance, however, it more than made up for in excitement. Auburn looked safe with a 27–7 lead early in the fourth quarter, until Bayou Bengal quarterback Jamie Howard came off the bench to lead LSU to three touchdowns and a 28–27 lead, with 1:43 to play. White led Auburn back down the field, and Scott Etheridge, a junior who had never been in such a situation before, drilled a forty-three-yarder, his fifth kick of the game, with eight seconds to play, for a 30–28 Auburn win.

Southern Miss was next to visit, and the Tigers were wary of suffering a third consecutive upset at the hands of the Golden Eagles. Again, Etheridge was called on regularly, and he delivered with three field goals, as Auburn improved to 3–1 with a 16–8 win.

Vanderbilt followed on the schedule, and the Commodores seemed to be headed in the right direction under Gerry DiNardo. Auburn held the Vandy wishbone attack to sixty-seven yards on thirty-seven carries, while Bostic and Tony Richardson broke late touchdown runs to seal the victory, 31–7.

Another road trip to Mississippi pitted the Tigers against Mississippi State. White connected with Orlando Parker for a long score to bring Auburn ahead, 7–6, but State returned a punt sixty-three yards for a touchdown early in the fourth quarter and two late interceptions doomed the Tigers, 14–7.

Facing Florida in Gainesville is always a struggle for Auburn, but in 1992 their chances looked good. The Gators were only 2–2, having been embarrassed by both Tennessee and Mississippi State earlier in the season, each time on national television. Steve Spurrier had openly criticized his team for its performances and he finally saw some inspired play against Auburn. Florida coasted, 24–9, in a game that featured twenty-one penalties.

Southwestern Louisiana came into Auburn with a 2–5 record and very little respect from the Tigers. After building a 24–10 halftime lead, the Ragin' Cajuns had earned a bit of attention. In the second half, however, the Auburn defense woke up and shut out USL for a thrilling 25–24 victory decided in the last fourteen seconds. The Tigers were now 5–3 and in prime position for a bowl berth.

Arkansas made its first visit to Jordan-Hare the following week. Three Auburn turnovers, including an interception returned eighty-five yards for a touchdown, helped Arkansas escape with a 24–24 tie. On the interception, which came just before the half, many observers felt that Stan White had given up in pursuit of the Arkansas defender running for the touchdown. Dye confronted White before going into the dressing room, and the Jordan-

Hare stands echoed with chants of "We Want Nix!" a reference to redshirt freshman quarterback Patrick Nix, White's understudy.

The following Wednesday, ten days before the traditional meeting with Georgia, the NCAA's formal letter of inquiry finally arrived on the Auburn campus. The football program was charged with nine violations, one of which implicated Dye directly. The NCAA had determined that Dye had knowledge of the "extra benefits" given to Ramsey and did not report them to university officials. Dye made a bad situation worse by telling reporters from the *Huntsville Times* that he did indeed know of violations and that he might be held responsible. Auburn president William Muse was not pleased with his head coach, both for what he said to the reporters and for not previously admitting knowledge of the wrongdoing to Muse.

Traditionally, the NCAA has been lenient in applying sanctions to schools that had taken measures to remove those involved in rules violations. Thus, speculation across the state about the possibility of Dye's resigning became louder and louder. At a news conference held just after receipt of the letter, Dye was asked if he planned to step down. He said no and deferred all other questions to Muse, who refused to comment. Talk continued among Auburn and Alabama people alike that Dye, at best, had three games left in his coaching career.

Finally, after one of the most turbulent weeks in Auburn history, Ray Goff's Georgia Bulldogs came to town, ranked twelfth in the country. The battle with Georgia on this day would be one of the best in the history of the South's oldest rivalry. With nineteen seconds left in the game, Georgia was leading by a score of 14–10, and the stage was set for a remarkable ending.

Auburn had a second and goal on the Georgia one-yard line. White turned to hand off to Bostic, but his lead blocker, Tony Richardson, bumped the ball out of White's hands. Bostic caught the fumble in midair and fell for no gain. Nevertheless, he stretched the ball into the end zone. Some of his teammates, thinking he had scored, began to celebrate. Bostic, who knew better, was trying to get out from under the pile of Georgia defenders in time to run another play. A defender grabbed the ball from Bostic, claiming he had recovered a fumble. Another defender disputed an official's ruling about the "fumble." Meanwhile, the clock continued to run, and before the Tigers could line up for a last chance, the game was over. Goff and Dye embraced at midfield, where Goff told the beleaguered, confused Tiger coach that he hated to see a game end that way. Both coaches jogged off the field, and the stunned fans on hand wondered if Dye were leaving Jordan-Hare Stadium for the last time.

ALABAMA STARTED 1992 in Tuscaloosa against Vanderbilt with Palmer in uniform but serving his private one-game suspension on the sidelines. His absence was sorely felt by the anemic Tide offense. Thanks partly to three Michael Proctor field goals, however, Bama secured a 25–8 win. Amazingly, Palmer had not learned much from his suspension. Less than twenty-four hours later he was again charged with driving under the influence. This time Stallings suspended his sophomore star "indefinitely," which most people took to mean "as long as we keep playing teams we should beat anyway."

Southern Miss was one of these teams, but it did not leave Legion Field quietly the following Saturday. Capitalizing on two turnovers, the Golden Eagles led, 10–7, in the third quarter, before Proctor tied the game and Chris Anderson pulled the Tide ahead with a fourth-quarter touchdown run, salvaging a 17–10 victory.

The Tide visited Arkansas in Fayetteville the following week. A month prior to his presidential election victory, Gov. Bill Clinton, a Razorback alumnus, made a brief visit to the game but left early, with good reason, as the Tide coasted to a 38–11 win.

Stallings, on the advice of psychologists who suggested that Palmer needed football more than Alabama needed Palmer, reinstated the sophomore for the next game, against Louisiana Tech. The Deuce showed that he was still one of the most exciting players in the country, and the timing of his return was perfect for the Tide. With Bama clinging to a 6–0 lead early in the fourth quarter, Palmer exploded for a sixty-three-yard punt return to put the game away, 13–0.

The story was different the following week, as South Carolina received a rude welcome to the SEC in Tuscaloosa. Alabama rolled over the Gamecocks, 48–7, with five different players scoring touchdowns. A trip to New Orleans to play Tulane resulted in a 37–0 victory.

By now, Bama was 6–0 and ranked fourth as it faced the SEC East front-runner, the Tennessee Vols, headed by Johnny Majors, who had just recovered from preseason heart surgery. The Crimson Tide dealt Majors more misery, beating the Vols, 17–10, in a game that wasn't as close as the score indicates. The win marked the Tide's seventh consecutive beating of Tennessee, and its seventeenth straight win overall. It also marked Majors's final game against Alabama. At the end of the regular season, Majors, under fire from Tennessee boosters, announced his resignation, and Philip Fulmer replaced him immediately, coaching the Volunteers in the Hall of Fame Bowl. After sixteen years, and twelve losses to Alabama, one of the last of the SEC old guard was gone, and it is clear that the Volunteers' long dry spell against the Tide hastened the departure of Majors.

PAUL W. BRYANT MUSEUM

The 1992 Alabama defense, led by All-American end Eric Curry (80), ranks as one of the greatest in college football history.

Ole Miss next made its first visit back to Tuscaloosa since the infamous Homecoming weekend of 1988. This time, a 31–10 win virtually sealed Alabama's place in the first SEC championship game. After a week off, the Tide traveled to Baton Rouge, to face a reeling LSU team. The Tigers had lost six games in a row, and Alabama wasn't willing to stop the trend, cruising to a 31–11 win behind 301 rushing yards.

At 9–0 and second only to Miami in the national polls, Bama felt that all was right in the crimson world. On Thursday, November 12, however, just one week after Auburn heard from the NCAA about Ramsey's allegations, former Tide star Gene Jelks made headlines of his own.

In an interview with the *Atlanta Journal-Constitution*, Jelks claimed that Jerry Pullen, who had been his eighth-grade coach and had been given a full-time position on Ray Perkins's staff when Jelks entered college, rewarded the freshman with a $2,100 "signing bonus" for enrolling at Tuscaloosa. Jelks also claimed that Pullen helped him make payments on his car. Jelks supported these claims by recording phone calls with Pullen, during which the former assistant seemed to acknowledge having supported Jelks. Additionally, Jelks claimed that Rocky Felker, at the time an Alabama assistant, gave him cash in high school to buy Christmas presents and for each playoff game his Gadsden high school team won.

Jelks also alleged that he received cash through the mail in white envelopes, with no return address, while at the university. Finally, he claimed that two Gadsden businessman paid him for work he rarely completed and that they also paid for two shopping sprees at a Gadsden clothing store, a claim that the owner of the store denied. Jelks backed up his assertions with copies of checks written to him on the personal account of Harold Simmons, a Gadsden food distributor, two of which were written during the 1989 football season, months after any summer work would have been completed.

At first, Jelks's mother, Doris, and his sister, Audry, both refuted his charges. Audry Jelks, in fact, said that an Auburn booster had put Jelks up to making the claims. The allegations eventually prompted a defamation lawsuit from Pullen, who claimed the negative publicity was preventing him from getting work as a coach. Pullen insisted that Jelks, who was unemployed, was bitter and looking for easy money.

Jelks denied that he had followed Ramsey's lead or was "put up" to making his allegations by Auburn boosters. "I want kids to know that Tide Pride is not what they say it is," he said. "They buy and sell it. And when they're through with you, they kick you to the curb." Jelks said that he retained Stan Kreimer, an Atlanta attorney, after lawyers in Alabama refused to get involved.

In a brief statement, Bama athletic director Hootie Ingram said, "Our policy is to check everything out, document everything, and turn it over to the SEC and the NCAA." Stallings said that he had never met Jelks. Bill Curry and Ray Perkins flatly denied any suggestion that they had broken the rules. The NCAA sent an investigator to interview Jelks the day after the story broke.

Whatever his motives, Jelks had placed a potential detour on the Tide's pursuit of glory. As Ramsey had done a year earlier, Jelks waited until just before his former team went on a tough road trip to make his claims. For Bama, the trip was to Starkville to face Mississippi State, which was 7–2 and ranked sixteenth in the national polls. The Tide was focused from the outset, winning, 30–21, in a game that was closer than the score indicates. For the second time in four years, Alabama was 10–0, rolling into the Game.

IN THE first year of the SEC's divisional format, the preseason favorites had emerged as the top teams in their respective divisions. Thus, as had been predicted, Bama and Florida were set to meet in the inaugural SEC championship game, December 4, 1992, nine days after the Iron Bowl.

In retrospect, the actual Game between Alabama and Auburn in 1992 was not as compelling as all the subplots involved. The Crimson Tide was undefeated, had won twenty consecutive games, and was in prime position to play for the national championship. The Jelks controversy, however, would not go away. Auburn fans were understandably heartened by the possibility of scandal in Tuscaloosa and the fact that it had been started by an Alabama hero. Yet foremost on their minds was Pat Dye. From the day the Ramsey story broke, fourteen months earlier, Dye had insisted he was not going anywhere. Now the NCAA was clearly on the way to handing down sanctions on his program, and speculation held that Dye would either jump or get pushed.

For the first time since the days of Doug Barfield and Bear Bryant, the Game looked to be a mismatch. Alabama was installed as a fifteen-point favorite over the 5–4–1 Tigers, whose bowl chances had vanished with the loss to Georgia. Following the form of the previous two years, the matchup was one of two predominantly defensive-minded teams. The key to the Tide's success was its penchant for forcing turnovers, and its plus-sixteen margin in that category was the best in the country. The defense came into the Game looking to become only the second squad in NCAA history, after Oklahoma in 1986, to lead the nation in all four major defensive categories: points allowed (8.8 per game leading up to the Iron Bowl), total yards (187.4 per game), rushing yards (61), and passing yards (126.4).

Although the Tide boasted one of the premier defensive groups in the history of college football, Auburn's defense was also capable of great play. The Tigers were fourth in the nation in total yards allowed (257 per game). Its offense, however, had given up numerous interception and fumble returns for scores, so Auburn was only sixth in the SEC in points allowed (18.8).

After a six-year break, ABC once again would broadcast the Game but insisted on moving it to Thanksgiving Day, two days earlier than originally scheduled. The decision would help the Tide in its preparation for the SEC title game, giving the team an extra couple of days to heal and come down from the emotion of playing Auburn, regardless of the outcome. For supporters of both state schools the move to Thursday wrecked innumerable holiday plans and in many cases created the ultimate southern dilemma: football versus family. Even worse, ABC decided to send the revered Keith Jackson to Lincoln to cover the Nebraska-Oklahoma game and put Brent Musberger and Dick Vermeil in Birmingham to cover the Game.

On the eve on the Game, big news broke in Birmingham. Auburn hastily arranged a 10 P.M. news conference, covered live by television stations throughout the state. Saying "there is a time to fight, and there is a time when to fight would cause more destruction than the other," Pat Dye announced that he would resign as the Tigers' head coach after the Game. Despite Dye's constant claims to the contrary, the announcement was not unexpected, but the timing was interesting. Dye and Auburn president Muse had been discussing the situation since the Georgia game and had decided that the move was best for all involved. The resignation would be looked upon favorably by the NCAA as it continued its investigation of the Tiger program, and some hoped it would also give Auburn an emotional boost in its attempt once again to derail Alabama's national championship hopes. Others were not so sure, wondering how the Auburn team could not be adversely affected by such a massive and sudden distraction.

As the faithful began filing into Legion Field on a cloudless Thanksgiving Day, Dye surveyed his troops one last time during their warm-up drills. Soon after shaking hands with Stallings at midfield, the usually stone-faced Dye lost his composure and began sobbing. The end was finally at hand after twelve unforgettable years, and the realization was taking its toll on him. Stallings put his arm around Dye in a noble attempt to console the fallen warrior, and Dye soon regained his self-possession.

The emotion was cutting for everyone involved. How would Dye and Auburn football fare without one another? What lay ahead for the young men to whom Dye had sold the message of the Plains? Long-term questions, however, were of secondary importance to the Game at hand. Tiger fans simply hoped that Dye's farewell would be enough to inspire his outmanned team to allow the coach to collect his one hundredth win against his favorite opponent.

For several memorable minutes, Dye drifted in the middle of the playing field, head down in contemplation, seemingly studying the huge logo commemorating Alabama's one hundredth year of football. It was a poignant scene. Who could have imagined such a fate for the man who had saved the Orange and Blue? The Auburn players entered Legion Field at a slow, dignified walk, holding their helmets high above their heads in a solemn, moving tribute to the departing coach. Many wore black tape on their arms and wrists, and the word "Dye" was written on dozens of shoes and wristbands.

AUBURN WON the toss, and Dye chose to defer the choice to the second half. Alabama took the ball. Palmer returned the opening kick to the 19, but a penalty moved the ball back to the six-yard line. Mal Moore scripted a running offense using Lassic, Palmer, and Houston to move the ball out to a more comfortable field position. After making two first downs on the ground, Barker dropped back to pass, saw Auburn in a linebacker blitz, and ran the ball ten yards upfield, garnering another first down. Following an attempt at some razzle-dazzle with Palmer, the drive bogged down and the Tide surrendered the ball to Auburn.

Neither offense could move the ball, and the first half became a game of dueling punters. The Auburn defense was matching the top-ranked Tide defenders step for step. On the half's most memorable play, James Willis nearly decapitated Palmer on a short third-down pass for a two-yard loss.

Finally, the Tiger offense seemed to come to life as Bostic charged through the Alabama line for seventeen yards on two carries. A sack and an incompletion later, on third down and fourteen, White tried to go deep, but felt the pressure of the defensive rush and sailed the ball to Tommy Johnson, a Tide defender, who returned the interception from the Bama 12 to the 27. It was the Game's first turnover. That was as close as the Tigers came to the Tide's goal line in the first half.

Auburn's Stan White led the Tigers in a scoreless effort.

The two teams wore out the field between the 20-yard lines. Neither team could sustain a drive, although Bama at least tended to make positive yardage and Auburn seemed to be stuck in reverse. The half saw three more turnovers, including a change of possession on two successive plays near midfield and an interception of a Barker pass in the Auburn end zone. The Tigers' deepest penetration in the second quarter was to midfield; the Tide came as close as the Auburn 16.

At halftime, the Game was scoreless. The Auburn fans were fired up that their defense had stymied Bama's offense and kept the Game close. Coach Dye had to like what he saw in the first half. Despite being prohibitive underdogs, Auburn was still in position to pull off the upset. The deadlock, however, had to be unsettling to Stallings. One of the trademarks of the Tide's success all year had been their ability to get on the scoreboard early and often. In the previous ten games Bama had outscored its opponents 172–18 in the first half.

THE SECOND half began at the Auburn 25, and the scoreless contest didn't stay scoreless for long. The Tigers began to move the ball effectively and consistently. Bostic and McMilion bulled the ball downfield for the first movement of the chains. After gaining two yards on the ground, White dropped back and found Thomas Bailey at the Bama 43. Bostic added four more, and the Tigers were in scoring position. On second and six, White dropped back again and saw Orlando Parker on the left sideline. It was a simple play designed for a short gain. Parker, however, never had a chance for the ball. Bama cornerback Antonio Langham stepped in front of the intended receiver, tipped White's pass, and ran under the deflection near the Alabama 40. The talented defender caught the ball directly in front of Coach Dye and had nothing between him and the goal line.

Langham sprinted down the sideline with only White in pursuit. The quarterback, despite having the angle on Langham, was no threat to catch him. Langham crossed the goal line, and Proctor added the point after. With 11:41 left in the third quarter, the Alabama defense had delivered where the Tide offense could not, pulling the Tide ahead, 7–0.

When Auburn owned the ball again, Bostic carried the ball well and White scrambled for good yardage, and the Tigers were again moving well. With the ball now at the Tiger 32, the Tide defense anticipated Auburn's taking to the air and sacked White for a ten-yard loss. The Tigers eventually faced a fourth-and-short situation on their own 38 and had to punt the ball twice after a penalty on the first attempt.

PAUL W. BRYANT MUSEUM

The Tide's Antonio Langham (43) intercepted a third-quarter Stan White pass and returned it for a sixty-one-yard touchdown.

Bama started at its own 40-yard line. Keeping the ball on the ground and passing only on third down with more than three yards necessary for the first, the Tide swept down the field to the Auburn 21 and scoring position. Although bent, the Tiger defense refused to break and shut down the Bama runners. Forcing a third-and-twelve play, the Auburn defenders sacked Barker for a ten-yard loss. Proctor returned to the field for a forty-seven-yard attempt, which barely cleared the crossbar, and Bama led, 10–0, with 3:04 remaining in the third.

The Tigers went back on offense at their own 21. Three Bostic carries yielded nine yards, and once again Auburn punted, this time badly, giving Alabama the ball at the Auburn 45. Stallings kept the ball on the ground and in the hands of Chris Anderson, Martin Houston, and Sherman Williams. In six plays, the Tide was poised on the Auburn 16-yard line. On the seventh play of the drive, the sophomore Williams sliced through the line for a sixteen-yard touchdown, which essentially iced the Game. Proctor added the point after, and Alabama's apparently insurmountable lead was 17–0, with 12:08 to go.

Down by three scores, Auburn had to score on this drive. White was sacked on the first play and the Tigers never came close to making a first down for the rest of the possession and White was almost intercepted again. Once more, the Plainsmen punted.

Having had such good success moving the ball on the ground, Bama began to drive from its own 24 and kept its backs busy. Lassic and Williams made nothing but positive yardage and moved the ball upfield. On the sixth play of the drive, Williams was stopped on a third-and-short carry, but he also fumbled the ball. Auburn's Karekin Cunningham recovered it at the Bama 41. It was too little, too late.

White had to throw and Alabama's defenders knew it. The pass rush was relentless. The Tiger quarterback was sacked for an eleven-yard loss. Two short passes set up fourth and three, and Frank Sanders caught a White pass at Bama's 25. A late hit penalty against Auburn set up first and twenty-five at the Tide 40. Bama was flagged offsides, and White threw incomplete on the next play. On second down, White found Thomas Bailey at the Bama 30. The Tide's John Copeland then sacked White, and in the process the junior quarterback was injured, lost to a separated shoulder. With 4:56 to

play, redshirt freshman Patrick Nix replaced White, throwing incomplete to Bostic and Frank Sanders on two attempts. Scott Etheridge came in for a forty-eight-yard attempt, but the kick was short, and Bama still led, 17–0.

Alabama ran the clock out on six carries by Houston and one apiece by Lynch and Craig Harris. On the last play of the game, Houston converted a fourth and one to complete the 17–0 man-handling—Alabama's first shutout of Auburn since 1975.

Dye made his last walk to midfield, congratulating Stallings and accepting the best wishes of several Alabama players. After-

Pat Dye was a very somber man on the sideline during his last game as head coach of the Auburn Tigers.

AUBURN UNIVERSITY PHOTOGRAPHIC SERVICES

AUBURN UNIVERSITY PHOTOGRAPHIC SERVICES

Alabama's Martin Houston (35) found daylight throughout the afternoon, gaining enough yardage on critical plays to keep the ball in Crimson hands.

ward, at an emotionally charged post-Game news conference, Dye showed the pain of a man losing his identity. He said that he chose not to fight for his job because "sometimes when you fight the destruction outweighs the other things. I didn't want to tear down what's been built." Surrounded by his players, Dye brought his wife, Sue, and their three children to the podium. He put his arm around cornerback Fred Smith, but the words wouldn't come. Dye sobbed, then turned and silently left the room with his family. With that, the Pat Dye era ended at Auburn University.

FOR ALABAMA, the emotional high of beating Auburn a third consecutive time was lost in the preparations for the inaugural SEC championship game, just nine days later. Despite the success that Steve Spurrier had brought to Gainesville, the Gators were cast as double-digit underdogs to the Tide, who would enjoy the advantage of playing the game in Legion Field.

The sellout crowd had to endure near-freezing temperatures on an overcast December day. This was not what SEC executives had had in mind when selecting Birmingham as the host city, and a Gator upset would make the whole thing disastrous. A Bama win, under provisions of a new bowl coalition system, would set up a number-one-versus-number-two Sugar Bowl matchup, Miami versus Alabama.

Florida showed little fear of the storied Bama defense, taking the opening kickoff and marching seventy-seven yards for a touchdown. The Tide answered immediately and built a 14–7 halftime lead. Derrick Lassic, with his second score of the day, gave Bama a 21–7 edge, and it looked as if the game would get out of hand. Quarterback Shane Matthews, however, led the Gators back into contention with two touchdowns, and only a strong stand by the Tide defense at midfield kept the score tied, 21–21.

With less than four minutes to play, fans began to ponder the overtime provisions of the game. Florida owned the ball at its 21 when Matthews attempted to throw to his receiver on the sideline near the 30-yard line. Antonio Langham, however, stepped in front of the intended receiver and returned the interception for the deciding score. As the clock expired, Bama had a ticket to New Orleans as the SEC champion, finishing the league's first title game with a thrilling 28–21 win and a sterling 12–0 record.

ON DECEMBER 17, Auburn announced its new head coach in a surprise press conference. North Carolina State's Dick Sheridan was an early favorite, along with Air Force coach Fisher DeBerry and favorite son Pat Sullivan, now at TCU. Sheridan declined after stories appeared in the press asserting that he had accepted the Auburn job and was negotiating terms, saying that the reports were destroying Wolfpack recruiting. Sullivan, only a year into a five-year contract, also bowed out, as TCU demanded that his remaining four years be bought out at an exorbitant price. Auburn assistant Wayne Hall lobbied for the job, but the committee was clearly looking for new blood.

On December 14, a dark horse rode into Auburn for what he called "the best interview of my life." Terry Bowden, age thirty-seven and the head coach of 1-AA Samford University in Birmingham, had an impressive record, 65–35–1, from stints at NAIA Salem College and Samford. He had taken the Bulldogs from Division III status in 1987 to Division 1-AA's playoffs in 1991 and 1992. He also had one of the most famous pedigrees in all of college football. Yet Bowden had never been a head coach in Division 1-A, and his team had been decimated, 55–0, at Auburn just three months before.

Bowden walked into his interview and impressed the committee with his confidence and positive attitude. "I told my father, 'I don't care what they do, but they just got the best I could possibly give them,'" he said afterward. "I told them in that interview, 'If I can coach you're going to love me because I can do all the other things. I can talk. I've got the academic background that you like. I've got the name.'" Three days later, by a unanimous vote, he also had a new job.

In his introduction to the media, Bowden said, "I'm coming not to take Auburn football where it has never been before, but to take it there again, and keep it there longer than before." Like Dye before him, Bowden acknowledged the most important task ahead of him. "I probably won't be accepted here until I beat Alabama. I know that. That's the way it is, and that's the way it should be."

The Dye era at Auburn truly ended at the year's seniors' banquet in Birmingham. Normally a homage to departing players, it became an emotional tribute to Pat Dye. Bo Jackson made a surprise appearance and gave a moving speech. "I've always had a father, but I never had a dad," the superstar said. "In my four years at Auburn, this guy was the closest thing I had to a dad. He's taught me how to be a man. He taught me how to be a father. He taught me how to love others and respect others."

Clearly moved by this and other tributes, Dye stepped up to address, not the past, but the future. Terry Bowden was there, still a stranger to most of the people in the room. "You can help Terry in his efforts to put our program back to where it was," Dye said. "If you choose to complain, if you choose to gripe, if you choose to make excuses, if you choose to be disruptive, then you're going to hurt Auburn. You're here because you love Auburn. If you can't be productive, then for God's sake, don't hurt us."

Dye stopped and looked to the long road ahead for what was no longer his team. "You don't have to worry about Auburn," he said. "The Auburn I know knows how to fight back. Get on with it." He left the podium amid thunderous applause.

FEW FANS across the country gave Alabama much of a chance against the mighty Miami Hurricanes in the Sugar Bowl. Miami was the defending national champion, had won twenty-nine consecutive games, boasted Heisman Trophy–winning quarterback Gino Torretta, and had subdued Bama only three years earlier in the same bowl game. The Hurricanes, installed as the favorite by more than a touchdown, strutted into the Crescent City with their usual arrogance. Senior wide receiver Lamar Thomas, who already wore two national title rings, asserted that winning a third would be "icing on the cake."

The Canes lived the high life in the French Quarter, openly ridiculing Alabama players and instigating fights. In the meantime, the Tide prepared quietly for the showdown, building a game plan designed to negate the lifeblood of the Miami offensive attack—the short pass. When the ball was lined up, the Superdome, almost completely awash in red and white, played host to one of the great humblings in modern sports history.

Behind the running of Derrick Lassic and the confusing defensive formations Bill Oliver was throwing at Torretta, Bama built a surprising 13–6 halftime lead. As the nation began paying attention in earnest, thirty of the most glorious minutes of Alabama lore transpired on the field. Tommy Johnson returned a Torretta interception deep into Miami territory, and Lassic scored soon after. On the Canes' next play, senior George Teague stepped in front of another short Torretta offering and went all the way, putting the Tide up, 27–6, and destroying Miami's chance to come back.

The greatest play of the game, and of the season, was yet to come. Torretta, finally taking advantage of the aggressive Bama defense, found Thomas, a member of the Hurricane track team, open along the sideline. The brash senior was in the clear, heading for an apparent ninety-yard score and possibly a momentum change. Thomas, closing on the goal line, slowed down slightly, while Teague rocketed toward him from the rear. In a flash, Teague reached around Thomas, stripped the ball, gained control of it, and reversed his direction without losing his balance. He returned the "fumble" five yards.

Alabama was offsides on the play, thus Teague's effort didn't stand, but it hardly mattered. His heroics galvanized the Tide defense, and the Hurricanes, still backed up, could do nothing with the ball. The exhausted Teague took a well-deserved rest, while Lamar Thomas retreated to the Miami bench and disappeared behind a towel curiously resembling a white flag.

A long fourth-quarter Bama drive culminated in Lassic's fourth postseason touchdown of the year. When it was over, Alabama had brought the Miami machine to a grinding 34–13 halt, claiming its twenty-third consecutive win and twelfth national championship.

The Tide defense staked its claim as the greatest unit of all time. John Copeland, Eric Curry, George Teague, and Antonio Langham all would become first-round draft choices, and several other Bama defenders went on to apply their skills in the NFL. Stallings was selected as the consensus collegiate coach of the year, having gone, within the span of three seasons, from 0–3 to a national championship. The Crimson Tide was flowing high once again.

Meanwhile, on the other side of the state, Auburn observed Alabama's glory with grudging respect and prepared to emerge from the darkness with a new leader. The challenge was great, the odds were long, but the Tigers dug in, searching for the means to return to glory. It would be a question of heart and work—and attitude.

ROLL TIDE

One More Hurdle

MOMENTS AFTER the 1992 Game was history, Gene Stallings was already letting everyone know that there was more work to be done. Florida was waiting, and after that, hopefully, Miami. When Stallings said that the Tide hadn't won anything by merely beating Auburn, he was right.

This year was the only one I can remember when the outcome of the Game was a foregone conclusion. When the inevitable was at hand, it was simply time to move on and aim a little higher.

Some members of the 1992 Tide said that Florida, in retrospect, gave them the greatest challenge on the way to the title. Others say it was probably Mississippi State. One school that is conspicuously unmentioned is Auburn. Pat Dye's last team had been only 5–4–1 at the time and, in the Iron Bowl, had never threatened the Bama goal line.

Obviously, the main story on that Thanksgiving Day was Dye's farewell. We couldn't have known then that Auburn was curing itself, but there were more important things to think about.

It was a magical time, my first year out of school. I remember what it meant to make those first fall visits back to campus. They've been great ever since, but that first year was the best.

My greatest memory of 1992, however, is looking down on the massive Sugar Bowl celebration in the French Quarter. It was like a dream, too beautiful to believe. After thirteen tough, bitter years, Alabama was back on top, having gotten there the hard way—one step at a time.—S.B.

WAR EAGLE
Dyeing Hard

LET'S GET something straight from the start. A recurring question among the Orange and Blue for the last decade was, "Are you a Pat Dye fan?" There has always been a minority at Auburn who didn't like Dye, who wanted somebody to do dumb things such as fumblerooskies instead of playing four yards and a cloud of dust, to promote touchdown dances instead of down-and-outs, to generally just do things differently. So let's just get the question out of the way right now and leave no doubts remaining. Will Collier is a Pat Dye fan.

How quickly some forget. Dye brought us back. Through skill and guile and work and sometimes through sheer force of will, he turned the Tigers around, and he turned the Tide, too. People griped when Auburn didn't go to the Sugar Bowl during Dye's last three years. Folks, before he came to town, we'd only been there once, and we lost that one big time. I'm not taking a thing away from Terry Bowden when I say that just about everything that Auburn football is today, we owe to Pat Dye.

Dye's leaving was hard and cruel. He was betrayed, raked over the coals, and condemned to slow torture. The Inquisition would have been kinder. Newspapers were probably the greatest offenders. Speculation across the Plains was that the strings were being pulled in Tuscaloosa. They couldn't beat Dye, so they decided to destroy him and hoped to take Auburn down in the process. Except the plan backfired. Dye, naturally, put it best. "A lot of people there felt that when they got rid of Pat Dye, they'd kill Auburn. But what it did was set up Auburn to hire the best young coach in the country. And it tickles me to death."

I'd like to remind the Alabama fans who hooted when Dye left and who've mocked him ever since of just one thing. If Dye hadn't come to Auburn, if he had stayed at Wyoming for another couple of years, *he* would have been the heir to the Bear. He'd still be in Tuscaloosa now, and he sure as hell wouldn't have taken twelve years to get the program back in the championship business. Remember *that* when you're having to hire your next coach.

Dye was not perfect. He made his share of mistakes. He was as stubborn as a whole team of mules. His bad relations with the press were at least partially due to his own impatience with reporters. A former AU athletic department employee said, "Dye was very unapproachable but absolutely adored by everyone. . . . Don't be mistaken: he was 95 percent football coach, 5 percent everything else. Dye didn't come to Auburn because of his witty repartee with reporters. He came because he was tough, because he had guts and character, and because he *was* football."

Pat Dye was—*is* a winner. A winner and a class act to the very core. The real Auburn people have not forgotten his legacy.—W.C.

1993

DRAMA AND DESTINY
PART 2

EARLY 1993 WAS A TALE of two cities in the Heart of Dixie. In Tuscaloosa, it was the best of times. The celebrations of the Tide's long climb back to the top went on and on. Victory parades were held and banquets were carried out with relish. Gene Stallings was named SEC and national coach of the year. He basked in the warm glow of unending praise from the press and the Alabama faithful. All involved predicted a banner recruiting year for the Tide, and Auburn appeared to be down for the count. Alabama coaches privately and sometimes publicly ridiculed the hiring of Terry Bowden. Offensive line coach Jimmy Fuller nicknamed the diminutive Bowden "Buster Brown," and the laughter from the Alabama gentry echoed throughout the state. Thousands assumed as a matter of course that the Tide would repeat as national champion.

At Auburn, in many eyes, it was the worst of times. The final verdict of the NCAA still hung over Auburn's head. The nonstop celebrating of Alabama fans rang in their ears. Eric and Twillita Ramsey graduated in an ugly scene, complete with obscene gestures from Twillita at the booing graduates. Still shell-shocked from Pat Dye's sudden departure, the Tiger faithful tried to imagine how to pick up the pieces with a rookie from Division 1-AA. Some old-time Auburn fans figured Bowden as an inexpensive caretaker, to be replaced by Pat Sullivan after the Heisman hero had accumulated some head coaching experience at TCU. The conventional wisdom held that Bowden might make a good accounting of himself, but there was no way that he could be in position to challenge the conference heavyweights for years to come.

Terry Bowden had a job to do, and he proceeded to ignore the distractions and get down to it. He quickly assembled a staff, starting by convincing Wayne Hall to stay on as defensive coordinator. Many, including Hall himself, thought that he wasn't welcome after waging his own battle for the head coaching job. He had cleaned out his office and was putting out feelers for a new employer. Bowden sat down with him and came to an understanding, asking him to stay on and help rebuild the Tigers to national stature. Hall accepted, but Bowden still had to fight to keep him. Auburn president William Muse and athletic director Mike Lude wanted Hall out, figuring that since the Ramsey case originated in the defense, then Hall must have been involved, or at least tainted by the scandal. Bowden insisted, however, and Dye's defensive genius unpacked his bags and settled back into life at the Auburn athletic complex.

Retaining the popular Hall was the first major coup for Bowden, and it went over well with Auburn people. When Bowden said he was looking to build "a Bobby Bowden offense and a Pat Dye defense," it went over even better. Bowden went on to call down two of his assistants from Samford, Jimbo Fisher as quarterbacks coach and his brother-in-law, Jack Hines, for the secondary. He stole the architect of Jackie Sherrill's imposing offensive lines, Rick Trickett, from Mississippi State. Dye incumbents Joe Whitt, Rodney Garner, and James Daniel were invited to stay on, as well as Terry's older brother Tommy, who was demoted from offensive coordinator (Terry would claim those duties for himself) to receivers coach. Daniel, however, accepted an offer to join the staff of the NFL's New York Giants under Dan Reeves, which sent Bowden looking for a former Auburn standout to take his place, former All-SEC linebacker Kurt Crain, who was the linebackers coach for Pat Sullivan at TCU.

When Bowden called with the job offer, Crain told him, "I've always wanted to come back to Auburn. And I want to come back and help you beat Alabama. We never lost to 'em when I was there, and I hate them bastards." The new coach seized the moment and replied, "Now wait just a minute. You know that I used to coach at Samford. If you're going to work for me, you're not going to use language like that. You say, 'I hate *those* bastards.'" The exchange became an instant alumni club anecdote.

Bowden introduced himself to the Auburn team in a meeting just before the winter quarter. Bowden knew that he could walk in and tell the young men that he was going to clean house, rebuilding from the ground up. He had a lot of latitude because this team hadn't been over .500 in two seasons and hadn't been really impressive since mid-1990. It was a tried-and-true coaching style, but Bowden didn't take that course. He told the returning players that they were close, that they had missed out on a great season by just a few plays, and that together they could correct the problems and move forward.

At the same time, Bowden wasn't going to make any excuses, and he left no questions about who was in charge. The first words Bowden said to the team established the discipline standards. This is my program, he said, and things are going to be done my way. In every team I've ever taken over, there have been one or two stars who thought they were more important to the program than me. Every time, I've had to kick them off the team. If you think you're more valuable to Auburn than Terry Bowden, speak up now and get out. To the defense, he said, you were third in the nation last year. You're doing your job. Keep it up, and we'll be fine. Offense, he said, you're not holding up your part of the deal. We're going to fix that.

WITH THE ground rules established and his new staff in place, Bowden joined the 1993 recruiting wars. At the outset, it was clear that Alabama was going to have a monster year. The success of 1992 opened up new areas of recruiting for the Tide, affording Stallings the potential for a national freshman class. The old sin of pride, however, began to work its wiles on Alabama again, just as it had in the early 1980s and at Auburn in the early 1990s. Tide coaches and players began to look on top recruits as their rightful bounty, not as young men who had to be convinced to come to school at Alabama. The weekend before national signing day, every top prospect in the region was invited to Tuscaloosa to witness the banquets, celebrations, and the grand parade commemorating the 1992 season. It was intended as the final overwhelming push toward a dominant recruiting class, a display of prestige that would override the objections of impressionable eighteen-year-olds. Things didn't necessarily work out that way, however.

To be sure, Alabama claimed a good number of blue-chip recruits in 1993, including quarterback Freddie Kitchens, lineman Chris Jordan, and linebackers Fernando Davis and Tyrell Buckner. Yet the display of conspicuous self-congratulation backfired on two of the state's most highly sought-after prospects. Lineman Willie Anderson and tight end Jessie McCovery, both from the traditional Alabama stronghold of Mobile, broke ranks and signed with Auburn. Both players were considered among the top two or three at their respective positions in the nation. Terry Bowden had been saying throughout the recruiting year that Auburn would have a few surprises on signing day, and the Mobile twosome, who had been considered by the "experts" as shoo-ins for Alabama, certainly came as a welcome bonus to Tiger partisans.

The surprise was not so pleasant in the environs of Bryant Hall. Alabama assistant Mike Dubose, who had been charged with securing Anderson and McCovery for the Tide, called both shortly after they committed to Auburn. Dubose was not happy, and according to the two players and their families, he accused the young men of taking illegal payments from Auburn. Bowden reacted strongly to the allegations. He called Stallings after the charges hit the newspapers, and sources on both athletic staffs indicated that it was not a courtesy call. Bowden was staking out his territory and meant to let Stallings know that he wasn't going to put up with unfounded allegations from the Bama camp. Dubose eventually apologized to the two players (but not to Bowden or Auburn).

BOWDEN, LIKE Pat Dye before him, set out to establish the personality for his team in his first spring practice sessions. Like Dye, Bowden did not seek to emulate his predecessor but to set a new tone for Auburn football. No one would compare Bowden's 1993 practices to Dye's 1981 boot camp in physical terms. The 1993 spring was not meant to weed out the weak but to begin teaching a new philosophy, particularly on offense. Bowden brought in his modified version of his father Bobby's Power I-Shotgun schemes and began drilling it into the returning players. Stan White, who had been the presumptive starting quarterback for three seasons, now found himself being strongly pressured by redshirt sophomore Patrick Nix.

Senior wide receiver Orlando Parker tried to test Bowden's disciplinary resolve and wound up looking for a new school. Parker had asked to be excused from spring practice to work full time with the Auburn track team. Bowden refused, insisting that Parker needed to start learning the new offense as soon as possible. When Parker didn't show up for the first day of spring training, he was kicked off the squad and out of the athletic dorm. Auburn had lost its deep-threat wide receiver, and Bowden had laid down the law of his new domain. By the time spring practice ended, Bowden said of his team, "We're not ready to play Ole Miss. All we're ready for is the two-a-days in August."

As the summer passed, the NCAA seemed no closer to resolving the drawn-out process of investigation, inquiry, and sanctions. Bowden took advantage of the period of indecision to cut a contract with ESPN for the season-opening Ole Miss game, but he had to move the game up to Thursday night, an anathema for most Auburn fans. It was the kind of nontraditional move that Dye never would have accepted, but Bowden needed something positive for his players and recruits, and a supposedly guaranteed national television slot for the season's opening game was as good as he could get.

DESPITE A general silence on the matter, Alabama was still dogged by the Gene Jelks controversy during 1993. In January, Hootie Ingram had stated to the media that the NCAA had "no case" against Alabama. In February, however, the university reluctantly released a letter from the infractions committee dated December 3, 1992, in which enforcement director Mark Jones said that NCAA investigators would visit the Alabama campus to help determine whether a preliminary letter of inquiry, similar to an indictment, would be necessary. The NCAA extended the deadline to March for delivery of such a letter or ending the case, an occurrence that caused unease among Bama boosters.

In June, after being interviewed by NCAA investigators, Jelks's sister, Audry, recanted her earlier denials of the story. "I told them Gene wasn't lying," she said in a press interview. "I provided them with the information they asked for. . . . A lot of influential people were kind of afraid of him coming out with his story, so they tried to ensure he wouldn't."

A lawsuit that would drag into 1995 added to the drama. Jerry Pullen, who had lost his job at Clemson, sued Jelks for slander. At first, this was seen as a foolish move on the part of Pullen and his supporters. Jelks's attorney, Stan Kreimer, was delighted at the idea of getting the principals on the stand and under oath. "I have subpoena power and the NCAA doesn't," he said. "That should open a few more doors to me than have been opened to the NCAA." Jelks said, "Jerry messed up. I think he will be in for a rude awakening. I like Jerry. I have nothing against him personally. But he has caused himself a major problem." An NCAA investigator said of the suit, "Certainly if testimony is given and NCAA rules are indicated to have been broken, we'd take that information." Under oath, Jelks's mother recanted her earlier denials of her son's accusations and substantially confirmed his charges. In June 1995 an Atlanta judge ruled that Jelks had told the truth regarding Pullen and dismissed the suit.

MOST OF the "experts" discounted Auburn and Bowden during the 1993 preseason hype. Sportswriter Paul Finebaum of the *Birmingham Post-Herald* weighed in with a blisteringly negative prediction, figuring the Tigers to do no better than 5–6 in 1993. *Sports Illustrated* ranked Auburn as the forty-sixth best team in the nation and predicted a 4–7 finish. Virtually all of the preseason magazines picked the Tigers to finish at or near the bottom of the SEC West. Alabama, however, was a unanimous choice to win the West, a split decision to win the conference (with Florida as the heir-presumptive), and was picked by many to repeat as national champion.

As Auburn's August practice sessions opened, there was still no word from the NCAA. A few days later into the practices, the team was dealt what looked like a crushing setback. Senior cornerback Fred Smith, the Tigers' 1992 defensive player of the year, went down with a season-ending knee injury. Then, less than two weeks before the start of the season, after nearly two years of investigation, the NCAA hammer fell on Auburn.

It was a heavy blow. The Tigers were banned from television for one year and from postseason play for two. Fortunately, since the violations were not related to recruiting, the team received only token scholarship restrictions, losing two for the 1994 season. With that exception, the penalty was comparable to Florida's 1984 sanctions—which stemmed from more than a hundred major violations, as opposed to Auburn's six. For recruiting purposes, Auburn elected to take the television ban in 1993, but it was too late to reschedule the Ole Miss game. It would still be played on Thursday, September 2, but the ESPN telecast was scrubbed with an agreement that Auburn would play a Thursday game in 1994 for the network.

While the final NCAA report concluded that assistants Larry Blakeney and Frank Young and booster Corky Frost had knowingly violated the rules, the verdict was more circumspect regarding Pat Dye. The investigators noted that Dye, who had faced a life-threatening illness during the period in question, possibly was unaware of much of the wrongdoing. The committee found no proof to Ramsey's accusation that Dye had arranged the loan from a Montgomery bank but determined that the loan itself, approved by an Auburn alumnus, was a violation. Although the former head coach was not found guilty of any overt violations in the report, it was Dye's job as athletic director to stay on top of compliance, and his omissions were cited by the NCAA as a basis for the deadly "lack of institutional control" infraction. The NCAA noted that Auburn had received "no competitive advantage" from any of the violations.

Former defensive assistant Steve Dennis was cleared by the committee, noting that the tape used by Ramsey to implicate Dennis had been rere-corded and spliced many times.

For many observers, the verdict looked like a heavy nail in Auburn's 1993 coffin. For the Auburn players, coaches, and fans, the sentence was something of a relief. Few had expected to be dealt with so harshly, but all were glad to see the matter settled. For Auburn, the long trial was finally over.

ALABAMA'S NATIONAL title defense began with a sleeper in Birmingham over lowly Tulane, and the Tide cruised to a 31–17 victory. In Nashville the next week against old punching bag Vanderbilt, Alabama's superior talent and depth won out for a 17–6 victory and the team's twenty-fifth consecutive victory. Then came one of Bama's best efforts of 1993, a 43–3 shellacking of Arkansas in Birmingham. After a 56–3 dismantling of Louisiana Tech, Alabama paid a visit to Columbia, South Carolina, for a rematch with the Gamecocks. It was a 17–6 victory that wasn't as close as the score.

Finally, in September, the NCAA enforcement committee sent a pre-liminary letter to Alabama president Roger Sayers, stating that the NCAA believed there was sufficient evidence to conduct a formal investigation. This was very bad news for Alabama, as the "preliminary letter" leads to sanctions more than 75 percent of the time.

A total of four ranked teams met in Alabama on October 16, 1993, two of them colliding in Legion Field: Alabama and Tennessee. The Vols, desperate to break seven years of frustration, brought in a great team, led by vaunted quarterback Heath Shuler, who turned a 9–7 halftime deficit into a 17–9 lead, despite fumbling twice inside the Alabama five-yard line. Late in the fourth quarter, Tennessee seemed ready to break two streaks, their own losing streak to the Tide and Alabama's twenty-eight-game winning streak against everybody. With no time-outs remaining, the Tide offense, led by Jay Barker, came to life with 1:44 left to play. Barker directed a text-book eighty-three-yard drive for a touchdown to pull within two points. David Palmer lined up at quarterback for the two-point conversion. Every-body in the stands and everybody watching on television knew what was coming: quarterback draw to the right. Presumably, the Vol defense knew it too, but they still couldn't stop Palmer, who ducked into the corner of the end zone to seal a 17–17 tie. The winning streak was over, but Tennessee would not end Alabama's unbeaten streak.

Ole Miss, with nation-leading defensive numbers but a sub-par record, looked to upset the Tide the following week in Oxford. It was a tough, gritty game from start to finish, but Alabama prevailed, 19–14. A 40–0 blowout of Southern Miss in Tuscaloosa was another sleeper, but starting quarterback Barker went out with an ankle injury.

Of course, nobody expected the loss of Barker to be a problem in the Tide's next game, against LSU, which had been blown out at home by Auburn and Florida and now had to face Alabama in Tuscaloosa. Alabama went in a twenty-five-point favorite, ranked fifth. It looked like a sure thing, number thirty-two on the unbeaten Bama hit parade, but it didn't work out that way.

Neither team scored in the first half. In the third quarter, LSU scored two touchdowns. Having failed to move the ball with two quarterbacks, Stallings installed Palmer at quarterback for the next series, and the old Deuce magic seemed to revitalize the Tide offense. Then Palmer became the third Bama quarterback to throw the ball away, ending a Tide drive inside the Tiger 20-yard line with an interception that led to an LSU field goal. Trailing 17–7 and desperate now, Palmer and the offense managed a nice drive for a touchdown, closing the gap to 17–13. LSU, presumably having watched the Tennessee films, stopped Palmer short of a two-point conversion and picked up the ensuing onside kick to seal the biggest upset of the 1993 season.

The Alabama players and coaches watched the LSU celebration in stunned shock. This was the first Tide loss in more than two years, since a 35–0 shellacking at Florida in 1991. Now there would be no defense of the national championship.

The recovery was difficult for Alabama, but the return of Jay Barker, still undefeated as a starter, helped the Tide to pull out a messy 36–25 win over Mississippi State at home. It wasn't pretty, but it was what Alabama needed, a win in the conference. With the West Division of the SEC clinched for the second straight year, the Tide prepared to make the trip to Auburn for the second time in its history. Before the season, it had looked like a walk in the park for the mighty Tide, a chance to get even for 1989 and put some fear into Buster Brown. In 1993, however, you couldn't take anything for granted in college football. In 1993, Auburn was having a year for the ages.

WITH THE NCAA probe finally settled, the Auburn players and coaches turned their full attention to Ole Miss, which returned twenty starters from the squad that had embarrassed the Tigers, 45–21, the previous year. Remembering the blitz that had disrupted Auburn's passing game in 1992, and figuring the Rebel coaching staff would expect a wide-open attack from the son of Six-Gun Bobby, Terry Bowden decided to turn the tables and go at Ole Miss with a straight-up running attack, old-style Auburn power football. On a hot, muggy Thursday night, the reversed strategy paid off. The

Tigers walked to the dressing room with a 16–12 SEC victory. The win was like a tonic for the coaches and fans, and it gave the team confidence that they could win again. Just as the shocking loss at Oxford had shattered Auburn's early hopes in 1992, the gritty win at home against the Rebels would set the tone for Auburn in 1993.

After a deja-vu game with Samford (Terry Bowden remarked during warm-ups that he knew the Samford players far better than his own team at that point), which was mercifully handled 35–7, the Tigers flew southwest to Baton Rouge. Auburn had not won in Tiger Stadium since 1942, mainly because of the scarcity of Auburn-LSU matchups prior to divisional play in the SEC. LSU had upset Mississippi State the week before and was a slight favorite. In the first quarter, the LSU offense roared downfield for a quick score, but the eastern Tigers came to life afterward, tacking on twenty-one unanswered points in the first half. Stan White was brilliant, throwing for 282 yards and becoming Auburn's all-time leading passer that night, eclipsing his mentor, Pat Sullivan. When it was over, Auburn carried home a huge 34–10 win, the team gaining confidence with each passing day.

Auburn came out flat against Southern Miss the next week, finishing the game with a comfortable 35–21 margin, but a trip to Nashville was very nearly a disaster. Gerry DiNardo had brought Vanderbilt up to a level of respectability, at least in home games, and the Commodores gave Auburn all they wanted in a low-scoring slugfest. The 14–10 win on the road, however, was a sweet victory for the defense and another confidence-builder.

It was surely a bonus for Bowden that his toughest 1993 games were played in the friendly environs of Jordan-Hare Stadium, and the first-year coach was appreciative of the boost his team got from the noisy Auburn stands. The Mississippi State game at home didn't start well for the Tigers, but halfway through the second quarter, the offense roared to life. It ended as a 31–17 Tiger manhandling of a very physical football team.

The story of this one didn't end on the field. MSU head coach Jackie Sherrill contacted the SEC front office after the game, accusing Auburn of filling its footballs with helium to allow the nation-leading punts of Terry Daniel to fly higher and farther. The next week the SEC confiscated the ball from Daniel's first punt, had it analyzed in Birmingham, and found it to be correctly inflated with air.

Auburn had outdone the two previous years' records in only six games, and the Tigers were riding high. But the real tests were yet to come. The next opponent, the Florida Gators, were 6–0, ranked number four in the nation, and looking for the school's first national title. Florida was loaded with talent and favored by a touchdown.

In the first quarter, it seemed the experts were right. Florida moved the ball virtually at will, scoring a touchdown and a field goal, and was about to go ahead, 17–0. Florida's Danny Wuerffel lofted a soft pass into the end zone, but Auburn's Calvin Jackson, one of the "Dillard Five" from Fort Lauderdale and a sophomore cornerback, picked it off at the four-yard line and sped down the sideline for an electrifying ninety-six-yard touchdown return. The Auburn offense scored on its next possession, putting the Tigers up 14–10. Florida responded, however, scoring seventeen unanswered points to take a 27–14 halftime lead.

In the second half, a perfect drive led to a twenty-three-yard White-to-Richardson touchdown, and the lead was cut to 27–21. The defense stuffed the Gators again, and Auburn headed down the field with a chance to take the lead. The drive made it all the way to the Florida four before the Gator defense stiffened. On fourth down, James Bostic took a pitchout in the backfield and was immediately grabbed by linebacker Dexter Daniels, a good seven yards short of glory, and two more Gators closed in from the outside. Bostic blasted forward, leaving Daniels without even a handful of jersey, and roared through the line of scrimmage and into the end zone for a momentous touchdown. Auburn had come back from thirteen down to lead by a point, 28–27.

On Florida's next series, Auburn's Chris Shelling, following the lead of his Dillard teammate Jackson, picked off an interception and ran sixty yards to the Gator nine-yard line. Bowden seized the initiative and caught the Florida defense napping with a reverse on the next play from scrimmage. Frank Sanders, another former Dillard Tiger, carried the reverse untouched into the end zone to put Auburn ahead by eight, 35–27.

Florida still had some fight left, however. An eight-play, eighty-one-yard lightning drive, led to a Wuerffel-to-Jack Jackson touchdown and the Gators' first score of the second half. Trailing 35–33, Spurrier called for the two-point conversion, and the game was tied at 35 with 5:54 left to play.

It looked like Auburn was going three snaps and out before White found Frank Sanders on a crossing route on a crucial third down. On the next set of downs, White and the Tiger offense couldn't move. White was forced to pass in desperation on fourth and long, going for Sanders on the far sideline. The ball sailed far over Sanders's head untouched, but Florida free safety Lawrence Wright came blasting in from the outside and leveled Sanders out of bounds. It was an instant fifteen-yard penalty. The Tiger drive stayed alive, and Auburn started to move. On fourth down, Scott Etheridge ran out for the biggest field goal attempt of his life. On the sidelines, Bowden didn't even look at the ball, but watched the Auburn students behind the goalposts. When they went into a wild, screaming frenzy, he knew the forty-one-yard attempt had sailed through. Auburn, ranked nineteenth in the nation, written off by virtually every "expert" in the land, had just gone ahead of mighty fourth-ranked Florida, 38–35, with 1:21 left. Florida made it back only to its own 34 before time ran out.

Bowden's players drenched him with ice water (Gatorade wasn't really appropriate) and carried him to midfield, yelling and waving his fist in the air. The Auburn fans in Jordan-Hare stayed in the stands, celebrating long after the final buzzer had sounded. In the end, Bowden led the students in a roaring "War Eagle" before the crowd would leave the stadium. Larry Guest of the *Orlando Sentinel* said that the celebration "suggested a national title [had been won], or maybe a cure for Yankees had been discovered." On Monday, the Associated Press voters vaulted the Tigers up to number nine, Auburn's first appearance in the Top Ten since 1990.

After a week off, Auburn flew to Fayetteville, Arkansas, for a matchup with the Razorbacks and their new head coach, Danny Ford, late of Clemson and Alabama. Despite near-zero temperatures and blowing snow flurries, Auburn broke a 7–7 halftime tie and marched smartly to a 31–21 win. New Mexico State was dispatched, 55–7, for Homecoming, and Auburn was an amazing 9–0, bound for Athens.

Despite the two teams' respective records (Georgia was 4–5 at the time), the bookies made the 'Dawgs a one-point favorite. Georgia's sensational quarterback Eric Zeier had a huge day with 426 yards passing, but Auburn maintained a comfortable fourteen-point lead for most of the game, moving the ball virtually at will. When it was over, Auburn had won, 42–28, and silenced much of the national carping about "playing above their heads."

FOR THE first time in memory, there was no open date before the Auburn-Alabama Game. Rather than scheduling a home game during the Thanksgiving break, Auburn officials had elected to move the Game up to the week after Georgia, and their Alabama counterparts readily agreed. Even so, the buildup for this Game was no less intense. NCAA regulations allowed a team visiting an opponent on probation to beam a closed-circuit broadcast of the game to one location at their campus. Florida had arranged for a large-screen television to be set up in Florida Field for the Auburn game, and some eighty-five hundred fans had bought tickets to sit in the rain and watch the Gators fall. Alabama officials, figuring that they could get the six thousand needed to break even, arranged for two Jumbotron screens to be erected in Bryant-Denny Stadium for the Game. The response was more than anyone anticipated. The full allotment of forty-five thousand tickets, priced at twelve dollars apiece, sold out in one day. For the first time in history, one football game had sold out two stadiums. Within days, scalpers were selling tickets for the television broadcast for forty dollars or more, while actual seats at Jordan-Hare were going for upwards of five hundred dollars apiece.

Auburn defensive lineman Randy Hart, rarely described as shy or quiet, fired the first volley in the pre-Game war of words. "I'm foaming at the mouth for Bama," he said. "To tell you the truth, we're going to blow Alabama out. We're not going to let them move the ball. I guarantee it."

Alabama players, naturally, had a few things to say about that. Willie Gaston said he had a "personal vendetta" against Auburn, adding, "To me, they're not the best in the SEC. Until they play us and beat us, they can never say that they're the best in the SEC."

Auburn went in as a point-and-a-half favorite. Most of the state sportswriters went with Auburn. The Tigers would enter the Game without cornerback Otis Mounds, who had suffered a serious knee injury against Georgia. Alabama's Palmer would labor under a bruised shoulder and was not expected to play at quarterback, and running back Sherman Williams had a similar shoulder injury. Conventional wisdom held that Auburn would need to contain Palmer and keep the pressure on Barker to win. Conversely, Alabama figured to go after Stan White and hope to slow down the power running of Auburn's Bostic, Davis, Richardson, and McMilion. While the Tide had the nation's best cornerback in Antonio Langham, questions remained about Alabama's defensive effectiveness against the run. Ole Miss, Tennessee, and LSU had all run well against the vaunted Tide defense, and the defensive line wanted badly to regain its stingy reputation against its greatest rivals.

THE UNTELEVISED Game was carried on Armed Forces Radio to American troops in 130 countries. A telephone services company had carried Auburn Network broadcasts for listeners around the nation, setting new sales records during the season, but this time, the desire to hear the Game was too much. The switchboards were flooded with more than fifty thousand calls, blowing out circuits and shutting down the company's computers. Many faraway fans responded by calling their families in the state, having the telephone receiver placed in front of a radio, and paying long-distance charges for the duration, just to keep up with the Game.

The day was clear, cool, and beautiful for the one o'clock kickoff. The Auburn seniors came onto the field in a stately walk, holding their helmets high above their heads, following the tradition established by their 1992

Terry Bowden, Auburn's new head coach, leads his team onto the field with his sights on an unprecedented 11–0 season.

predecessors. The Alabama players and the Auburn underclassmen then followed at the customary full run, Auburn won the toss and deferred to the second half, and the Game was on.

The two defenses proved that they were ready for the Game by limiting the first three possessions to three plays and a punt. Neither quarterback was having a particularly good afternoon, so the Game became a rushing contest. The Tigers had the advantage in field position and began their second drive of the day from their own 38.

Keeping the ball on the ground, Auburn moved to midfield, where the Tigers faced third and nine. White connected with Tony Richardson in the flat, and he advanced the ball to the Alabama 36, a fifteen-yard gain. The Tigers lost yardage on the next play, and a second-down completion set up third and nine. White had to throw the ball away on third down, and Bowden sent in his field goal unit for a fifty-two-yard attempt with the wind. The ball was well short, but the Tide drew a flag for fifteen yards, giving Auburn a break and a new set of downs. Starting from the Alabama 20, Bostic lost yardage. White took the next snap in the shotgun and ran up the middle to the 11-yard line, just short of the first down. On third down, the Auburn line pushed the defenders back, and White carried the ball to the seven-yard line and a first down. A run up the middle went to the six, followed by an incompletion. On third and goal, White found Frank Sanders in triple coverage but still threw the ball to him. Sanders was ruled out of bounds, and the pass was incomplete. Scott

Etheridge came out with the field goal unit again and this time nailed the short attempt to give the Tigers a 3–0 lead with just under two minutes left in the first quarter.

The two teams exchanged punts on successive possessions, and Alabama's offense returned to the field in the second quarter with the ball at its 19-yard line. Two plays later, in a second-and-two situation, Barker pitched the ball to Sherman Williams on a sweep to the left. Williams, in turn, gave the ball to Kevin Lee on an end-around, and Lee had a clear field for sixty-three yards and an Alabama touchdown. Instantly, the Tide seized the lead and the momentum in the Game. The point after by Proctor was perfect, and Alabama led, 7–3, with ten minutes left in the half.

Auburn tried to answer the score, even after making a first down at its own 39, but the drive went no farther than the 45. Palmer called for a fair catch on the following punt, but he never touched the ball. Taking an Auburn bounce, it was called dead at the Alabama three-yard line.

Taking the snap on his own goal line, Barker threw long for Lee, but the pass went incomplete. Incredibly, Bama offensive coordinator Mal Moore called another pass from the end zone. Barker tried to call an audible from the line, but nobody heard him over the crowd. The Alabama quar-

Stopping Alabama's versatile David Palmer (2) was the top priority of the Auburn defense on the afternoon.

terback dropped back, then ran right, away from a strong rush. Auburn's Andre Miller grabbed Barker's ankle, and Jason Miska roared over the line to complete the tackle, dropping Barker for an Auburn safety. The play resulted in the unusual score of 7–5, Alabama, and the Tide was forced to kick to the Tigers from their own 20-yard line.

Again the two teams went through three possessions and exchanged punts, Bama getting the edge on field position and taking the ball on its own 47. Quick to capitalize on having the ball at midfield, Barker hit Lee for a thirty-four-yard gain to the Auburn 19. From the I formation, Chris Anderson took an outside toss sweep, turned inside, and darted into the end zone. Another two-play drive, and Alabama led 14–5 with barely a minute left in the half.

Auburn made a last run at the end zone with time running out. Bostic darted outside for a nice gain to the 35 and a first down in Auburn's longest running play thus far in the Game. White found Sanders for a fourteen-yard gain. The Tide was slapped with a personal-foul call on the other side of the field, giving the Tigers a first down on the Alabama 35 with less than thirty seconds remaining in the half, but they failed to capitalize on the opportunity and time expired.

Assessing the first half, the biggest surprises for Auburn had been the poor performance of the Tiger running backs and the strong scrambling of Stan White. Auburn had held the ball for nearly twenty minutes in the first half. If they could duplicate that in the third and fourth quarters, they had a strong chance of winning. The Alabama defense had responded to the Auburn ground attack and held it in check. Conversely, the Alabama offense had responded with three big plays, but otherwise was unimpressive. The Alabama players knew that they would need more than three plays to win.

THE TIGERS started the second half inauspiciously, going three downs and out on incompletions. Alabama was able to gain some yardage and move the ball into Auburn territory, but a holding penalty and two sacks drove the Tide back to its own 27. Alabama's Bryne Diehl executed a forty-two-yard punt, but Auburn's Thomas Bailey returned the ball twenty-five yards to the Alabama 45, where he was dragged down by Diehl, saving a touchdown.

This time the Tigers ran a two-play drive, the difference being the drive ended, not with a touchdown or a field goal, but with an interception that was returned to the Alabama 28. Neither team was allowed to exult in either big play. Following the turnover, an official invoked what had become

known as the "Miami rule," interpreting Gaston's celebration of his interception as taunting. The flag moved Bama back to the 12, and Barker once
again had to deal with poor field position. The Tide held the ball for only
three plays and gave it back to Auburn, outkicking the Tigers' coverage but
giving them the ball at their own 27.

The Auburn offense didn't exactly move at will. An incompletion
and a Bostic carry for four yards gave White third and long. The senior
quarterback couldn't find an open receiver and had to tuck the ball in and
run with it. He was hit at the 30, broke another tackle at the 35, and carried the ball to the 42 and an Auburn first down. Suddenly, the offense
began to execute flawlessly. White found his tight end, Derrick Dorn, on
the sideline for a gain to the Auburn 46. Reid McMilion carried through
the line, falling into Alabama territory for a first down at the Tide 46.
White rolled out to his right and rifled a pass to Frank Sanders, who beat
Langham's coverage for the reception and another first down at the
Alabama 30. Bostic tried to slip outside, but could only make two yards
before being pulled down. As quickly as things had started to go smoothly
for the Tigers, they began to misfire. White rushed a throw and sailed the
ball out of bounds. On third down, White went into the shotgun, and
Alabama sent the kitchen sink into the backfield. White took a hit that
knocked the quarterback off-balance. As he fell, he wrenched his knee. He
threw his last pass in desperation, but the officials ruled him down as the
ball fell incomplete.

A sudden hush fell over the Auburn crowd when White did not get up.
He had severely sprained his right knee, and the four-year starter was carried
from the field. To Auburn, it looked like a death-blow. Facing fourth and
fifteen after the team's only sustained drive of the Game, the Tigers had lost
their quarterback.

On the sidelines, White's understudy, sophomore Patrick Nix raced
from Bowden's side to the bench for his helmet and onto the field. Bowden
faced a tough decision. He had lost his senior quarterback. His team was
looking at fourth and long on the Alabama 29. The Tide defense was fired
up. A punt would do him no good. With those options to choose from, the
rookie coach signaled in his play and rolled all the dice.

In the huddle, Nix called a go-route for Sanders on the short side of
the field. He looked at his receiver and said, "Frank, go catch it." From the
bench, Stan White craned his neck to see what would happen. In the press
box, receivers coach Tommy Bowden couldn't believe his good fortune.
Bama's Langham, who had shadowed Sanders all day, had lined up on the
wide side of the field.

Nix took the snap in the shotgun. Alabama blitzed, but the Tigers' protection kept the pressure off their quarterback. The sophomore lofted a high, soft pass toward the left corner of the goal line. Sanders was in perfect position. He and Bama's Tommy Johnson both leaped for the ball, colliding just as it reached Sanders's hands. The Auburn receiver pulled the ball in, landed on his feet at the four and dove across the goal line—touchdown. Etheridge's kick sailed through, and the Alabama lead had been cut to 14–12.

The Alabama sideline knew that its next possession was crucial. Even though Auburn's kickoff went out of bounds and the Tide returned to offense at its own 35, Alabama struggled to go three and out, giving the Tigers the ball at the Auburn 40.

The Tigers began to build a drive that looked unstoppable. In two plays, Richardson and Bostic carried the ball to the Alabama 32-yard line. Bostic would have broken the run for a score had it not been for Langham.

Auburn's Patrick Nix came off the bench, replacing an injured Stan White, to face a critical fourth-and-fifteen play. The sophomore quarterback did not disappoint the crowd.

Nix rolled the pocket to the right on the next play and found Sanders on the sideline for a gain to the 26. Richardson and McMilion moved the ball to the 21 for another first down. Bostic carried on a sweep to the left side to the Bama eight-yard line and first and goal. The Tide defenders dropped him for a four-yard loss on the next play and allowed only a yard gain for McMilion. With the ball on the 11, the third quarter ended.

Regrouping at the other end of the field, Nix gave the ball to Bostic, but the runner was tripped up at the eight-yard line. On fourth down, Etheridge came on to try to put Auburn ahead. His kick was good, and the Tigers took the lead, 15–14.

Bama went back on offense at its own 22. Barker threw to Lee, who had to leave the game with an injury. On second down, the Tide ran the ball, creating a third-and-two situation. Barker tried to hit Toderick Malone for the first down and more, but the wind caught the ball and it was intercepted by Auburn's Brian Robinson, who returned it to the Tide 43. As had happened throughout the game following turnover, a penalty after the play moved the ball back. It was exactly what Alabama didn't need. Not that Auburn was able to do much with the ball offensively, but time was no longer a Crimson ally.

The Tigers ran three plays and moved only as far as the Tide 49. Their punt rode the wind into the end zone for a touchback.

Having been disappointed by his team's passing proficiency, Stallings kept the ball on the ground. Putting the pressure on his running backs, Williams carried three times, coming very close to a first down at the 30-yard line. The measurement showed barely a foot to go to move the chains. Facing fourth down, deep in his own territory, and trailing with ten minutes left to play, Stallings elected to go for the first down. The Auburn defense brought everyone to the line during the snap count and knocked the Tide offensive line back a good two yards at the start of the play. Barker gave the ball to Tarrant Lynch, who dove at the pile, but Auburn's defenders were waiting for him and knocked the Alabama fullback down well short of the 30. With 8:55 left to play, Auburn had the ball on the Bama 29.

The Tigers tried to work the ball downfield on the ground, but Bostic was stopped for no gain. They turned to the air, and Nix floated a pass across the middle to Richardson, who took it to the 20, just short of the marker. On third and one, Nix was able to sneak the ball for two yards and the first. The Tide defenders were playing on their heels, and Auburn's running backs were beginning to find the lanes. Richardson avoided a tackle in the backfield and slipped through the line to the 16. Bostic hit the line and carried the ball to the three-yard line. He lost three yards on the next play, but made five on the following carry. Richardson advanced the ball just short of the goal line. Electing for the field goal, Bowden sent Etheridge out again.

Auburn's Brian Brinsfield was the best long snapper in the country, never recording a bad snap in all of 1993. On this attempt, he was perfect again, but holder Sean Carder bobbled the ball. Carder tried to run for the goal line rather than pass to Etheridge, but Alabama's Lemanski Hall dragged him down at the goal line. It was a break for the Tide, but they had placed their offense on the worst place on the field, ninety-nine yards away from the Tigers' goal line.

Throwing on his first two plays, Barker finally connected with Palmer near the 24-yard line. The Deuce had to dive for the ball, and he reeled it in for a badly needed first down and his greatest contribution to the Game. With a little more room with which to work, Barker threw again, incomplete, but the Tigers were flagged for interference. Having thrown on three consecutive plays, Alabama tested Auburn's run defense and wished they hadn't. Lynch was stopped at the line of scrimmage on first down. The Game was going to depend on Barker's arm. He overthrew his receiver on second down and almost connected with a wide-open Chris Anderson. Anderson had slipped Auburn's coverage and could have gone the distance for a Game-changing touchdown, but his hands turned to stone and he couldn't hold on to the ball.

With 2:33 remaining to play, Alabama had no choice but to go for it. Barker threw long for Toderick Malone, but Auburn's Dell McGee had the coverage and he made the interception. Had McGee considered the field-position questions, he would have served the Tigers better had he dropped the ball. An incompletion would have given Auburn possession on the Bama 24. As it was, the Tiger offense went back to work at its own 30.

Alabama's coaches expected Auburn to keep the ball on the ground and not risk a turnover, so they employed the strategy that had worked well for them against Miami the previous January. By bringing all their defenders to the line of scrimmage, they strove to contain Auburn's running game and force a punt, maybe giving the Bama offense a minute or so to work a miracle. Auburn did run, but the strategy didn't work.

Bostic hit the line just as his blockers had cleared the way for him, and there were almost no Tide defenders left in the area to attempt a tackle. The Tiger running back turned Langham inside out, leaving the All-American on the ground. Another defender barely touched Bostic's shoulder pads near the Bama 20, and another followed Bostic into the end zone for a shattering seventy-yard touchdown. The point after was good, and Auburn assumed a commanding lead, 22–14, with 2:19 left to play.

Palmer received the following kickoff at his five-yard line and almost broke free of the coverage. Barker returned and went back to the air. He overthrew a wide-open receiver and then was sacked for a one-yard loss. On third down, he found Chad Key for a fourteen-yard gain, keeping Bama hopes alive at their own 40. Barker, who had never lost a college game as a starter, took the next snap and was almost immediately caught in the backfield for another loss. This time the loss was not only yardage, the Tide had also lost a quarterback. Barker lay on the turf, his left leg twisted grotesquely below the knee and protruding out from his body. Auburn and Alabama players both called for the Tide trainers and doctors as he writhed on the field.

Sophomore Brian Burgdorf came in for Barker and managed to make the first after losing nine yards on a third-down sack and a twenty-nine-yard completion on fourth. It was the last hurrah for the Alabama offense. The Tide relinquished the ball on downs, and the Tigers had completed a perfect 11–0 season.

BOWDEN, THE first Division 1-A coach to go undefeated in his first year, jogged to midfield for a brief handshake with Stallings and then ran to the Auburn student section, followed by many of his players. He then turned to the other side of the stadium to thank the alumni and one man who had never attended a class at Auburn.

Pat Dye had watched the Game from a skybox and had made his way down to the Auburn sideline. He held out a victory cigar to his successor, and Bowden took it and then pulled the retired coach onto the field. The players and the coaches stayed on the field for thirty minutes after the Game, savoring the victory. On paper, Alabama was the West Division champ and slated to face Florida two weeks later in the title game, but Auburn had won the 1993 Southeastern Conference championship on the field.

In the dressing room, Bowden said to the team, "Today, you have set the standard. The greatest football team ever to play at Auburn University, 11–0. Because of what you did on the field, 11–0, it's never been done before. There's better teams maybe, but you have done something nobody else can do, and no one will ever take it [away]. You'll be the benchmark that they look to. And one more thing," Bowden said. "Today I became an Auburn man." He had a final word for Alabama, specifically Jimmy Fuller. "From now on, it's Buster Brown, *Sir*."

Auburn had not figured into Alabama's 1993 plans any more than LSU had. The frustration of the season, compounded by Alabama's second-half offensive blues, didn't sit well with Stallings, who had harsh words for the officials. "In the second half, penalties killed us, for whatever reason. . . . I was very disappointed with some of the things I saw on the field. I'm very disappointed in what I saw on the field, other than our players. I think the penalties really hurt us and I feel bad about that."

AUBURN'S SEASON ended with the Game, a fact that Alabama fans pointed out quickly. "Eleven and O and nowhere to go," was a popular refrain, along with "home for the holidays," but the Tiger faithful didn't seem to mind. T-shirts reading "No TV, No Bowl, No Problem" and "We Should Be on Probation More Often" sold briskly. Alabama would face two more opponents, and the first was the Florida Gators in Birmingham.

The week before the SEC championship game (quickly dubbed the Loser Bowl by gleeful Auburn fans, having vanquished both participants during the season), the Tide's Antonio Langham became embroiled in controversy. A letter from Alabama athletic director Hootie Ingram to the SEC office was intercepted by a mailroom clerk and forwarded to the media (the clerk, an Auburn fan, was later convicted of tampering with the mail). The letter stated that Langham's eligibility had been compromised when he signed with a sports agent hours after the 1993 Sugar Bowl in a New Orleans nightclub, also accepting a check for four hundred dollars. After the publication of the letter, Alabama declared Langham ineligible and immediately petitioned the NCAA to have the player's eligibility restored in time for the SEC game.

The NCAA refused, declaring Langham ineligible for the playoff and the bowl game. In addition, the NCAA indicated that it was unsatisfied with Alabama's explanation of the affair. At the time, Stallings was more angry that the matter had been made public than at charges of wrongdoing. The University of Alabama has a long tradition of settling disputes behind closed doors, and Stallings was deeply incensed that his program's dirty laundry was being made public.

The losses of Langham to questions of eligibility and of Barker to injury didn't help Alabama, but the Tide played well against the Gators in the first half. Alabama's first possession was pure precision and magic, a march downfield for a swift touchdown. The drive, however, was most of Bama's offense for the day. Steve Spurrier's offense turned up the heat and eventually coasted to a 28–13 win.

Alabama went on to, ironically, the Gator Bowl. Behind the strong passing of Burgdorf, the Tide cruised to a 24–10 victory over North Carolina. Alabama finished the season at 9–3–1, a more-than-impressive finish anywhere but Tuscaloosa.

Bowden took Stallings's place as the unanimous national and SEC coach of the year. Even without a bowl game, Auburn was a major story for sportscasts all over the country during the holidays. Terry's father, Bobby, claimed his first national championship by edging an undefeated Nebraska in the Orange Bowl. Notre Dame, which had beaten FSU during the regular season, moved past Auburn to number three. Nebraska gained respect with the sportswriters and held on to number two. The Tigers, despite being the only undefeated, untied team in the nation, garnered only four first-place votes and finished number four in the final Associated Press poll. Stan White started for the South at the Senior Bowl in Mobile and won the game's MVP trophy. Coincidentally, White threw the game-winning pass to Alabama's Kevin Lee.

ROLL TIDE

Apples and Oranges

I SUPPOSE IT was only natural that Auburn follow Alabama's undefeated year by doing the same thing. To rise from the ashes, as it were. I draw the line, however, when someone like Terry Bowden proclaims his team to be national champions.

It takes more than winning eleven games to qualify for the crown. In the SEC, for instance, it takes thirteen, as Alabama proved a year earlier. The two simply don't compare. Of course, the pollsters know that, the players know that, most coaches know that, but the fact seems lost on the fans. Auburn supporters by the barrelful claimed to have been robbed when the season was over.

There are other reasons why the Tigers were overlooked. First, before claiming to be the best team in the land, it's a good idea to beat more than two teams with winning records. It's even better to beat some winning teams on the road, which is something Auburn didn't do in this year.

Also, there's the matter of probation. The idea here is to punish someone for breaking the rules, not reward them. For years, Auburn fans mocked Florida as "the best team money can buy." When the tables were turned, however, the party line became "Oh, that stuff happens everywhere," and a team serving sanctions suddenly became some sort of victim. The stigma is stronger now than in the 1950s, when the Tigers claimed their only national title (under probation, of course).

Going undefeated in any league, let alone the SEC, is an impressive feat. No one could have expected Bowden's first year at Auburn to go like it did. He could have ended up 6–5 and been lauded as a savior. What they did was amazing and a credit to all involved, but to suggest that a national championship was merited is foolish. Try it when you're playing for real.—S.B.

WAR EAGLE

Perfect Justice

OW DO you capture magic in words? How can you distill three months of fiery emotion into ink and still let the fire show? How do you describe a dream come true?

In 1973, David Housel introduced the Amazin's of 1972 in *Saturdays to Remember*, saying: "This is the story of a football game, but it is something more. It is a story in the finest tradition of the American Dream, a Horatio Alger story of the first degree. . . . This is the story of an entire football team who refused to accept the lot handed them by a pragmatic world that does not believe in dreams or miracles. . . . This is the story of how an Auburn football team sought greatness, found it, then reached into the sky and slew a football giant."

Those words were written about Auburn's most famous win ever, the "Punt Bama Punt" Game. Apparently, Housel is not only a great writer and all-around good guy, he's prescient, too, because those same words ring just as true twenty years later. Amazin's of 1972 meet your direct descendants, the Believers of 1993 (of course, Housel coined that name, too).

They say nobody loves an underdog like an American. I give you a hundred-odd underdogs, a bunch of guys maligned by virtually everybody. Players called overrated. Coaches called incompetent. Fair-weather fans leaving for warmer climes. I give you a team saddled with an unbearable burden. I give you a coach with a legion of doubters in his corner. I give you the 1993 Auburn Tigers. Untelevised. Unbowled. Unbowed. Unafraid. Unbeaten. Unbelievable.

Take that, you NCAA goons with your platitudes and selective enforcement. Take that, Kevin Scarbinsky and Paul Finebaum, take that and your snide columns and stick 'em. Take that, Eric Ramsey and Donald

Watkins. Take that, all you Alabama boosters who paid their bills (you know who you are). Take that, Steve Spurrier and Gene Stallings. Take that and tattoo it on your foreheads. You might as well, 'cause we're never going to let you forget it.

One thing that made this season so much fun was the childish reaction of opposing coaches to Auburn's success. Spurrier and Stallings were the two most egregious offenders, whining about the refs and offended at the very idea that their mighty teams had lost to this kid from Samford. While Spurrier still holds the title for all-time ego-driven classless behavior, I must say I got the biggest kick out of Stallings's stupid suggestion that Auburn fans should sit on their hands and whisper while Alabama had the ball. Maybe he just misses that nice, quiet stadium in Phoenix.

I highly recommend going undefeated. It makes for one fun year. Not just for a season, mind you, but for a whole year. There are a number of Alabama fans (and one of them has his name on the cover of this book) who will sniff that the triumph of 1993 was incomplete, because the Tigers were not declared the national champions. What a pile of bull. Auburn couldn't win the national championship, and neither could anybody else, because there ain't no such animal. There never has been, and there never will be, until Division 1-A has a playoff. Until then, it's all just talk. As long as we cling to the old system, the 1993 Tigers have as good a claim to number one as anybody. Better than most, if it comes to that.

After the Game, Pat Dye said, "Sometimes justice is done, and this is justice." How true. How right. After two years of struggle, two years of attacks, when everyone has counted you out, going undefeated is perfect justice.

You may notice that I haven't mentioned any individual players. I'm not going to. The Auburn Tigers of 1993 were a team in the truest sense of the word, living proof that the whole is greater than the sum of its parts. There have been more talented Auburn squads. There has never been, nor will there ever be, a greater Auburn *team* than the Believers of 1993.—W.C.

1994

THE END OF THE LINE

A LABAMA'S FALL FROM GLORY in 1993, much like Auburn's of 1985, claimed casualties. Since Gene Stallings's arrival, Tide fans had grumbled that the offense lacked creativity. Despite the amazing versatility of David Palmer, the Bama attack had become sluggish, and the chief villain, at least in the eyes of the fans, was offensive coordinator Mal Moore. His conservative nature was keeping the attack in low gear, said the faithful. After the three losses of 1993, in which Bama averaged only thirteen points, and when Palmer made an early departure to the NFL, something obviously had to be done.

In response, Homer Smith, who had returned to UCLA after Bill Curry's departure in 1990, was contacted about re-assuming his duties as offensive coordinator. He accepted the offer, and Moore was booted upstairs in the athletic department.

Smith's first duty was to settle on a starting quarterback. Jay Barker, whose knee had been badly damaged in the 1993 Game, was fighting through grueling rehabilitation, and Brian Burgdorf spent the spring preparing to enter the season at starter. Regardless of who lined up behind center, the cornerstone of the Bama attack would be Sherman Williams, returning for his senior season at tailback. Despite being short in stature, Williams was a shifty, effective runner, who figured to get the ball often to compensate for the loss of Palmer. Tarrant Lynch, who had lost more than thirty pounds in the offseason at Stallings's demand, would lead the way at fullback. Curtis Brown and Toderick Malone returned as receiving threats, and Marcell West showed promise as well. The offensive line was a huge question mark, with only Jon Stevenson returning as a regular starter.

The defense drew early comparisons to its historic 1992 predecessor. The front line, despite lacking the presence of a Curry or Copeland, was as deep as any in the country, with ten players rotating into the first wave of Bill Oliver's new 4–3 scheme. Dameian Jeffries and Shannon Brown were the most prominent returnees, but the ability to substitute reliable performers gave line coach Mike Dubose a valuable tool.

The linebackers, with the exception of Michael Rogers, were young, but names such as Ralph Staten, Tyrell Buckner, and Dwayne Rudd would soon become familiar. In the secondary, Sam Shade, Tommy Johnson, and Willie Gaston returned for their final season, but the loss of Antonio Langham would be telling.

Langham's name still lingered. The results of the preliminary NCAA investigation into his signing with an agent, as well as the claims of Gene Jelks, were due in mid-September. In contrast to Auburn's Eric Ramsey controversy, the Langham investigation had not drawn constant media attention, but the prospect of impending sanctions hovered over Alabama as the season began.

HOW DO you improve on perfection? That was the not-unpleasant dilemma facing Terry Bowden in 1994. The Tigers still had to serve one more year of probation and were banned from postseason play, but they could now appear on television. Bowden elected to focus on Auburn's possession of the nation's longest winning streak and on the possibility of extending it to twenty-two wins. He instituted a new motto for the season, Audacity, with emphasis on the AU. The pundits were unimpressed. Bowden said, "It's not likely that we'll go 11–0 again, but that's what we're going to shoot for."

James Bostic made an early departure to the NFL, making Stephen Davis the Tigers' top tailback. Seniors Frank Sanders and Thomas Bailey returned as the heart of a breakaway receiver corps, and senior Joe Frazier would take the place of the departed McMilion and Richardson at fullback. The offensive line was highlighted by center Robique and tackle Anderson, as well as rotating tight ends Andy Fuller and Jessie McCovery.

With the graduation of Stan White, the quarterback position became a point of controversy for the first time in four years. Patrick Nix was the hero of the 1993 Alabama Game, but he came under heavy pressure from sophomore Dameyune Craig. Bowden was unwilling to start a freshman on the road in a conference game and elected to stick with the more experienced Nix. Fans speculated that Craig might come along well enough to take over before the big games against Mississippi State and Florida.

Auburn's defense looked to be excellent, returning nine starters from 1993 and one from 1992, All-SEC cornerback Fred Smith, who had missed the 1993 season with a knee injury. The secondary was as talented as any in the nation, with Chris Shelling, Brian Robinson, Dell McGee, and Otis Mounds returning, and freshman safety sensation Ken Alvis working his way into the rotation. The all-senior front line, led by tackles Gary Walker and Mike Pelton, along with ends Willie Whitehead and Alonzo Etheridge, was fast and powerful. Linebackers Anthony Harris, Marcellus Mostella, and former walk-on Jason Miska were not as talented but nearly as experienced. All-American punter Terry Daniel returned, but junior Matt Hawkins would have to step up as place-kicker. Defensive coordinator Wayne Hall expected great things from his squad, but with a schedule that included Mississippi State, Florida, and Alabama on the road, he knew the season would be tough.

For the first time since 1990 the Tigers entered the season in the Associated Press rankings, at number twelve, as they took on Ole Miss. The Rebels had been shorn of long-time coach Billy Brewer during the summer, the victim of an NCAA investigation. His replacement, former defensive coordinator Joe Lee Dunn, faced the daunting task of rebuilding an Ole Miss team facing sanctions. Nicknamed the Probation Bowl by more than one pundit, the contest ended as a 22–17 victory for the Tigers. To no one's surprise, Auburn buried Northeastern Louisiana, 44–14, the next week.

The following game held some of the biggest surprises in the history of college football. Although LSU came into Jordan-Hare Stadium a big underdog, the Tigers' cousins from the West jumped out to a 10–9 halftime lead. In the second half, the Auburn offense was even worse, and LSU kept scoring, running out to a 23–9 third-quarter lead. The fourth quarter was, without exaggeration, unbelievable. Craig had replaced Nix, but the offense was still held in check by the LSU defense, so the Auburn defense took over. LSU quarterback Jamie Howard was intercepted by Ken Alvis, who returned the turnover for a touchdown, cutting the deficit to 23–16. Then Howard was picked off again, this time by Fred Smith, who returned the ball for a touchdown, tying the game at 23.

Howard moved LSU on a clock-eating drive to the Auburn five, but the Bengals had to kick a field goal to take the lead again, 26–23. Auburn had five minutes left to score, but the LSU defense again smothered the Tigers. The Bengals looked ready to run out the clock. On third and four, with 1:55 to play and Auburn out of time-outs, LSU coach Curley Hallman made the worst possible call, a pass over the middle. The pass was intercepted by Brian Robinson and returned for a touchdown. Auburn escaped with a 30–26 victory in a game that drew national headlines: five fourth-quarter interceptions, three returned for touchdowns.

East Tennessee State, replacing Southern Miss on the Auburn schedule, was dispatched the next week, 38–0. Five days later, Bill Curry coached his first game in the state of Alabama since leaving for Lexington, and Auburn picked Kentucky apart, 41–14, in a Thursday night ESPN game. As in 1993, many had picked Mississippi State to knock off the Tigers in Starkville, but Patrick Nix came into his own against MSU, racking up 311 passing yards and three touchdowns as the Tigers buried the Bulldogs, 42–18.

The Tigers' next game, also on the road, was against the number-one-ranked team in the nation, the Florida Gators, and Auburn was a sixteen-point underdog. The largest football crowd in the history of the state of Florida and a national audience watched a game for the ages.

Auburn came out on fire, stuffing the vaunted Gator offense, then driving sixty-eight yards toward a Nix-to-Bailey touchdown on their first possession. It marked the first time in 1994 that the Gators had trailed in a game. Gator quarterback Terry Dean, considered a leading candidate in the Heisman race, fumbled his first snap after Florida got the ball back. Auburn converted it into a field goal and led, 10–0, in the first quarter. Dean recovered, throwing a forty-two-yard bomb to All-World receiver Jack Jackson to get back in the game. The Tigers answered with a forty-three-yard Hawkins field goal, but the Gators took their first lead, 14–13, with another Jackson touchdown. With three minutes left in the half, Dean was intercepted. The Tigers subsequently moved fifty-seven yards for a touchdown, only to fail on a two-point conversion try. Dean was intercepted again, and Hawkins kicked another field goal to give Auburn a 22–14 halftime lead.

Early in the third quarter Dean was replaced by sophomore Danny Wuerffel, who brought a spark back to the Gator offense and passed for a quick touchdown on his first possession, then another early in the fourth quarter, giving the Gators a 26–22 lead, but two-point conversions failed on both scores. Nix and Auburn finally answered after a scoreless third period, scoring on a thirty-yard toss to Andy Fuller. Now trailing, 29–26, Wuerffel led the Gators downfield again and hit Jackson on a twenty-eight-yard strike to regain the lead, 33–29, with 5:51 left to play. It looked like Auburn's dreams of glory were over.

With just over a minute left, Florida was on its own 29, facing third and fifteen. The smart play would have been to run the ball and exhaust the clock, but Florida went for a long pass. Wuerffel's throw was intercepted by Brian Robinson and set up a classic drive. On first and goal with thirty-one seconds left, Nix threw the ball to Sanders in the corner of the end zone. In a picture-perfect catch that would grace sports pages nationwide, Sanders pulled it in. Auburn had come back to beat the number-one Gators, 36–33, raising its two-year record to 18–0 and breaking a school record for consecutive wins.

The ten thousand Auburn faithful present began chanting "We're Number One!" over and over to the shell-shocked Gator partisans. On the field, Terry Bowden told a reporter, "They were preseason number one based on what they did last year. Well, we beat them last year. Everybody said [this year] they were the number one team in the country. You ask me, should we be number one, I say, 'Yes!'" Auburn defensive tackle Gary Walker found an ESPN camera and made the case to the nation. "We're the best!" he shouted. "They can't play with us! *Give us our respect!*"

On Monday, despite having pulled off the biggest upset of the season, the Tigers were not ranked number one, but number four. Apparently the pollsters couldn't bring themselves to vote for a team on probation.

Disappointed but determined to go on proving their point, Auburn returned to Jordan-Hare Stadium for a game with Arkansas. The Razorbacks carried a 14–10 lead into the dressing room at halftime, but Auburn's Stephen Davis exploded for three fourth-quarter touchdowns to lead the Tigers to a 31–14 final. Homecoming foe East Carolina was having a fine season, but the game ended as a 38–21 Auburn win and number twenty in "the Streak."

The 5–4 Georgia Bulldogs rolled into Auburn the next week, and just about everybody thought they would be number 21. When Davis rumbled forty-one yards on a brilliant run to put the Tigers up 23–9 early in the third, it looked like the Dawgs would go quietly. Then things started to go wrong for Auburn. A long Nix-to-Sanders pass was intercepted. Three plays later, Georgia quarterback Eric Zeier showed why he was a Heisman candidate. He rifled a seventy-nine-yard touchdown to Juan Daniels, getting the Dawgs back in it. After Auburn went three downs and out, Zeier and running back Terrell Davis marched fifty-eight yards to forge a 23–23 tie with 13:06 left. Auburn had plenty of opportunities late, but couldn't convert crucial third and fourth downs. In the end it came down to a Matt Hawkins forty-four-yard field goal attempt with seconds left. His kick sailed wide right.

The streak ended with an unexpected tie. The players and coaches, their confidence shaken for the first time since 1992, would have to regroup and regain their composure in just seven days. The Game was next, and this time, there was more than one undefeated team in the program.

ALABAMA BEGAN 1994 in Birmingham against the Moccasins of Tennessee-Chattanooga. Though the Division I-AA Mocs posted two second-quarter scores to stay in the game, the Tide pulled away easily in the second half for a 42–13 win.

Vanderbilt was next, in Tuscaloosa. The Commodores controlled the line of scrimmage for the better part of the game and outgained the Tide in total yardage. Undaunted, Sherman Williams eventually took over, leading Alabama to a 17–7 victory. Coming off this shaky home performance, the Tide traveled to Fayetteville for a date with Arkansas and escaped with a close one, 13–6.

The following Thursday, the NCAA's long-anticipated letter of inquiry arrived in Tuscaloosa. It formally charged the university with two major violations of NCAA rules. To the surprise of many, Gene Jelks was named in only one, and it was not a part of his 1992 allegations. Birmingham sports agent Jerry Albano had loaned Jelks more than ten thousand dollars during the spring of 1990, and the loans were determined to be an improper benefit. NCAA enforcement director David Berst indicated in the letter that Jelks's other charges fell outside of the organization's four-year statute of limitations.

The other violation was potentially more serious. The NCAA charged that Alabama had allowed Antonio Langham to participate in eleven games in 1993, despite knowing that he had signed with an agent on January 1 of that year, and that he had cashed a four-hundred-dollar check in return for his signature. Although Alabama would have a chance to respond to the charges, sanctions were expected, the first in the history of the University of Alabama.

The next week the Tide hosted Tulane in Birmingham. The Green Wave led, 10–3, in the second quarter before Dameian Jeffries returned a fumble for a touchdown to tie the game at halftime. Fans could rest easy only when Proctor connected with three minutes left, sealing a 20–10 decision that most wanted to forget.

At 4–0 and ranked eleventh in the country, Alabama had done little of which to be proud. With Georgia and Zeier coming to Tuscaloosa, the first legitimate test of the year was at hand. In one of the most entertaining SEC games in years, Zeier and Barker dueled it out under the lights and in front of a national ESPN audience. Behind Zeier's cannon arm and a surprisingly effective running game, the Dawgs built a 21–10 halftime lead. In the third quarter, Barker threw a thirty-five-yard touchdown that trimmed the deficit to five. Then Proctor made it 21–19 with a short field goal.

With the Tide closing, Zeier went back to work, firing another touchdown late in the third quarter for a 28–19 edge, becoming the SEC's all-time passing yardage leader in the process. Barker was quick to respond with a forty-nine-yard touchdown reception to Toderick Malone to get within two points. Georgia had a chance to ice the game, but James Warner couldn't hold on to a Zeier pass that would have allowed the Dawgs to pick up a first down and run out the clock. Proctor drilled a twenty-nine-yard field goal, and Bama claimed an amazing 29–28 win over Georgia.

After the emotional victory, the Tide hosted Southern Miss the next weekend. Bama was again outgained by an inferior opponent but three blocked kicks and a fumble return for a touchdown were the saving graces in a boring 14–6 victory.

Tennessee was waiting next in Knoxville for what would be another classic confrontation. After a 3–3 first half, Alabama's Barker threw a twenty-nine-yard scoring pass to Marcell West. The Vols responded quickly to tie it, then went ahead, 13–10, early in the fourth quarter. Up against the wall, the Tide offense put together its finest drive to date, culminating in a Sherman Williams score. In the end, the Tide escaped again, winning 17–13, for its fifth consecutive victory in Neyland Stadium.

The next week in Tuscaloosa, Ole Miss came to town. The Rebels were ahead, 10–0, in the second quarter when a severe lightning storm suspended the game for twenty-five minutes. Some Bama fans suggested it was divine intervention, but it was just the "spark" the Tide needed. Alabama rebounded nicely, coming back for a 21–10 triumph.

After an open week, the Tide traveled to Baton Rouge to settle a score with LSU. The Tigers, still reeling after the Auburn debacle, lost this one virtually before it began, an eventual 35–17 slaughter.

Now at 9–0 and ranked sixth in the nation, Bama took on Mississippi State in Starkville. Despite the earlier humbling at the hands of Auburn, the Bulldogs were in position to win the SEC West title with a victory over the Tide. Behind a mammoth offensive line and rugged runners Michael Davis and Kevin Bouie, State ran roughshod for three and a half quarters, leading the Tide, 25–15, in the fourth quarter.

Barker took over with 7:57 to play and threw a forty-two-yard scoring pass to Curtis Brown to make it 25–22. Again it was up to the defense to come through, and again it did, stopping the Bulldog running game and giving Barker another chance. He made the most of it, moving the ball to the Bulldog 16 and then giving it to his running backs. Freshman Dennis

Riddle scored from a yard out with fifty-one seconds to play. The Tide won, 29–25, clinching the SEC West yet again. For the third time in six years, Alabama was headed to the Iron Bowl at 10–0.

FOR THE first time since 1971, the Game would be waged between two undefeated teams. For Alabama, ranked fourth, a victory would mean a chance to move into contention for a shot at the national title. A third consecutive SEC championship date with Florida was looming on December 3, and the Gators, despite losing to Auburn, had climbed back up to the third spot in the polls. Although the Tide was undefeated, the top two teams in the rankings, Nebraska and Penn State, were dominating the headlines. As a result, consecutive wins over sixth-ranked Auburn and the Gators would be needed to keep Bama in the running for another national crown.

For the Tigers, a Game victory would do much more than redeem the Georgia tie. Doubters far and wide had grumbled that Bowden rode luck and perseverance through 1993, and the LSU miracle hardly silenced their scoffing. Beating Florida in Gainesville, however, sent a clear message that Auburn was a force, and the opportunity to make it through two full seasons without a loss (and to ruin Alabama's year in the process) was strong motivation.

The keys to the Game were relatively simple. Auburn hoped to establish the running of Davis, the SEC's leading ground gainer. Equally powerful options were the deep threats of Sanders, the league's premier receiver, and Bailey. Alabama hoped to counter this daunting combination by using its bountiful supply of defensive substitutes. The Tide had given up only one fourth-quarter touchdown all year, that coming in the lopsided LSU win. Thus, the armchair quarterbacks opined, if Bama could contain the Tiger offense early, defensive coordinator Bill Oliver would keep fresh defenders in the Game to the end.

Offensively, the Alabama burden clearly fell on Williams. Rated second only to Davis among SEC backs, Williams had tailed off somewhat late in the season but would be expected to keep the Auburn defense honest. Incredibly, Barker had thrown only two interceptions all season in 190 attempts. The Auburn secondary, generally considered to be the nation's best, figured to change that if the Tide were forced to throw regularly. Bama had committed only twelve turnovers for the season, easily the best in the league, and had to continue this trend to have a realistic shot at beating the opportunistic Tigers.

The national attention accorded this clash of unbeatens was second only to the 1989 Game. Legion Field hosted ESPN's hour-long *College Gameday*, which dedicated several features to the rivalry and afforded the faithful on both sides of the field opportunities to cheer for their favorite. At long last, after an eight-year absence, ABC's Keith Jackson had returned to the site of so many Iron Bowls to call the action of the Game.

WHEN SATURDAY arrived, the Birmingham skies were beautiful, and a stiff breeze filtered through the southern end of Legion Field. Auburn went three and out on its first possession. Alabama, however, put together a six-play drive, all on the ground, that stalled at the Tigers' 16. Proctor came on for a field goal attempt, but the kick was wide right. Although lacking points on the scoreboard, Stallings saw that his running game had gotten off to a good start.

Auburn again went three and out, but then so did Bama. Neither team was making progress in field position or in pinning its opponent deeper into its own territory. Thus far, the Game was essentially a draw. Momentum would depend on who committed the first turnover. That honor fell to Auburn. On the second play of the Tigers' next drive, Davis lost the ball as he was being tackled in the backfield. Alabama recovered the fumble at the Auburn 47.

RICH ADDICKS, ATLANTA JOURNAL-CONSTITUTION

Jay Barker, Alabama's all-time winningest quarterback, confers with head coach Gene Stallings during warm-ups for the 1994 Game.

Bama's Michael Rogers (52) forces a fumble from Auburn running back Stephen Davis (48), which Sam Shade (31) recovered, leading to the Tide's first score.

The Tide's Toderick Malone (80) breaks free for Bama's second score, a seventy-four-yard touchdown reception, avoiding a diving Auburn Tiger, Chris Shelling (4).

With the short field in front of them, the Tide assembled an eight-play drive that culminated with a thirteen-yard scoring run by Williams. Proctor added the point after, and Alabama was on top, 7–0, with 2:38 to play in the first quarter.

In response, Auburn went three and out again, starting the possession on its 24 but losing yardage to 18, mostly by way of a penalty. The Tide went back on offense at its 30. It seemed as if Alabama would go the way of the Tigers when it drew a flag on its first play. Still officially a first-down play, Barker went back to pass. He looked for his tight end, Patrick Hape, and the Auburn defense followed the quarterback's eyes, shifting in Hape's direction. At the last moment, Barker looked away and saw Toderick Malone over the middle. The Tide signal caller hit him at the Alabama 45, and Malone was alone and en route to the end zone. The seventy-four-yard touchdown reception on the last play of the first quarter, along with Proctor's point after, gave Alabama a 14–0 lead going into the second quarter.

Auburn made a first down on its next play from scrimmage, but three plays later, the Tigers punted again. This time, the Tide was fairly close to the shadow of its goalpost, taking the ball on its own 13. The ensuing drive, however, seemed to have a charmed life.

On first down, the Tigers limited Williams to a one-yard gain. Then Bama tried to run a reverse. Barker handed off to Williams, and the tailback gave the ball to Chad Key coming around from the side. Unfortunately for Alabama, Key bobbled the exchange and lost the ball. Unfortunately for Auburn, the ball bounced back to Key. Unfortunately for Alabama, Jason Miska was bearing down on Key in the end zone. Unfortunately for Auburn, Key hurled an improvised pass to Barker, and the quarterback-turned-receiver advanced the ball to the 24 for a first down. It was the Game's most remarkable play.

Taking advantage of the unusual play, Bama began to run the ball and make positive yardage. Lynch gained nine up the middle, then powered for four more and a first down at the Bama 37. Williams charged through for fourteen yards and across midfield to the Tiger 49. The Tide then lined up in the I-formation, usually a strong sign of an upcoming run. Not this time. Barker dropped back to pass and threw deep down the middle for Marcell West. The Tide receiver was a step ahead of the coverage. He caught the ball at the Tiger 20 and blew into the end zone for a forty-nine-yard score. Proctor added another point after, and with 10:25 left in the first half, Alabama was punishing Auburn, 21–0. The margin was the largest lead enjoyed by either team in the fourteen years recounted in this book. Auburn's radio play-by-play announcer, Jim Fyffe, a man not known for either praising

Alabama or disparaging Auburn, said that the Game looked like men playing with boys.

The remainder of the second quarter was an exchange of punts, with
the Tigers losing field position to the Tide. The kicking game was such a part
of both team's offense, it was fitting that the last play of the half was a punt.

Bama had utterly dominated the first thirty minutes. Auburn managed
just three first downs to the Tide's eleven, and 76 total yards to 278. Big plays
were obviously the difference, as time of possession favored Alabama by only
two minutes.

ALABAMA LOOKED good as the second half started. Beginning on his own 38,
Williams took the first carry of the third quarter for twenty yards. Riddle
then picked up four, and Williams added seven more en route to another
Bama first down. The carry put the senior over a hundred yards on the day,
and again the Tide was threatening to score. Barker's attempt to Key, however, was broken up, and Williams was wrapped up on the next play for no
gain, bringing up third and 10.

Barker found his primary options covered and threw short to Hape,
who lumbered down to the Auburn 17. The Tiger defense responded
strongly, stopping Lynch after a short gain and tagging Riddle for four-yard
loss. Facing third and twelve, Barker was forced to scramble and he lost the
ball. Auburn recovered at the Tiger 28, but the team did more than recover
the ball. Along the way, the Tigers found their offense.

Davis charged up the middle for nineteen yards. Two more runs yielded
six yards. On third and four, Nix found Bailey for a first down at the Tide 41.
It was the Tigers' first successful third-down conversion of the afternoon.
Davis then added five more yards. Nix went looking for Sanders, but the
brunt of the Bama rush forced him to throw the ball away. On third down,
a well-designed screen pass to Beasley advanced the ball to the Bama 21.
Nix found Bailey for another nine, then gained three more yards and an
Auburn first down on a keeper.

On first and goal from the eight, fullback Harold Morrow carried to the
five. Nix then rolled to his right, looking for Sanders in the end zone. His
pass was tipped and went incomplete. On third and goal, Nix threw over the

Both teams pressured each other's quarterback throughout the afternoon. Above,
the Auburn defense, led by Mike Pelton (50), swarms Alabama quarterback Jay
Barker in the first half. Below, constant pressure from the Alabama defense had
Auburn's Patrick Nix (10) rattled early in the Game.

middle to walk-on Hicks Poor, but while he collected the ball he was stopped just short of the goal line.

Trailing by twenty-one points, Auburn had no choice but to go for it. Nix followed his linemen and lunged into the end zone, and Auburn had finally gotten on the scoreboard. Matt Hawkins added the point after, and with 5:03 to play in the third quarter, the Tide lead was 21–7. The thirteen-play drive showed that the Tigers still had a little life in them and might make the Game live up to its billing.

Bama took the ball on its 20 and began to use Williams to punch the ball down the field and punish the Tigers in the process. Williams gained only two yards on his first carry, but he more than made up for it on his next, gaining sixteen yards to the Bama 38. On his next carry, he picked up five more before being forced out of bounds. Offensive coordinator Homer Smith hadn't forgotten that he had other runners at his disposal. On second and five, Riddle managed a four-yard gain, and on third down he gained three more yards and another Bama first down.

Given the reprieve of a two-play "rest," Williams gained nine yards on the next two carries, setting up a third and one so that Riddle could gain two yards and keep the drive alive. Lynch carried for a gain of three, and the Tigers finally nailed an Alabama runner for a loss when Riddle was brought down for a short loss. Facing third and six, the Tide went to the shotgun formation, and Barker found Curtis Brown at the Auburn 26, good for another first down as the quarter ended.

Auburn wide receiver Hicks Poor reaches for the end zone as the Tigers fight back from a twenty-one-point deficit.

The offense was working the clock to perfection. On first down, Williams added nine yards to the Tide's offensive tally. Lynch was held just short of the first down. Williams was tripped up on the third-down play before he could dive over the pile. With fourth down and inches to go, Stallings chose to go for the first down. Barker carried the ball on a sneak and made just enough yardage for the down. On first down and with the ball on the Auburn 15, Williams cruised to the four-yard line.

With their backs against their own end zone, the Tigers stiffened and stopped Williams for a loss of three. A second time they dropped the senior for a two-yard loss. On third and goal, Barker took the snap from the shotgun and rolled right. He tried to get the ball to Curtis Brown in the end zone, but safety Brian Robinson picked the ball off and returned it to the Auburn 19, with just over ten minutes to play. The nineteen-play Bama drive had been memorable, and more importantly time-consuming, but the effort had also been fruitless and the Tigers were still alive.

Auburn looked to capitalize immediately on the turnover as Nix came back on the field and found Bailey for a forty-eight-yard gain to the Bama 33. The Tigers battled the hard way for the next first down, getting three yards on a sweep by fullback Joe Frazier but losing one on the following carry. On third and eight, Nix connected with his tight end Andy Fuller, who moved the ball into scoring position at the Bama 16. Auburn returned to its running game, but Davis was stacked up for a two-yard loss, forcing Nix to throw on the next down. The pass was intercepted by Dameian Jeffries and returned to the Bama 30, ending the Tigers' threat. The Auburn offense left the field knowing that time for unlikely heroics was getting short.

Sherman Williams returned and added to his running stats, gaining fifteen yards and a first down on two carries before losing a yard on his third. As was the pattern, however, when Williams had been stopped, the Tide turned to Riddle to carry the ball. The freshman gained six yards on the fourth play of the drive but made the mistake of taking the ball out of bounds and stopping the clock. On third and five, Riddle streaked to the Auburn 36, but the play was called back for a clipping violation, setting up a third and eleven at the Tide 39. Riddle gained only six on the replay, and Alabama had to punt for the first time in the second half.

Nix came back on the field looking like a man with a mission. Forced out of the pocket, he managed to gain six yards and get out of bounds. He threw incomplete on second down but connected with Poor on a third-and-four play from the 32. Poor collected the first down at the Auburn 37 and stopped the clock. Successive passes to Bailey were broken up, and Nix again faced a third-and-long situation. Remembering previous success,

Bowden called for a screen to Beasley, and the played worked to the Bama 47 for a first down, with 3:21 to play. Another short attempt to Poor worked for eight yards, then Nix hit Sanders over the middle. It was the senior's fourth reception of the Game, and he advanced the ball to the 30 for another Auburn first down. With less than three minutes left in the Game, the Tigers again ran the screen to Beasley, this time making only three yards on the play. Bama, however, drew a flag for having too many players on the field. The step-off gave the Tigers a first down at the Alabama 13, with 2:53 on the clock. Nix's first-down pass was almost an interception, and on second down he found Sanders over the middle. The star receiver lunged as far as the Bama one-yard line. Facing first and goal, Nix followed his line over the goal line for his second score of the game. Hawkins's point after pulled the Tigers to within a score, 21–14. The clock showed 2:23 still left in the contest.

Bowden decided to try an onside kick, but Bama covered the ball at the Auburn 46. The Tiger defense came to life and held the Tide short of a first down, both through the efforts of the defenders and a little penalty yardage. Alabama punted the ball at the 2:02 mark. Things looked to be going Auburn's way until the punt took a peculiar bounce and was downed inside the Tigers' one-yard line. If there were to be a miracle finish, it would take a ninety-nine-yard drive. For good measure, Auburn drew a delay-of-game penalty, which marked the ball half the distance to the goal line.

With 1:45 to play, Nix threw long and incomplete for Bailey, who was streaking down the sideline for a potential ninety-nine yard score. The Tigers returned to the screen play that had worked so well for them earlier. Beasley caught the ball and took it to the 15, going out of bounds with 1:29 left. From the shotgun, Nix threw over the middle to Bailey at the Tiger 27 for another first down, then he dumped the ball over the middle to Sanders, who carried the ball out of bounds at the 36. A little more than a minute was left. On the following play, Nix scrambled to midfield. His next two attempts were incomplete, one had been batted down, the other thrown away. On third and ten, the Tigers returned to the reliable screen to Beasley, who took the ball out at the Alabama 43, stopping the clock with thirty-eight seconds remaining but three yards shy of the first.

The Tigers had to go for it. Nix found Sanders slanting over the middle and hit him with the ball at the 40, where he was brought down almost immediately. The officials marked the ball and called for the measurement. It looked as if Sanders had just enough yardage for the down, but the chains showed that the Tigers were an inch short. It was Alabama's ball.

The Auburn bench was beside itself. After a twenty-one-game unbeaten streak, it was hard not to see that Sanders's catch had kept the drive and the dream alive. Both Nix and Bailey exploded at the official's call, and the Tigers were penalized a total of thirty yards for unsportsmanlike conduct, giving Bama the ball at the Auburn 30, with thirty-one seconds remaining to be played. The Tide ran the clock out, taking the Game, 21–14.

In a post-Game interview, Jay Barker, now 3–1 as a Game quarterback, responded, as usual, with class: "This is a game that, if you've never seen one, you need to come down here and experience it. . . . When you grow up in Alabama like I did, the braggin' rights as a kid—you know those kids at home want to go back to school and tell their friends that Alabama won. I know that, and I realize the importance of this game. The state of Alabama has so much to be proud of with the two teams that they have in Alabama and Auburn, because both teams play with a lot of class, and a lot of intensity."

Barker's mother had been Terry Bowden's secretary at Samford, and the Auburn head man had known the Tide quarterback as he was growing up. After the Game, Bowden said, "He had a great game today. I hope Auburn fans know how much I wanted to win this game, but I love Jay Barker."

IN A somber Auburn locker room, Bowden faced for the first time the worst part of being a coach—consoling his players. He advised them to focus on how they had managed to get back into the Game and to let the bright memories from Gainesville soften the pain of losing.

Meanwhile, the Alabama players celebrated the victory and the snapping of Auburn's streak. In the duel between the SEC's top runners, Williams clearly bettered Davis, whose offense was forced to throw early and thus limited his running.

After twenty-one games, Bowden's honeymoon at Auburn was finally over. The Tigers knew that as 1995 approached and the specter of probation was removed, their horizons would be bigger and brighter. Looking ahead, Bowden declared, "Next year we'll go for the national championship; we'll go after it every year. It starts with the first game and ends up in the Iron Bowl. We'll just have to take them one at a time." The Streak was history, but the Bowden era at Auburn had barely begun.

For Alabama, the SEC championship game showdown with Florida was next. After two years of poor weather and sagging ticket sales, league officials elected to move the game to Atlanta, which obviously neutralized the home-field advantage Bama had enjoyed in the first two matches with the Gators.

The winner of the 1994 title game would play in the Sugar Bowl against Florida State, which had managed a shocking tie with Florida in Tallahassee just one week earlier. The Gators were itching for a rematch, while the Tide needed a shot at beating the 'Noles to stake a claim to the national title.

Before a capacity crowd in the Georgia Dome, Curtis Brown put Bama ahead with a seventy-yard touchdown reception, but Florida quarterback Danny Wuerffel responded with a scoring pass and a keeper for another touchdown, pacing the Gators to a 17–10 halftime lead. Two Proctor field goals put the Tide within reach, then freshman Dwayne Rudd returned a Wuerffel interception twenty-three yards midway through the fourth quarter for a score.

Leading 22–17, Stallings elected not to go for the two-point conversion, instead calling on Proctor to extend the lead to six. Wuerffel promptly led Florida back down the field, and a couple of trick pass plays, with the point after, gave the Gators a 24–23 conference title victory.

Forced to lower its sights somewhat, Bama headed to the Citrus Bowl to take on Ohio State. In keeping with the entire Tide season, the game was close throughout, but Sherman Williams was the difference. Playing in his final collegiate game, he produced 359 all-purpose yards, 50 of which came on a game-clinching reception in the closing seconds. The thrilling 24–17 victory closed the Bama season at 12–1, one point short of another potential national title, and gave the senior class a school-record forty-five career wins. Barker's thirty-five victories placed him at the fore of the legendary line of Alabama quarterbacks, and the humble senior finished fifth in the Heisman voting.

With 1994 in the books, there was no time for rest in either Auburn or Tuscaloosa. Both programs had enjoyed successful years by any standards, but recruiting season kicked into full gear in January, followed by spring practice and summer drills. As always, the Tide and the Tigers feverishly prepared for each step, longing for the start of another season and another November Saturday.

ROLL TIDE

Not So Fast

A S AUBURN rumbled through its 1994 schedule, the whole nation watched in awe. Terry Bowden suddenly was a football genius along the lines of his father. The Tigers were gaining support by the week as the best team in the country. After stunning Florida in Gainesville, the world seemed infatuated with this "poor little team on probation."

Alabama, meanwhile, was plodding along, struggling past Tulane and Southern Miss, and generating a massive wave of indifference in the process. Fantastic games with Georgia and Tennessee were written off as luck, the other team being responsible for losing more than the Tide was for winning.

On and on it went, Auburn picking up steam, while boring ol' Alabama did nothing but win. When the 1994 Game approached, many people felt that Bowden was about to punch a hole in the Tide mystique to last for decades. Well, twenty-one points later, this was revised somewhat. The Streak was over. And so was the constant talk about Auburn's taking control in the state.

Recognition of the historic 1994 Alabama senior class is in order. How can you begin to describe what Jay Barker meant to the University? Thirty-five wins? A national championship? Three Iron Bowls? Each of these things will always be associated with him, but when I think of Barker I think of someone whose character and sincerity shone through in an era of ego and shallowness. He was a credit to the school, and it will be a while before another one like him comes along.

What about Sherman Williams? How many great victories would have gone up in smoke were it not for his courage and guile? And Jon Stevenson, Tarrant Lynch, Michael Rogers? Simply the greatest class in the history of the Crimson Tide. What of the Game contributions of Dameian Jeffries, Sam Shade, and Tommy Johnson? How would 1994 have ended without them?

This was one of my favorite years as an Alabama fan, regardless of the Florida heartbreak. The 1994 Tide team lived on the edge for the whole year and made every game enjoyable. They stared defeat in the face time after time. They found ways to win. They made us proud. And they put Buster Brown in his place.—S.B.

WAR EAGLE

Two Steps Forward . . .

ALL RIGHT, just to get it out of the way, of course, Frank Sanders made the first down. You're just not going to get that call in Legion Field. But it shouldn't have come down to that.

Sanders shouldn't have had to catch a pass in the closing seconds to keep a desperation drive going. There shouldn't have been a desperation drive to begin with. Auburn never should have gotten down 21–0 at the half. But they did. I don't know why. Terry Bowden said afterward that Patrick Nix was so nervous before the Game, he could barely tie his own shoes. This from the same guy who came off the bench and rallied Auburn back a year before. You figure it out.

The whole team short-circuited in the first half. Nothing went right. All-Americans missed tackles and dropped passes. Alabama's offensive line, which had been blown over by the likes of Tulane and Vanderbilt, played like they were All-Pro. I'm hard-pressed to remember one team dominating another as thoroughly as Bama did the Tigers for thirty minutes.

When we left Legion Field that night, Auburn fans were holding their heads high. It was a feeling unlike any I've experienced after losing the Game. Sure, it hurt. But Auburn showed everybody what they were really made of in the second half. The Auburn defense bowed up and shut out a team that was hitting on all cylinders. The Auburn offense came to life and came within inches of pulling it off. They, and we, had nothing to be ashamed of.

There was something there that we had been missing during the dark early 1990s, a conviction that all was not lost, an assurance that Auburn was far from vanquished, a knowledge that the Tigers would roar back without missing a beat. How can you not be optimistic when you have the best coach on the planet? After the experience of the last five years, how can you doubt that Auburn will return to the top? It's a long road, and no one travels it without stumbling along the way. Two steps forward, three steps back, and you keep fighting every day. There is always another day, another year, another Game to fight for.

The Auburn spirit is indomitable. It comes from wide-eyed kids and strong young men and stout-hearted elders. It comes from red clay and city streets. It comes from the top of Sand Mountain and the marshes of Robertsdale. It comes from the heart and from the soul. It comes from the dream of America. It is everywhere, even in the face of temporary defeat.

You can't beat the Auburn people. All you can do is hope to slow them down. Go ahead, take your best shot. We'll be back. Ever to conquer. Never to yield.—W.C.

FINALE

A ROAR LIKE THUNDER

IT IS JANUARY IN Montgomery. Basketball teams are forming at the YMCA. An airman from Maxwell Air Force Base has volunteered to coach a team of twelve- and thirteen-year-olds. After the squads have been chosen, the coach, a lieutenant from Pennsylvania, polls the boys for a name for the team. After a heated debate, War Eagles has been selected. The coach watches in astonishment as three of his players immediately jump to their feet and demand to play for another team.

It is early March in Mobile. A seventeen-year-old boy wrestles with his future and his heart in a dilapidated housing project. His telephone rings incessantly with calls from Tuscaloosa and Auburn. After a brilliant season playing linebacker for Vigor High, he thought that everything would be easy. He has survived the drugs and the dangers of his impoverished life. He has kept himself more or less out of trouble. He has a promising future as a college football player. The young man grew up an Alabama fan. Bright posters, collected over the years, cover the faded wallpaper of his room with images of Bobby Humphrey, Cornelius Bennett, and David Palmer. Yet he has found a quiet home in a visit to Auburn that is unlike anything he has ever known in his life. He has found a bond with an Auburn coach who is already, if not like a father, then at least like an uncle to him. His family has always followed Alabama. He has always said that he wanted to play for the Crimson Tide. Trembling with indecision, he winces as the telephone rings again.

It is May in Birmingham. The senior class of Hoover High School graduates with aplomb and enthusiasm at a suburban stadium. It is a joyous occasion for nearly everyone in attendance, except for one father, who watches with tears in his eyes, tears, not of joy, but of sadness and growing horror. His only daughter has just told him that she is determined to go to Alabama in the fall. Despite his pride in seeing his child to near adulthood without a major mishap, he can't help feeling that he has failed, somehow, somewhere in raising her. He is an Auburn graduate.

It is June at a nursing home in Selma. Two elderly men sit in their shared room, one in bed, the other in a wheelchair. The man in the wheelchair is watching a birthday gift from his grandson, a videotape of the last Auburn-Alabama game. His companion, whose team came out on the losing end this year, watches as well, offering acerbic commentary on every play. A passerby smiles. The two men are both obviously having a wonderful time.

It is the Fourth of July at a Gadsden church barbecue. The minister, a divinity degree holder from Vanderbilt, is amazed as two of his parishioners, middle-aged women who never went to college, argue with unfailing courtesy and considerable venom the outcome of a football game played seven months ago. Their children play in a pick-up softball game, wearing too-large jerseys, one blue and bearing the number 34, the other red with a single number 2 on the back.

It is late August in Greenville. A first-grade class meets for the first time. After lunch, the children go out to the schoolyard for recess. It is still blindingly hot and humid, but they run and play as if the temperature were a breezy 72 degrees. Sweltering under the bare shade of an old pine tree, the young teacher notices an argument over a toy football between two of her charges. One of them wears navy shorts trimmed with orange, the other, a brilliant crimson T-shirt. She walks over to them and hears: "You can't have it! You're for Alabama!" "Give me the ball! Auburn fans aren't good enough to play!" "Uh uh! Auburn's the best!" "Is not!" "Is too!"

It is September in Enterprise. Two close friends meet after a long separation. They are glad to see each other, but within an hour they are arguing bitterly. When the weekend ends, they part still friends, but each is angry and determined to prove the other wrong. They are twenty years old and college juniors, one at Auburn, the other at Alabama.

It is October, somewhere in the deep woods of Chilton County. A group of deer hunters has been up since long before dawn. The early dew has fallen on their shoulders, barely noticed. The forest is still, and the robins twitter in the tall pines. In a cramped deer stand, one hunter elbows his partner. With a grimace, the latter carefully lays down his shotgun, takes a set of earphones off of his head, and hands a portable radio over. The first hunter eagerly puts the headset on, then frowns in annoyance, hearing the voice of

Jim Fyffe calling the play-by-play of an Auburn game. He quickly changes the station, tuning in the kickoff from Tuscaloosa.

It is a late autumn day in Birmingham, maybe Auburn, depending on the year. The streets are virtually deserted, the churches empty, the stores closed. In the distance, the rumbling sounds of a huge multitude can be heard. The noise becomes a distinct chant, rising in pitch and volume. Surrounded by anxious people, television and radio speakers across the state amplify the chant borne on the southern wind until it becomes a roar like thunder.

Roll Tide!

War Eagle!

ALL-UNCIVIL TEAM

Auburn		Alabama
	Offense	
Reggie Slack	QB	Jay Barker
Bo Jackson	RB	Ricky Moore
Lionel James	RB	Bobby Humphrey
Tommie Agee	FB/TE	Lamonde Russell
Frank Sanders	WR	Joey Jones
Lawyer Tillman	WR	Al Bell
Ben Tamburello	C	Wes Neighbors
Ed King	OG	Jon Stevenson
Jeff Lott	OG	Doug Vickers
Wayne Gandy	OT	Larry Rose
Steve Wallace	OT	Terrill Chatman
Al Del Greco	PK	Van Tiffin
	Defense	
Dowe Aughtman	NG/DE	Eric Curry
Ron Stallworth	DT	Jon Hand
Tracy Rocker	DT	Willie Wyatt
Willie Whitehead	DE	John Copeland
Kurt Crain	MLB	Keith McCants
Aundray Bruce	OLB	Cornelius Bennett
James Willis	OLB	Derrick Thomas
Kevin Porter	CB	Antonio Langham
Chris Shelling	CB	Jeremiah Castille
Bob Harris	S	George Teague
Tom Powell	S	Tommy Wilcox
Terry Daniel	P	Chris Mohr

Most Uncivil Moment

Alabama: 1985, Van Tiffin's 52-yarder to win the game
Auburn: 1982, Bo Over the Top. The shot heard 'round the world.

APPENDIX

A STATISTICAL HISTORY OF THE GAME, 1981–94

1981

AUBURN	0	7	7	3—17
ALABAMA	7	0	7	14—28

Scoring Summary:

ALA—Gray 1 run (Kim kick)
AUB—Peoples 63 run (Del Greco kick)
ALA—Bendross 26 pass from Coley (Kim kick)
AUB—James 2 run (Del Greco kick)
AUB—Del Greco 19 FG
ALA—Bendross 26 pass from Lewis (Kim kick)
ALA—Patrick 15 run (Kim kick)

	AUBURN	ALABAMA
First downs	15	14
Rushes-yards	56–188	53–199
Passing yards	123	80
Att-comp-int	21–8–3	11–4–1
Punts	7–39	7–46
Fumbles-lost	0–0	5–4
Penalties	8–80	4–40

1982

AUBURN	7	7	0	9—23
ALABAMA	7	6	9	0—22

Scoring Summary:

ALA—Jones 22 pass from Lewis (Kim kick)
AUB—James 14 run (Del Greco kick)
ALA—Kim 37 FG
AUB—Campbell 2 run (Del Greco kick)
ALA—Kim 33 FG
ALA—Carruth 8 run (pass failed)
ALA—Kim 18 FG
AUB—Del Greco 23 FG
AUB—Jackson 1 run (run failed)

	AUBURN	ALABAMA
First downs	11	27
Rushes-yards	47–193	53–256
Passing yards	64	251
Att-comp-int	14–6–0	33–18–2
Punts	6–46	3–42
Fumbles-lost	1–1	2–1
Penalties	2–11	5–66

1983

AUBURN	0	10	13	0—23
ALABAMA	0	14	6	0—20

Scoring Summary:

AUB—Jackson 69 run (Del Greco kick)
ALA—Jones 20 pass from Lewis (Tiffin kick)
AUB—Del Greco 29 FG
ALA—Carter 3 pass from Lewis (Tiffin kick)
AUB—Del Greco 26 FG
AUB—Del Greco 34 FG
ALA—Moore 57 run (pass failed)
AUB—Jackson 71 run (Del Greco kick)

	AUBURN	ALABAMA
First downs	15	19
Rushes-yards	59–355	46–289
Passing yards	39	62
Att-comp-int	14–5–0	22–5–2
Punts	4–33	7–32
Fumbles-lost	3–2	2–1
Penalties-yards	3–25	3–15

1984

AUBURN	7	0	0	8—15
ALABAMA	0	7	10	0—17

Scoring Summary:

AUB—Jackson 2 run (McGinty kick)
ALA—Carruth 6 run (Tiffin kick)
ALA—Carruth 4 run (Tiffin kick)
ALA—Tiffin 52 FG
AUB—Fullwood 60 run (Jackson run)

	AUBURN	ALABAMA
First downs	16	13
Rushes-yards	59–215	46–180
Passing yards	113	73
Att-comp-int	20–8–1	11–6–1
Punts	6–47	7–43
Fumbles-lost	0–0	2–0
Penalties-yards	6–34	5–35

1985

AUBURN	0	10	0	13—23
ALABAMA	10	6	0	9—25

Scoring Summary:
ALA—Turner 1 run (Tiffin kick)
ALA—Tiffin 26 FG
ALA—Tiffin 32 FG
AUB—Jackson 7 run (Del Greco kick)
ALA—Tiffin 42 FG
AUB—Johnson 49 FG
AUB—Jackson 1 run (Del Greco kick)
ALA—Jelks 74 run (pass failed)
AUB—Ware 1 run (pass failed)
ALA—Tiffin 52 FG

	AUBURN	ALABAMA
First downs	17	20
Rushes-yards	49–175	40–239
Passing yards	159	195
Att-comp-int	17–8–1	28–14–1
Punts	7–49	5–52
Fumbles-lost	2–1	1–0
Penalties-yards	2–15	5–37

1986

AUBURN	0	7	0	14—21
ALABAMA	7	7	3	0—17

Scoring Summary:
ALA—Stafford 2 pass from Shula (Tiffin kick)
AUB—Fullwood 18 run (Knapp kick)
ALA—Humphrey 7 pass from Shula (Tiffin kick)
ALA—Tiffin 29 FG
AUB—Fullwood 26 run (Knapp kick)
AUB—Tillman 7 run (Knapp kick)

	AUBURN	ALABAMA
First downs	25	19
Rushes-yards	39–225	50–340
Passing yards	153	53
Att-comp-int	30–19–3	24–9–1
Punts	3–45	6–38
Fumbles-lost	4–1	1–0
Penalties-yards	5–31	7–72

1987

AUBURN	0	7	0	3—10
ALABAMA	0	0	0	0— 0

Scoring Summary:
AUB—Mose 5 run (Lyle kick)
AUB—Lyle 23 FG

	AUBURN	ALABAMA
First downs	20	10
Rushes-yards	39–185	59–136
Passing	128	47
Att-comp-int	18–14–1	15–7–2
Punts	6–40	6–37
Fumbles-lost	3–1	1–1
Penalties-yards	5–36	3–39

1988

AUBURN	5	3	7	0—15
ALABAMA	3	0	0	7—10

Scoring Summary:
AUB—Lyle 25 FG
ALA—Doyle 20 FG
AUB—Safety, Smith tackle in end zone by Stallworth
AUB—Lyle 22 FG
AUB—Harris 1 run (Lyle kick)
ALA—Payne 12 pass from Smith (Doyle kick)

	AUBURN	ALABAMA
First downs	19	16
Rushes-yards	47–130	27–12
Passing	220	255
Att-comp-int	26–13–1	35–20–2
Punts	6–45	5–43
Fumbles-lost	3–1	2–0
Penalties-yards	14–112	7–48

AUBURN UNIVERSITY PHOTOGRAPHIC SERVICES

AUBURN UNIVERSITY PHOTOGRAPHIC SERVICES

1989

AUBURN	7	0	10	13—30
ALABAMA	3	7	0	10—20

Scoring Summary:

AUB—Joseph 1 run (Lyle kick)
ALA—Doyle 27 FG
ALA—Battle 18 pass from Hollingsworth (Doyle kick)
AUB—Joseph 2 run (Lyle kick)
AUB—Lyle 22 FG
AUB—Williams 12 run (Lyle kick)
AUB—Lyle 31 FG
ALA—Battle 15 pass from Hollingsworth (Doyle kick)
ALA—Doyle 23 FG
AUB—Lyle 34 FG

	AUBURN	ALABAMA
First downs	21	23
Rushes-yards	47–167	32–87
Passing	274	340
Att-comp-int	26–14–1	50–27–2
Punts	4–36	3–42
Fumbles-lost	2–1	2–1
Penalties-yards	8–51	4–20

1990

AUBURN	0	7	0	0— 7
ALABAMA	7	3	3	3—16

Scoring Summary:
ALA—Jones 1 run (Doyle kick)
ALA—Doyle 31 FG
AUB—Baxter 8 pass from White (Von Wyl kick)
ALA—Doyle 40 FG
ALA—Doyle 40 FG

	AUBURN	ALABAMA
First downs	11	13
Rushes-yards	32–52	43–92
Passing	185	102
Att-comp-int	31–17–3	28–14–0
Punts	9–35	9–42
Fumbles-lost	3–2	2–2
Penalties-yards	8–65	6–50

1991

AUBURN	0	3	0	3— 6
ALABAMA	3	7	3	0—13

Scoring Summary:
ALA—Wethington FG 39
AUB—Von Wyl FG 26
ALA—Palmer 11 run (Wethington kick)
ALA—Wethington 27 FG
AUB—Von Wyl FG 23

	AUBURN	ALABAMA
First downs	15	14
Rushes-yards	46–113	38–125
Passing	232	161
Att-comp-int	27–13–2	18–7–1
Punts	5–39	6–46
Fumbles-lost	3–1	2–1
Penalties-yards	9–100	6–59

1992

AUBURN	0	0	0	0— 0
ALABAMA	0	0	10	7—17

Scoring Summary:
ALA—Langham 61 interception return (Proctor kick)
ALA—Proctor 47 field goal
ALA—Williams 15 run (Proctor kick)

	AUBURN	ALABAMA
First downs	8	17
Rushes-yards	28–20	51–199
Passing	119	63
Att-comp-int	25–14–2	14–5–2
Punts	8–42	5–39
Fumbles-lost	3–1	1–1
Penalties-yards	8–74	7–44

1993

AUBURN	3	2	7	10—22
ALABAMA	0	14	0	0—14

Scoring Summary:
AUB—Etheridge 23 FG
ALA—Lee 63 run (Proctor kick)
AUB—Safety, Barker tackled in end zone by Miska
ALA—Anderson 19 run (Proctor kick)
AUB—Sanders 35 pass from Nix (Etheridge kick)
AUB—Etheridge 26 FG
AUB—Bostic 70 run (Etheridge kick)

	AUBURN	ALABAMA
First downs	21	10
Rushes-yards	13–255	26–148
Passing	133	156
Att-comp-int	29–14–1	20–10–2
Punts	7–41	7–47
Fumbles-lost	0–0	0–0
Penalties-yards	4–37	12–117

1994

AUBURN	0	0	7	7—14
ALABAMA	14	7	0	0—21

Scoring Summary:
ALA—Williams 13 run (Proctor kick)
ALA—Malone 74 pass from Barker (Proctor kick)
ALA—West 49 pass from Barker (Proctor kick)
AUB—Nix 1 run (Hawkins kick)
AUB—Nix 1 run (Hawkins kick)

	AUBURN	ALABAMA
First downs	17	22
Rushes-yards	24–86	56–227
Passing	247	188
Att-comp-int	42–23–1	18–9–1
Punts	7–46	6–42
Fumbles-lost	0–0	0–0
Penalties-yards	10–82	6–77

SCOTT BROWN and **WILL COLLIER** grew up as best friends in Enterprise, Alabama—until the time came for them to attend college. Scott chose the University of Alabama and received a degree in computer science in 1991. Will is a third-generation Auburn University graduate, receiving a degree in aerospace engineering in 1992. Their friendship is intact, though strained at least once per year. Scott now lives in Atlanta. Will resides in Fort Walton Beach, Florida.